State and Cap

A Marxist Debate

State and Capital

A Marxist Debate

Edited by John Holloway and Sol Picciotto

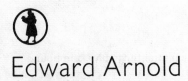

Edward Arnold

© John Holloway and Sol Picciotto 1978

First published 1978 by
Edward Arnold (Publishers) Ltd
25 Hill Street, London W1X 8LL

Chapter 5 © 1974 Sukrkamp Verlag, Frankfurt am Main. All Rights Reserved

ISBN Cloth 0 7131 5987 1
      Paper 0 7131 5988 X

Text set in 10/11 pt IBM Journal, printed by photolithography, and bound
in Great Britain at The Pitman Press, Bath

Contents

Acknowledgements

We gratefully acknowledge the assistance of the contributors to this volume, who have not only granted permission for the publication of their articles, but have, with comradely advice and friendship, helped us through the labyrinth of the German debates. Our thanks go also to the journals in which these articles were first published: *Probleme des Klassenkampfs* (the articles by Müller and Neusüss, Altvater, and Blanke, Jürgens and Kastendieck) and *Gesellschaft* (Reichelt, Gerstenberger and Braunmühl); and to Suhrkamp of Frankfurt for permission to publish the article by Joachim Hirsch. For undertaking the arduous task of translation, we must thank Robin Mann (who translated Claudia von Braunmühl's article) and Martin Sohn-Rethel (who translated the article by Blanke, Jürgens and Kastendieck). The responsibility for the other translations as well as overall responsibility for the translations remains with the editors. For assistance with the typing we thank Mrs Celia Hamilton and especially Joan Ludvick, without whose constant help nothing would be possible. The ideas in the Introduction owe much to the discussions with our comrades in the Conference of Socialist Economists, which have helped greatly not only to bring us together but also to form our ideas. Finally, our thanks to Catherine Hoskyns, Olga Stassinopoulou Holloway, Anna and Aidan.

John Holloway
Sol Picciotto
August 1977

I

Introduction: Towards a Materialist Theory of the State

John Holloway and Sol Picciotto

The present crisis of capitalism appears, more than ever before, as a crisis of the state. Attention has been focused, in Britain and elsewhere, not just on the usual failure of the state to 'manage the economy' but on the need to reduce and restructure state expenditure and consequently to restructure the state apparatus itself. For the first time since the War, the usefulness of large parts of the state administration has been seriously called into question. Faced with these developments, people are being forced to modify their views on both the strength and the weakness, the possibilities and the limitations of the state and many of the widely held views of a few years ago have been shown to be illusory. Those who believed in a 'new capitalism' which might still be oppressive, but in which the problem of economic crisis had largely been solved by state intervention, are now confronted by the return of high unemployment, wage cuts and the reduction of state expenditure. Those, on the other hand, who believed that a return of high unemployment and a general fall in living standards would pose a mortal threat to the political system should be no less embarrassed by the actual course of development: for the crisis has brought to light not only the limits of state activity, but equally the remarkable ability of the state to weather crises.

In short, the present crisis has shown the urgent need for an adequate understanding of the state and its relation to the process of capitalist accumulation and crisis. In the past, Marxist theory, in so far as it has dealt with the state at all, has too often confined itself to showing that the state acts in the interests of capital and to analysing the correspondence between the *content* of state activity and the interests of the ruling class. For an understanding of political development and the possibilities of political action, however, such an analysis is inadequate. In a period characterized on the one hand by the serious questioning of state interventionist policies and on the other by the rise of communist parties in some countries of Western Europe, the whole question of the limits to state action becomes crucial: limitations on

the ability of the state to solve the problems of capital, on the one hand;
limitations on the possibility of using the state to effect a transition to socialism, on the other. At the same time, the decline of parliament and the
erosion of civil liberties in even the most stable democracies raise the question of the development of state forms: is parliamentary democracy to be
seen as the ideal norm for the capitalist mode of production as a whole,
individual deviations from which should be seen as such, or was liberal
democracy merely the ideal counterpart of a certain stage of accumulation
which has now passed? In a period which has just witnessed the extraordinary
success of the state in Britain in persuading the workers to sacrifice their
interests for the good of 'society as a whole', it is essential to analyse why,
if the state is a class state, it is nevertheless seen by so many as a neutral
instance acting for the good of society. In a period in which it has become
commonplace for the leaders of capitalist industry to inveigh not only against
particular decisions but against the state in general, the whole question of
the capitalist nature of the state's activity is posed afresh, and more particularly the question of the necessary 'functionality' of state actions for
capital. It is our argument and the argument of this book that all these questions can be answered only by developing a materialist theory of the state,
i.e. by analysing the relation between the capitalist state and the form of
production in capitalist societies.

This book is intended as a contribution to the development of a materialist
theory of the capitalist state. In the Federal Republic of Germany (and
West Berlin), the last few years have seen a new departure in the Marxist
theory of the state in an intense and coherent debate generally referred to
as the 'state derivation' ('Staatsableitung') debate. The aim of this debate —
which is part of the general resurgence of interest since the late 1960s in
elaborating the scientific categories developed by Marx for an analysis of
modern capitalism — has been systematically to 'derive' the state as a political
form from the nature of the capitalist relations of production, as a first step
towards constructing a materialist theory of the bourgeois state and its
development. In this book we present some of the major contributions to
the German 'state derivation' discussion; but we present them not simply
as an interesting phenomenon, not simply as a 'German school' to be ranged
beside other 'schools', but as a fundamental critique of those theories often
considered in Britain to represent the Marxist theory of the state.

One of the aims of this introduction is to make that criticism more
explicit. We shall start by looking at the way in which the state is analysed
by those authors, political theorists and economists, who currently exert
influence on Marxist discussion in this country. In our view, there is a dichotomy underlying the debate in Britain. Some analyses pay little or no attention to the specificity of the political and argue (or more often assume) that
the actions of the state flow more or less directly from the requirements of
capital: such analyses are sometimes accused of 'reductionism' or 'economic

determinism'. Other analyses, in over-reaction to this approach, have insisted on the 'relative autonomy' of the political, denying (or more often overlooking) the need for theorists of the political to pay close attention to the conditions of capital accumulation: this tendency may perhaps be termed 'politicist'.[1] What both poles of this dichotomy — which does not, of course, always present itself as more than an underlying tendency — have in common is an inadequate theorization of the relation between the economic and the political as discrete forms of capitalist social relations. The only way forward, we shall suggest, is to break out of this dichotomy by developing an adequate theory of this relation, a theory which founds both the specificity of the political and the development of political forms firmly in the analysis of capitalist production. This is precisely the aim of the current German debate. After elaborating our critique of state theories current in Britain, we shall go on to outline the course of this debate, explore some of its weaknesses and suggest ways in which the analysis should be carried further.

'Marxist political theory' and the analysis of the state:

The discussion in Britain of the Marxist theory of the state has tended to become stuck in the rather infertile rut of the Miliband-Poulantzas debate. This debate has given rise to an illusory polarity between the approaches of these two authors, between what has sometimes been called the 'instrumentalist' and the 'structuralist' approach (cf. Gold, Lo and Wright 1975; Poulantzas 1976a), a false polarity which has done much to delimit and impoverish discussion. The 'state derivation' debate presented in this book falls outside this constricting framework and makes clear that it is quite wrong to regard Miliband and Poulantzas as representing polar alternatives in the Marxist analysis of the state, that, for all their real differences, that which Poulantzas and Miliband have in common is at least as significant as that which separates them. In contrast to the German debate, which focuses on the analysis of the inter-relation, the unity in separation of the different spheres; and insists that such a focus is central to a materialist understanding of the political, both Miliband and Poulantzas focus on the political as an autonomous object of study, arguing, at least implicitly, that a recognition of the specificity of the political is a necessary pre-condition for the elaboration of scientific concepts. To some extent this difference in focus is a question of emphasis: clearly neither Poulantzas nor Miliband denies the validity of Marx's famous dictum that 'political forms' can be understood only when related to the 'anatomy of civil society' (Preface to the Critique of Political Economy, MESW vol. 1 p. 503), but neither of them considers it important to analyse this relation with greater precision. An important consequence of this is that neither tries to build *systematically* on the historical materialist categories developed by Marx in his analysis of that 'anatomy' in *Capital* in order to construct a Marxist theory of the state. On the contrary, for

Poulantzas (explicitly) and for Miliband (implicitly), *Capital* is primarily (although not exclusively[2]) an analysis of the 'economic level' and the concepts developed there (value, surplus value, accumulation, etc.) are concepts specific to the analysis of that level. In the same way as *Capital* analysed the economic as an 'autonomous and specific object of science' (Poulantzas 1973, p. 29), the task of Marxist political theorists, in this view, is to take the political as an 'autonomous and specific object of science' to elaborate new concepts specific to the 'political level' (concepts such as 'hegemony', 'power bloc', 'governing class', etc.). In so far, therefore, as these authors base themselves on Marx's writings, they consider it necessary to develop not the 'economic concepts' mentioned above, but the 'political concepts' developed in fragmentary fashion in Marx's 'political writings' and the more 'political' parts of *Capital* (the discussion of the Factory Acts, etc.). This project, referred to by Poulantzas as the attempt to construct a 'regional theory of the political', is justified by reference to the 'characteristic autonomy of the economic and the political' in the capitalist mode of production (1973, p. 29). The assumption that the political can be constituted as an 'autonomous and specific object of science' — more fully theorized by Poulantzas, but shared equally by Miliband — and the interpretation of Marx's *Capital* on which it is based stand in sharp contrast to the approach elaborated in the debate presented in this book. The 'state derivation' debate, receiving much of its inspiration from a revival of interest in *Capital* in the late 1960s, sees in Marx's great work not an analysis of the 'economic level' but a *materialist critique* of political economy, i.e. a materialist critique of bourgeois attempts to analyse the 'economy' in isolation from the class relations of exploitation on which it is based; consequently the categories elaborated in *Capital* (surplus value, accumulation, etc.). are seen not as being specific to the analysis of the 'economic level' but as historical materialist categories developed to illuminate the structure of class conflict in capitalist society and the forms and conceptions (economic or otherwise) generated by that structure. From this it follows that the task is not to develop 'political concepts' to complement the set of 'economic concepts', but to develop the concepts of *Capital* in the critique not only of the economic but also of the political form of social relations. To this we shall return later; for the moment we are concerned only to contrast the two approaches and to argue that the assumptions common to both Miliband and Poulantzas have the effect of cutting these authors off from any possibility of elaborating a materialist analysis of the development of the state, of its possibilities and limitations.

Miliband's book, *The State in Capitalist Society*, is useful in providing a clear introductory critique of bourgeois sociological and political thought; but it is too deeply rooted itself in the British empiricist tradition. Miliband's principal fault, as indeed Poulantzas has pointed out, is that, in combating bourgeois theory, he does little more than show that the bourgeois theorists have got the facts wrong. Thus, defending himself against Poulantzas, he relates that 'having outlined the Marxist theory of the state, I was concerned to set it against the dominant, democratic-pluralist view and to show the latter's deficiencies in the only way in which this seems to be to be possible, namely in empirical terms' (1970, p. 54). While it is certainly important to show that bourgeois theory cannot give an adequate account of empirical development, a Marxist critique must surely go beyond exposing its 'deficiencies' in empirical terms: to understand the genesis and development of the bourgeois conceptions and to understand the development of the capitalist state, it is surely necessary to develop a materialist analysis of the relation between state, society and bourgeois ideology. One consequence of Miliband's approach is that, since he does not found his critique in a systematic analysis of capitalist society, he is unable to develop an analysis of the state which would show the relation between its development and the developing contradictions of the capitalist mode of production. Thus, when in the final chapter of his book he comes to the 'largest of all questions about Western-type regimes . . . how long their "bourgeois-democratic" framework is likely to remain compatible with the needs and purposes of advanced capitalism' (1969, p. 267), his answer to this important question remains necessarily speculative and vague, since he has no theoretical approach which can relate the process of accumulation to the development of the form of the state.

Poulantzas rightly criticizes Miliband for neglecting the essential structural links between the bourgeoisie and the capitalist state. What makes the state in capitalist society a capitalist state is not the class composition of the personnel of the state apparatus but the position occupied by the state in the capitalist mode of production:

> The relation between the bourgeois class and the State is an *objective* relation. This means that if the *function* of the State in a determinate social formation and the *interests* of the dominant class in this formation coincide, it is by reason of the system itself: the direct participation of members of the ruling class in the State apparatus is not the *cause* but the *effect*, and moreover a chance and contingent one, of this objective coincidence. (1969, p. 73.)

The task of state theory, therefore, is to analyse this 'objective relation' or, returning to Marx's dictum, to analyse the relation between political forms and the anatomy of civil society: to analyse how and to what extent the nature of 'the system' (Poulantzas refers presumably to the capitalist mode of production) brings about an 'objective coincidence' between the 'functions of the state' and the 'interests of the dominant class' and how and to what extent changes in the system affect both the interests of the dominant class and, hence, the function of the state.

Poulantzas fails, however, to focus on the relation between political forms and the 'anatomy' of civil society. His view, stated at the beginning of his first major book (1973, p. 29), that capitalist society is characterized by a relative autonomy of the economic and political 'instances' which allows one to make each instance a separate and specific object of study leads him to neglect the all-important question of the nature of the separation of and relation between these instances. Naturally he accepts that the separation of the two instances is not total, but he relegates their unity to a problematic 'in the last instance', never dealing with the relation between them in more than an allusory and cursory fashion.

As a result, the central problems of the Marxist theory of the state, the problems of the development of the state form, of the structural limitations and possibilities of state action, which can be approached only through an analysis of the relation between the state and the contradictions of capitalist accumulation, are necessarily passed over in Poulantzas's work, in the interests apparently of greater scientific rigour. The implications of the structuralist acceptance of the surface fragmentation of bourgeois society into relatively autonomous structures, which in this view can be examined in relative isolation, become clear. Not only does it mean that the question of the inter-relation between the structures (and hence the source of movement within the structures) is neglected, but the structuralist starting point has a fatal immunizing effect. On the one hand, the laws of motion of capital and the tendency for the rate of profit to fall are accepted, or, more accurately perhaps, they are taken for granted; on the other hand, taken for granted and relegated to the economic sphere, the analysis of the political can proceed in isolation from the necessities and limitations imposed on the political by precisely those laws of motion. The 'anatomy of civil society' being taken for granted, the 'political forms' can be examined, *pace* Marx, in their relative autonomy. This insistence on the 'relative autonomy' of the political may reflect a partly justifiable reaction against 'economism' or 'reductionism', i.e. against the common over-simplification of the relation between the economic and the political which presents the political as a mere reflection of the economic. But the 'reductionist' approaches have the merit of trying to provide an answer, however crude, to a real problem, the problem of how we come to a materialistic understanding of political development, of how we relate political development to the contradictions of capitalist production: it is no improvement at all simply to sidestep the problem.

How important is this concept of the 'relative autonomy of the political' for Poulantzas's work and what are its consequences? It seems to us that Poulantzas's false point of departure imposes severe limitations on his analyses. The principal consequence is that, by severing his study of the political from the analysis of the contradictions of accumulation, that is to say of the relations of capitalist exploitation, he cuts himself off from the principal source of change in capitalist society — the development of those contradictions, powered by the revolutionary struggle of the working class.

It follows that, although he is able to give penetrating insights into particular features of the bourgeois state, his analysis does not rise above the level of perceptive description. There is no analysis of the development of capitalist society, of the changing forms of state—society relations and of the state itself. Because there is no systematic analysis of the relation between the capitalist state and its basis, capitalist exploitation of the working class in the process of accumulation, so too there is no analysis of the constraints and limitations which the nature of capitalist accumulation imposes upon state action. Further, his failure correctly to problematize the nature of the separation of the economic and the political leads to his identification of the economic with production relations,[3] and even, despite statements and formulations to the contrary, to a continual tendency to identify class struggle with the realm of the political.

The merits but also the weakness of Poulantzas's analysis can be seen in his treatment of European integration. One of the main purposes of his essay on 'The Internationalization of Capitalist Relations and the Nation State' (1975, p. 38) is to criticize the over-simplified, 'economistic' view exemplified by Mandel's thesis that the success or failure of European integration depends on the form taken by the international centralization of capital. Poulantzas correctly points out that:

> the state is not a mere tool or instrument of the dominant classes, to be manipulated at will, so that every step that capital took towards internationalization would automatically induce a parallel 'supra-nationalization' of states . . . . The problem we are dealing with . . . cannot be reduced to a simple contradiction of a mechanistic kind between the base (internationalization of capital) and a superstructural cover (national state) which no longer 'corresponds' to it. (1975, p. 78.)

While this criticism of Mandel's over-simplification undoubtedly has some force, Poulantzas fails totally to give us an alternative analysis of the material basis of European integration. His emphasis is on showing that the internationalization of capital merely has the effect of transforming national political structures, on denying that it creates pressures for political organizations on a European level. This view stems from his emphasis that 'the task of the state is to maintain the unity and cohesion of a social formation divided into classes' (1975, p. 78) and his implication that there must therefore be a necessary congruence between state organization and the form of the class struggle. Since 'it is still the national form that prevails in these struggles, however international they are in their essence' (1975, p. 78), he comes to the conclusion that 'the current development in no way encroaches on the dominant role of the state in the monopoly capitalist stage' (1975, p. 81). We are thus left without any explanation at all of the impetus to European integration, of the tensions between new forms of capital accumulation and existing state structures.

The same failings can be seen even more clearly in Poulantzas's treatment of fascism. In his book on that subject (*Fascism and Dictatorship*, 1974) he is again concerned to attack the over-simplified 'economistic' interpretations of fascism which attribute fascism simply to the over-ripeness of monopoly capitalism. The book has many critical insights to offer, but Poulantzas again avoids the fundamental question of the relation between fascism and the contradictions of capital accumulation. To understand the origins of fascism and its relation to the continued existence of capitalism, it is surely necessary to examine the reorganization of social relations, and particularly of relations of exploitation, which takes place under fascism, to ask to what extent such a reorganization is made necessary by the contradictions of accumulation as the basic form of class struggle in capitalism, and to ask why the reorganization was carried out in this particular manner. Given that we live in a capitalist society characterized by the same contradictions of accumulation and by the consequent periodic and often violent reorganization of social relations in the interests of the continuation of accumulation, these are surely the questions that are politically important. Without assuming *a priori* the functionality of fascism for capital, the problem is surely to locate the phenomenon in the social process of accumulation and crisis, i.e. of the 'expanded reproduction of capitalist contradictions' (Bukharin 1972a, p. 264). Mandel poses the problem clearly, if sketchily and assertively, when he writes:

> The rise of fascism is the expression of a severe social crisis of late capitalism, a structural crisis which can, as in the years 1929 to 1933, coincide with a crisis of over-production, but which goes far beyond such conjunctural fluctuations. Fundamentally, it is a crisis in the very conditions of the production and realization of surplus value . . . . The historical function of the fascist seizure of power is to change suddenly and violently the conditions of the production and realization of surplus value to the advantage of the decisive groups of monopoly capital. (1975, p. xix.)

This is clearly not a complete analysis of fascism, but it has the great merit of posing very clearly the question of the relation between the rise of fascism and the contradictions *inherent* in capitalist class exploitation (i.e. accumulation) and of the function of fascism in relation to that process of exploitation. It is extraordinary that in all his long analysis of fascism, Poulantzas does not even pose the problem in these terms. Where he discusses the economic contradictions underlying fascism, he does so only in the context of the dominant classes — contradictions between big and medium capital, capitalists and land-owners etc.; to isolate the discussion of these contradictions is in any case very strange when one bears in mind that in Marx's analysis (cf. e.g. *Capital* vol. 3, ch. 15) the intensification of conflicts between individual capitals or groups of capitals can be understood only in relation to a general crisis of the extraction of surplus value, i.e. only on the basis of the fundamental contradiction of the capital-labour relation.[4] But when Poulantzas comes to talk of the relation of fascism to the working class, the contradictions of the relation of exploitation and the attempt to overcome those contradictions through fascism are hardly mentioned at all: the whole question is discussed in terms of a 'politico-ideological' crisis. Poulantzas thus performs the most extraordinary feat of writing a long 'Marxist' analysis of fascism and class without relating fascism to the fundamental core of class struggle in capitalism, the process of accumulation and exploitation. No doubt this is because the contradictions of accumulation are supposed to operate on a different level and can thus be 'taken for granted'.[5]

It seems in many ways to be due to its very limitations that Poulantzas's theory has provided a framework seized upon by a growing band of 'Poulantzians'. In place of theories based on the analysis of accumulation and class struggle, they utilize the political concepts of Poulantzas — 'power bloc', 'hegemony', 'governing class', etc. — like pigeon-holes which can be filled with the relevant contents from a political analysis of the class structure of any given state. The relation of general theory to political practice is seen as something very similar to bourgeois 'model-building' — the 'abstract' theory is 'concretized', resulting in a prescription for political intervention. The result is a kind of political pragmatism, since the prescription depends on the 'content' supplied by the analysis of political class relations, and this is often dictated by the tactics and expediency of the political moment as directly experienced. Since the relationship to the 'economic' is always 'in the last instance', too little attention is paid to basing the analysis of class struggle on the actual dynamic of capital accumulation. It is also very characteristic of a 'Poulantzian' approach that, as we have seen, the global patterns of capital accumulation are either ignored or granted no real effect on the political, so that the bourgeois nation-state is always accepted as the *de facto* political field.

We have concentrated our discussion in this section on Poulantzas because of the present influence exercised by his writings, but similar criticism might have been made of some of the writings of Gramsci, who has also become influential among 'Marxist political theorists' and 'sociologists' in recent years. He too speaks of 'politics as an autonomous science', he too is sharply critical of Rosa Luxemburg's 'economistic' identification of economic and political crisis without providing any alternative analysis of the relation between the economic and the political, he too concentrates his attention on classes, class fractions and class hegemony. His general emphasis is also on playing down the problem of the relation between political forms and the conditions for the accumulation of capital, on dissociating the concept of political crisis from that of economic crisis.[6]

It is characteristic of the authors we have looked at so far that they start with 'political' categories, most notably with what they see as the central 'political category' of class. This is in stark contrast with the German debate presented here, which starts from an attack on those (in this case Offe and Habermas) who try to construct a specific theory of the political, and insists on the need to start from the materialist categories developed by Marx in *Capital*. Thus, Hirsch criticizes Engels's treatment of the state in 'The Origins of the Family, Private Property and the State' for just such a 'class-theoretical' approach:

> The failure to take as the starting point of his analysis the laws and historical development of the capitalist process of accumulation and reproduction leads Engels inevitably to a restricted 'class-theoretical' determination of the state, in which the state appears as a power standing above society and regulating class conflict. (1973, p. 207.)

Perhaps we can parrot and extend this by saying that the failure to take as the starting point of their analysis the laws and historical development of the capitalist process of accumulation and production leads authors such as Miliband, Poulantzas and Gramsci inevitably to a restricted 'class-theoretical' determination of the state, which has two consequences of fundamental importance: first, they are unable to analyse the *development* of political forms; secondly they are unable to analyse systematically the *limitations* imposed on state by the relation of the state to the process of capital accumulation.

'Marxist economics' and the State:

The political theorists are, of course, not the only ones concerned with the analysis of the capitalist state. In view of the increase of 'state interventionism', it is hardly surprising that a growing number of Marxist economists have turned their attention to the analysis of the state. It would be wrong to assume that the economists (i.e. those who take the analysis of the economic as their starting point) necessarily take an economically determinist or reductionist approach to the state. The distinction between the two tendencies which we mentioned at the beginning of this introduction (the 'economically determinist' and the 'politicist') depends not on the starting point of the analysis but on the conception of the social totality which underlies the analysis. Thus, the controversy which has so sharply divided Marxist economists in Britain in recent years, that between the so-called Fundamentalists and the Neo-Ricardians,[7] divides them also in the general principles of their analyses of state action. The Neo-Ricardians have generally taken a positivist view of the separate spheres of politics and economics which has led them into many of the same failings as the theorists we have examined already: starting from an acceptance of the fetishized surface forms of politics and economics, they are unable to develop an analysis of the interrelation of the two spheres. The Fundamentalists on the other hand correctly take the category of capital as their starting point, but short-circuit the whole problem of the specificity of the political and the role of the political system.

On the Neo-Ricardian side, the problem of the role of the state makes its appearance in a totally unproblematic and simplistic manner. In Glyn and Sutcliffe's book (1972) *British Capitalism, Workers and the Profit Squeeze*, and particularly in their chapters on 'The role of policy of the government', the state is portrayed quite simply as the instrument of the capitalist class in its fight against workers' militancy, as 'a central element in capitalism's fight to survive the profit squeeze'. In many ways, their analysis is the economic counterpart of Miliband's political analysis. The emphasis is on showing empirically how the state has acted in the interests of capital. The problem of the development of the state and the problem of what makes the state take particular actions is not raised, or is explained simply by reference to the class struggle. Most extraordinary of all, the problem of the limitations on state action and the contradictory effect of state expenditure in relation to the present crisis is not even mentioned.

Ian Gough, in his article on 'State Expenditure in Advanced Capitalism' (1975), focuses more centrally on the nature of the capitalist state and illustrates more clearly the similarity of approach between the 'Neo-Ricardians' and Poulantzas.[8] The Neo-Ricardian approach is characterized above all by an emphasis on surface categories such as price, profit, wages, etc. The materialist categories developed by Marx to explain the movement of these phenomenal forms are either rejected completely or considered to be 'mere abstractions', of no practical significance for concrete analysis. Following from this, they reject also the view that capitalist development can be explained as the outcome of any 'fundamental tendencies' and dismiss in particular the tendency for the rate of profit to fall.[9]

Starting as they do from surface categories, it is not surprising that the Neo-Ricardians accept as a positive datum the distinction between economics and politics. It is symptomatic that Gough begins his article with an economic analysis of state expenditure and then turns for an analysis of the general character of the state to the expert political theorists, Miliband and Poulantzas. He quotes them as authority for emphasizing the autonomy of the state:

> For both Poulantzas and Miliband the capitalist state is a relatively autonomous entity representing the political interests of the dominant classes and situated within the field of class struggle. (1975, p. 64.)

Since the state is thus liberated, on the authority of the experts, from the exigencies imposed by capital accumulation, Gough is thus also liberated from the need to analyse the limits imposed on state action by its structural relation to the processes of capitalist production. For him (and for the Neo-Ricardians in general), the limits of state action arise not from the logic of capital but from class struggle. For them, as for Poulantzas (e.g. 1975, p. 78), capitalist development is to be explained not in terms of the unfolding of the contradictions of capitalist production through class struggle, but by reference to class struggle even as a political process exogenous from economic relations.

While it is axiomatic that 'the history of all hitherto existing society is the history of class struggles' (*Communist Manifesto*), it is of decisive importance for understanding that history to realize that the *form* of class struggle, the *form* of class antagonism varies from one society to another, and that the form of class struggle has a central role in determining the dynamic of that struggle. The *form* which class antagonism, the *form* which class exploitation takes in capitalist society was the object of Marx's analysis in *Capital*. It is only on the basis of an understanding of the specific *form* of capitalist class exploitation, based on the extraction of surplus value, that we can understand the dynamic of class struggle *in capitalism* and hence of the social and political development of capitalist societies. To say that capitalist development is determined by class struggle is certainly true — indeed we could go further and say it is itself a process of class struggle. But first, it is wrong simply to counterpose this to an explanation of capitalist development in terms of the 'fundamental tendencies' of capitalist accumulation; and secondly, in so far as such a counterposition is implied, or in so far as the 'fundamental tendencies' are dismissed as irrelevant or peripheral, the statement is no more than a misleading banality which overlooks the decisive importance of the *form* of class struggle and which leads inevitably to an ahistorical view of capitalism and hence a utopian view of the transition to socialism.[10]

If we reject these approaches which start from the autonomy of the political, does this bring us back to the 'iron economic determinism' (Gramsci 1971, p. 233) which these authors criticize? If we insist on starting with the category of capital because it is the contradictions of the capital relation (as the basic form taken by class antagonism in capitalist society) which provide the basis for understanding the dynamic of social and political development in capitalism, the problem of the nature of the relation between the actions of the state and the accumulation of capital remains. Or should this problem simply be dismissed as being no problem, the autonomy of the political denied, the correspondence between the actions (and structure) of the state and the requirements of capital accumulation taken for granted? Certainly this assumption is present in the work of many Marxists, among them the so-called Fundamentalists. Thus Yaffe, for instance, has correctly laid great stress on the role of state expenditure in the present crisis; in criticizing the Neo-Ricardians, he has correctly pointed out that state expenditure is not a panacea which will cure the ills of capitalism, that there are limits to the extent and effect of state expenditure which result from its unproductive nature and hence the requirements of accumulation. All this is important and a great advance on the common 'leftist' view which gets no further than pointing to the capitalist content of state action. What is significant, however, is that, although he attributes great importance to state expenditure, Yaffe does not find it necessary to consider further the analysis of the state. What results is a rather monolithic view of the state, in which the growth of the state apparatus is attributed simply to the state's post-war commitment to full employment, and in which the effect of state expenditure is seen as being adequately grasped by its classification into the categories of 'productive' or 'unproductive' expenditure.

While Yaffe's analysis may be valid in crude outline, it leaves many problems unsolved. The problem of the way in which the interests of capital are established through the political system is not even posed. For him, 'the intervention of the bourgeois state arises directly from the needs of capital' (Yaffe and Bullock 1975, p. 33). But then how are we to understand the role of bourgeois democracy, and how are we to see individual state actions which apparently do not correspond to the interests of capital? Again, the problem of contradictions within the state apparatus is not posed: 'This apparatus is simply an increase of unproductive expenditure' (1975, p. 34). Yaffe's great advance on the analyses of the Neo-Ricardians is to point out that, although the actions of the state favour capital in their content, certain limitations are imposed on state action by the nature of its relation to the process of accumulation. However, Yaffe focuses exclusively on one aspect of these limitations, namely on the fact that state expenditure represents a deduction from total social surplus value and is thus limited by the competing claims of private capitals on that surplus value which must be met if accumulation is to continue. Within these limits it is assumed that the state acts rationally in the interests of capital. It is the argument of the essays in this book that this is only one aspect of the limitations on state action, that for a fuller understanding of the state it is necessary to analyse the other limitations on state action which arise from the nature of the structural relation between capital and state — limitations which greatly restrict or render impossible state action in the rational interests of capital, irrespective of the limits of state expenditure. These objections to Yaffe's analysis are not just academic quibbles: they may affect the interpretation of individual state actions, the assessment of contradictions within the capitalist class and of vital questions such as state expenditure cuts: simply to oppose state expenditure cuts without more ado implies a view of the state as being at least potentially beneficial to the working class rather than as a form of capitalist domination, a form impregnated through and through by its place in that system of domination.

Fine and Harris attempt to transcend the Neo-Ricardian — Fundamentalist debate and to take the analysis of the state a step further in their discussion of Gough (1976a) and their review of recent debates (1976b). Correctly they criticize Gough for not starting from the category of capital; correctly too they nevertheless emphasize the specificity of the political and the importance of developing a materialist theory of the state. They do not progress very far, however, in analysing the relation between capital and the state, basically because they appear to see capital simply as an economic category and adopt a simple base-superstructure model of society in which the economic base is determinant. Capital and the economic are thus posited *a priori* as being separate from the political, so that it is not clear how the unity (and inter-relation) of the separate spheres is to be analysed. We shall argue that this starting point is incapable of yielding a solution: what is required is not an economic but a materialist theory of the state. The economic should not be seen as the base which determines the political superstructure, but rather the economic and the political are both forms of social relations, forms assumed by the basic relation of class conflict in capitalist society, the capital relation; forms whose separate existence springs, both logically and historically, from the nature of that relation. The development of the political sphere is not to be seen as a reflection of the economic, but is to be understood in terms of the development of the capital relation, i.e. of class exploitation in capitalist production. It was on the basis of capitalist production in general that Marx developed his critique of economic forms; and it is also on the analysis of the development of relations of production as class relations that the critique of bourgeois political forms must be based.

Implicit in our account of the analyses of the state currently influential in British Marxist discussion has been a contrast between these analyses and the German debate which we present in this book and which we shall now go on to examine in greater detail. It may be helpful to reiterate our main points in order to underline the advances which we feel the German discussion has made in the analysis of the state. We have argued that the inadequacy of the theories current in Britain stems from a failure to focus on the relation between state and society, or, put more generally, a failure to analyse the articulation of the totality of capitalist social relations. On the one hand, we have seen the acceptance of the fetishized categories of bourgeois thought, the acceptance as a positive given of the fragmentation of bourgeois society into the economic and the political: this, we have argued, leads inevitably to an a-historical and therefore utopian analysis of capitalism and the possibilities of socialism. Here the separation of the economic and political spheres is emphasized, the unifying totality neglected. At the other extreme we have seen the reduction of politics to a mere reflection of the economic, an over-emphasis on the unifying whole which overlooks the real, though historically conditioned particularization of the generality of capitalist relations into political and economic forms: the result is an over-simplified view of the relation between the actions of the state and the requirements of capital accumulation.

The starting point of the whole German 'state derivation' debate is the critique of those theorists (Offe and Habermas) who divorce the study of politics from the analysis of capital accumulation. Instead of simply reiterating the connection between capital and the state, however, the contributions to the debate have accepted the separation of the economic and the political and have tried to establish, logically and historically, the foundation of that separation in the nature of capitalist production. In other words, the aim has been to derive the state (or the separation of economics and politics) from the category of capital. This was the essential departure made by the seminal essay of Wolfgang Müller and Christel Neusüss. In the course of the debate much criticism has been heaped upon this article, but the basic starting point, the emphasis on the need to found the separation of the political from the economic in the analysis of capital, has been universally accepted, has indeed come to be taken for granted as a commonplace. In our view, this simple step, which emphasizes simultaneously the unifying totality of capitalist-social relations and the historically conditioned fragmentation of those relations into fetishized forms, is an important step in creating the framework for a materialist analysis of the state. In the rest of this introduction it will be necessary to analyse the German debate to see what progress has been made in developing such a theory, and how the progress made might be developed further.

The State Derivation debate

Since the 'state derivation' debate often appears to be so abstract, it is good to emphasize from the beginning that it is a response to practical political problems. Events in the Federal Republic of Germany in the late 1960s presented political problems for which previous Marxist analyses provided no ready answers. There were three developments which pointed forcefully towards much the same question. First, the recession of 1966—67, the first major break in the West German 'economic miracle', had brought the Social Democrats (SPD) into office for the first time since the War, as minority partners in the Grand Coalition with the Christian Democrats; the governmental change was accompanied by the completion of an ideological shift from the post-war liberalism to an emphasis on state intervention and planning, and it was this change in policy which was accredited with the successful economic recovery in 1967 and 1968. Secondly, the elections of 1969 brought the SPD into office as the major partner in a socio-liberal government pledged to bring in sweeping social reforms. Thirdly, the intervening period had seen the rise and decline of a powerful student movement which, although theoretically more developed than the French or British movement, had yet never succeeded in establishing real contact with the working-class movement. All these three developments raised in slightly different form the same question — the question of the limits (and possibilities) of state action. The first development raised the question of whether the state could go on 'managing' crises and planning social development indefinitely, whether the state could continue without apparent limit to mould society in the interests of capital (as was implicit in the writings of

Marcuse and others influential in the late 1960s). The second development, the coming to power of the socio-liberal coalition, posed the problem of the ability of reformist governments to achieve meaningful reforms, i.e. the problem of the limits of reformism. Thirdly, the failure of the student movement to establish links with the workers posed the problem of understanding the material basis of the widespread faith in reformism. These are the main problems with which this German debate on the state is trying to grapple. Certainly there are other problems which play a role: as the crisis grows deeper in the mid-seventies and the state's policy becomes more repressive, the problems of the functionality of state action and the repressive nature of the state come more to the fore, but most of the debate which we reproduce here is concerned with the limits to state action and the basis of illusions in the power of the state.

For this task the existing Marxist theory of the state was found inadequate. The literature which had been politically important in the late 1960s (most notably Agnoli and Brückner's *Transformation der Demokratie*) had focused on the critique of bourgeois democracy. After underlining the political importance of this critique, Müller and Neusüss, in the article which started the whole debate in 1970, point out that it is not adequate to solve the problems with which they are faced:

> This critique, if it is taken seriously, must become a critique of the development of the various functions of the modern state . . . and of its concrete limits and contradictions. For by explaining and criticizing state institutions as the instruments of manipulation of the ruling class, it is not possible to discover the limits of that manipulation. These can only be revealed by an analysis which shows in detail the needs for and the limits to state intervention, arising from the contradictions of the capitalist process of production as a labour-process and a valorization process. (Below, p. 33.)

To understand the limits to state action it was necessary to analyse the relation between state and society; to understand this relation, it was seen to be necessary to analyse the source of the relation, the source of the particularization (Besonderung) of capitalist society into apparently autonomous spheres of state and society. Just as Marx's analysis of the relation between commodities and money was based on the analysis of the source of this relation or, in other words, on the derivation of the money form from the contradictions of the commodity, so, Müller and Neusüss argue (below, p. 35), the analysis of the relation between state and society must be based on the *derivation of the state form* (as a 'particular existence standing alongside and outside bourgeois society' (*German Ideology*, MECW, vol. 5, p. 92)) from the contradictions of capitalist society.

This approach rests on a certain understanding of the Marxist method, as exemplified most notably by *Capital*. Marx's great work as a 'critique of political economy' in which Marx sought to penetrate behind the categories of political economy to discover the social relations which they concealed, to show that categories such as exchange value, price, etc., are not objective eternal reality, but merely represent historically determined forms assumed by social relations in bourgeois society:

> The categories of bourgeois economy consist of such like forms (value, money, etc.). They are forms of thought expressing with social validity the conditions and relations of a definite, historically determined mode of production. (*Capital*, vol. 1, p. 80.)

Moreover, Marx did not simply seek to decipher those forms, his aim was to provide a *materialist* critique of the economic forms, i.e. to show *why* bourgeois social relations assumed the forms expressed in the categories of value, price, money, etc. Indeed he distinguishes his own theory from bourgeois political economy on precisely those grounds:

> Political Economy has indeed analysed, however incompletely, value and its magnitude, and has discovered what lies beneath these forms. But it has never once asked the question why labour is represented by the value of its product and labour-time by the magnitude of that value. (*Capital*, vol. 1, pp. 845.)

In his critique of the economic forms, therefore, Marx does not simply analyse one form after another: starting from the basic form of value and the social relations it expresses and from which it springs, he 'derives' the other forms from those social relations. For Marx, to analyse a form is to analyse its (historical and logical) genesis and development.[11]

In this perspective, it is clear that *Capital* is in no way an attempt to examine 'the economy in isolation' (Fine and Harris (1976a, p. 109); still less does it constitute the economic 'into an autonomous and specific object of science' as Poulantzas (1973, p. 29) would have it. It is an historical materialist critique of the forms of political economy which attempts to show the social relations which are concealed by, and give rise to, those forms. It follows that a study of the political must not be an attempt to develop some autonomous 'political science', but should rather be a critique of political science which attempts to decipher the political categories as forms of social relations. Since the object of study is bourgeois society, the social relations which are concealed by and give rise to these political forms will be essentially the social relations uncovered by Marx in his critique of political economy, the social relations of the capitalist mode of production. Logically, therefore, the German debate, which is concerned with the analysis of the form of the political, draws its inspiration less from Marx's overtly political writings than from *Capital* and the *Grundrisse*. And this does not stem from a position of economic determinism but, on the contrary, from a view which sees in *Capital* not an economic analysis but a materialist critique of the economic form. Just as the social relations of the capitalist mode of production have given rise to the economic form and the categories of political economy, so they have given rise to the political form and the categories of political science. Thus the investigation of the relation between the economic and the political begins not by asking in what way the 'economic base' determines the 'political superstructure' but by asking: what is it about social relations in bourgeois society that makes them appear in separate forms as economic relations and political relations?

This way of approaching the state was not entirely new: the problem had already been posed in those terms in 1923 by Pashukanis, whose masterly essay on 'The General Theory of Law and Marxism', although translated into English, has been very sadly neglected by Marxists in Britain.[12] Pashukanis, whose relevance to the German debate was realized only after the debate was under way, was concerned to derive the form of law and the closely related form of the state from the nature of capitalist commodity production. Although abstract in formulation, his argument aimed at making an important political point. Writing in the Soviet Union of 1923, he argued that the law and the state were forms which arose from the nature of social relations in bourgeois society; that, while it was undoubtedly necessary for a transitional society to use those forms in the interests of the proletariat, it was a travesty of Marxist theory to argue for the development of 'socialist law' or a 'socialist state'. He inveighed against Marxist theorists who had hitherto criticized the class *content* of the law and of the state without seeing that the *form* of the law and the *form* of the state were equally determined by the nature of capitalist society and could not simply be transposed to a new form of society. (The parallels with the modern critique of state monopoly capitalism theories should be clear.) Thus, he says of Stuchka's rival theory:

> It discloses the class content comprised in juridic forms, but fails to explain why this content takes such a form. For bourgeois legal philosophy — which regards juridic intercourse as an eternal and natural form of every sort of human intercourse — such a question does not arise at all. For Marxist theory — which strives to penetrate into the secrets of social forms and to reduce 'all human relationships to man himself' — this task must occupy first place. (1951, p. 140.)

In like vein, when he comes to the analysis of the state, he points out that it is not sufficient to indicate the class nature of the state: the state must be analysed as a *specific form* of class domination. Having traced the emergence of the separation of public and private, state and society, with the growth of capitalist production, he criticizes Engels's characterization of the state in *The Origins of the Family, Private Property and the State*, which relates the state simply to class conflict, and then he continues:

Behind all these controversies one fundamental problem lies concealed:

why does the dominance of a class not continue to be that which it is — that is to say, the subordination in fact of one part of the population to another part? Why does it take on the form of official state domination? Or, which is the same thing, why is not the mechanism of state constraint created as the private mechanism of the dominant class? Why is it disassociated from the dominant class — taking the form of an impersonal mechanism of public authority isolated from society? (1951, p. 185.)

This is perhaps the clearest formulation of the question tackled by the German debate: the question of the form of the capitalist state. Rather than look immediately at the answer which Pashukanis gave to this question, we shall go on to look at some aspects of the debate itself.

What progress has the 'state derivation' debate made in analysing the form of the state? Since most of the important contributions are presented in this volume, it is hardly necessary to give here a blow-by-blow account of the debate with all its nuances and points of controversy. We shall here follow the discussion only in so far as it is necessary to elucidate the main points at issue and thus the main problems that have arisen in the attempt to derive the form and the function of the state. The reader will find that a small number of important but seemingly obscure problems criss-cross the debate: the problem of just what the starting-point for the derivation of the state form from society should be, and particularly whether the derivation should be based on an analysis of the surface or of the essence of capitalist society; the problem of the relation between the derivation of the form and the derivation of the function of the state; and the problem of the relation between logical derivation and historical analysis. Finally — and this problem comes increasingly to the fore in the later contributions — all these questions throw up the problem of the limits of 'state derivation', of just how far this approach can usefully be pursued. Clearly any attempt at classification is an over-simplification which does injustice to the nuances of the different positions taken; nevertheless, for the sake of simplicity, certainly two, and possibly three, general orientations — though not clear-cut positions — can be distinguished.

First[13] — and this may perhaps be seen as the 'mainstream' approach to the problem — there are those who derive the necessity of the form of the state as a separate institution from the nature of the relations between capitals. Starting from the fact that capital can exist only in the form of individual capitals, these authors focus on the question of how the reproduction of capital as a whole — total social capital — is ensured. In general terms, they conclude that it is only due to the existence of an autonomized state standing above the fray that the social relations of an otherwise anarchic society are reproduced and the general interest of total social capital thus established.

Thus, Müller and Neusüss, basing themselves on Marx's analysis of the

Factory Acts in *Capital*, deduce the necessity of the state as a particular form 'alongside and outside bourgeois society' from the self-destructive character of capitalist society: capital, with 'its unrestrainable passion, its werewolf hunger for surplus labour' (*Capital.* vol. 1, p. 252), would destroy its own basis, the labour power of the workers, if it were not for the necessary intervention of the state, acting in the interests of capital in general (although under pressure from the working class) to protect the health of the workers (see below, p. 37). Stressing the welfare aspect of the state's activity as a necessary condition for the reproduction of labour power, Müller and Neusüss derive from the inability of the individual capitals to perform this function both the necessary autonomy of the state and also the material basis of the reformist belief in the socially benevolent nature of state activity.

The argument of Altvater in his essay on state interventionism, from which a short extract is printed here, takes a similar approach, although he puts the point in more general terms. He derives the state from the inability of capital, as a result of its existence as many mutually antagonistic capitals, to reproduce the social nature of its own existence: to secure its reproduction, capital requires a state which is not subject to the same limitations as individual capitals, and which is thus able to provide the necessities which capital is unable to provide (see below, p. 41). It follows from this derivation of the *form* of the state that the state *functions* derived by Altvater (and by all the authors who adopt a similar approach) are concerned with making good the deficiencies of private capital and with organizing individual capitals into a viable body. Thus the four general functions of the state which Altvater arrives at are all of this nature:

1 the provision of general material conditions of production ('infra-structure');
2 establishing and a guaranteeing general legal relations, through which the relationships of legal subjects in capitalist society are performed;
3 the regulation of the conflict between wage-labour and capital, and, if necessary, the political repression of the working class — not only by means of law, but also by the police and army;
4 safeguarding the existence and expansion of total national capital on the capitalist world market. (Below, p. 42.)

The essay by Blanke, Jürgens and Kastendiek is the most refined and most developed version of this approach. They too start from the fragmentation of social production into commodity production carried on by individual producers and derive the form and the function of the state from the need to regulate the relations between commodity producers by means of law and money. Regulation by these means is necessary to maintain relations of exchange between commodity producers and this regulation can come only from a body standing outside the relations of commodity production. In arguing thus they are following closely in the footsteps of Pashukanis who also related the development of the state as a separate form to the emergence of commodity exchange:

> Factual dominance takes on the distinct juridic character of publicity with the appearance — side by side with it, and independently of it — of relationships associated with the act of exchange: that is to say of private relations *par excellence*. Coming forward as guarantor of these relation-ships, force becomes social force, public force — force pursuing the impersonal interest of order. (1951, p. 183.)

Blanke, Jürgens and Kastendiek's development of Pashukanis's argument brings out clearly the close relation between the questions examined here and the concerns of Marxist legal theorists.[14]

This first line of approach has much to commend it and has thrown considerable light on the relation between the state and individual capitals. In particular, it offers a clearly elaborated alternative to the 'state monopoly capitalism' thesis of the fusion of monopoly capital and the state, an alter-native which emphasizes both the capitalist nature of the state and the essen-tial distinction between capital and state: it is this critique of state monopoly capitalism which lies behind such statements as Altvater's insistence that 'the state is . . . never a real material total capitalist, but always only an ideal or fictitious total capitalist' (see below, p. 42).[15] This approach has also contributed much to the analysis of nationalization and the public sector and the function of that sector in its discussion of state provision of the 'general conditions of production'.[16] Finally, the authors who share this broad line of approach have had much of interest to say on the central question of the limits to state action: see in particular Altvater's discussion of the relation of state activity to the accumulation of surplus value, and Blanke, Jürgens and Kastendiek's discussion of the limitations arising from the necessarily indirect or mediate nature of state action. We are thus being in no sense dismissive of these contributions when we point out that there are nevertheless three strong objections to this line of approach. First, in so far as[17] they present the state as the institutionalization of the interests of capital in general or as coming into being to satisfy the requirements of capital, they attribute to it a power and a knowledge which it cannot possess. In so far as the state is derived from the need to fulfil a function which cannot be fulfilled by private capital, the state's ability to perform this func-tion is already presupposed. This means, as Hirsch points out (below, p. 187), 'that the central problem of state analysis, namely the question whether the state apparatus is at all able — and if so, under what conditions — to carry out certain functions and what consequence this has, is conjured out of existence'. Hence the insistence of this school's critics that it is necessary to derive the functions of the state from its form, and not *vice versa*. The second objection goes more directly to the heart of this approach: starting from the fragmentation of social capital and the antagonistic relations obtaining between individual capitals or individual commodity producers, this approach has very little to say about the state as a form of class domination, about the relations of repression and legitimation existing between the state and the working class. It is in fact a remarkable feature of the German discussion that, with one or two exceptions, it has so far placed very little emphasis on the repressive nature of the state. In part this reflects the general orientation of the debate which sees itself as a critique of crude analyses which present the state simply as the tool of the ruling class; in part if probably represents a generalization from the West German experience in the early 1970s, when the working class was relatively quiescent and 'public discussion' centred on the problems of planning economic development. This leads us on to a third, and possibly the most basic objection, namely that this approach is fundamentally a-historical. It is a-historical because the motive power of capitalist development lies not in the antagonistic relations between individual capitals or individual commodity producers, but in the antagonistic relations between capital and labour, in capital accumulation seen as a process of class struggle. Consequently, in approaches of this kind, although historical analysis is of course admitted to be important, the history is always brought in from outside as something external to the analysis: a distinction is made, implicitly or explicitly, between logical and historical analysis. The distinction is implicit in all these analyses, but is raised explicitly by Blanke, Jürgens and Kastendiek: having defined 'form analysis' as the derivation of the state as a necessary form in the reproduction of capitalist society, they continue:

> On this level of abstraction, however, we can only give the *general points of departure* for the development of 'functions' of the reproduction process which must *take form* in such a manner that they stand outside the system of privately organized social labour. The question of how this process of formation actually occurs, of how it is translated in structure, institution and process of the state, can no longer be answered by form analysis. This question must be made the object of historical analysis. The precise demarcation and mediation between form analysis and historical analysis raises difficult problems, however. It depends on how one understands the historical determination of Marx's concept of capital in general. (Below, p. 119.)

Without wanting to deny the difficulty of the problem — and to this we must return — it does not seem to us correct to make such a rigid distinction between form analysis and historical analysis. If form analysis is to be understood as purely logical and historical analysis as empirical, this will not help us to develop an historical materialist theory of the development of the state. It is no coincidence that, when Blanke, Jürgens and Kastendiek come at the end of their essay to a sketch of the different phases of the development of state activity (below, pp. 142—146), their sketch is rather unconvincing and bears little relation to the analysis that has gone before.

A second line of approach, far less well defined than the first, is to be found in those essays which place their emphasis on the need to base the analysis of the state not on the essential nature of capital but on the forms of appearance of capitalist relations on the surface of society. This approach is best exemplified by the article of Flatow and Huisken — here represented only by Reichelt's criticism of it.[18] Pointing out that Altvater's 'society' appears to have no place for the working class, Flatow and Huisken argue that it is necessary not only to analyse the question why the state is not immediately identifiable with the capitalist class, but to ask how it is possible for the state, a form of class rule, to appear nevertheless as an institution standing 'alongside and outside bourgeois society'. In thus insisting on the importance of deriving not only the *necessity* of the form of the state but also its *possibility*, they return to one of the problems raised by Müller and Neusüss, the problem of the material basis of the acceptance by the working class of the state as a neutral instance. The answer must be, so argue Flatow and Huisken, not in the analysis of the 'essence' of capitalist society, of the essential relations of class exploitation, but in the analysis of the 'surface' of that society:

> It is the central thesis of our argument that it is only from the determinations of the surface of bourgeois society that those interrelations arise, which allow one to grasp the essence of the bourgeois state. (1973, p. 100.)

It is on the surface of society that the community of interest not just of capitals but of all members of society appears. Referring to the 'trinity formula' ('capital: profit, land: ground-rent, labour: wages' (*Capital*, vol. 3, p. 814) discussed by Marx [at the end of volume 3 of *Capital*] , they argue that all members of society have a (superficially) common interest by reason of their common status as owners of a source of revenue. It is this community of interest (albeit superficial) which makes the existence of an autonomous, apparently neutral state possible. When it comes to deriving the *necessity* of the autonomization of the state, however, Flatow and Huisken's answer is very similar to Altvater's. An autonomous state is necessary because the relations of competition existing between the different classes of 'property owners' (i.e. owners of the different sources of revenue) makes it impossible for them to realise their common interest other than through the state.

This second line of approach is even further from providing us with an historical materialist analysis of the state. By starting, not from one aspect of the structure of social relations (as did the first approach), but from the fetishized appearance presented by the surface of bourgeois society, such authors necessarily cut themselves off from an historical understanding of the state. The merit of Flatow and Huisken's article lies in drawing attention to the primary importance of an analysis of commodity fetishism, of the relations between essence and surface appearance, in any study of the problem of legitimation, of how it is that the state is able to appear as a neutral instance acting in the general interest. But the extent to which they carry their analysis and to which they separate the analysis of the surface from the analysis of the essential relations of society, does indeed suggest (as Reichelt argues) that they too fall prey to fetishist illusions, that they lose sight of the nature of the surface as a mere form, the development of which can be understood only through an analysis of the class relations which it conceals.

The third approach – in fact the major counterweight to the first approach[19] – is represented here principally by Hirsch (although Reichelt's discussion of Flatow and Huisken has much in common with Hirsch's approach). This approach again starts from the analysis of the basic structure of capitalist society – but focusing now not on the relations between commodity producers but on the nature of the capital relation, the relation of exploitation of labour by capital. Paradoxically, this approach too can be traced back to Pashukanis and his question:

> Why does the dominance of a class not continue to be that which it is –
> that is to say the subordination in fact of one part of the population to
> another part? Why does it take on the form of official state domination?
> (1951, p. 185.)

The answer to this question must surely lie in the nature of the relation of domination itself. Hirsch argues that the particular form of the state must be derived not from the necessity of establishing the general interest in an anarchic society, but from the nature of the social relations of domination in capitalist society. The form which exploitation takes under capitalism does not depend on the direct use of force but primarily on the dull compulsion of uncomprehended laws of reproduction. Indeed, the form of the appropriation of the surplus product in capitalism requires that relations of force should be abstracted from the immediate process of production and located in an instance standing apart from the direct producers. Thus, both logically and historically, the establishment of the capitalist process of production is accompanied by the abstraction of relations of force from the immediate process of production, thus constituting discrete 'political' and 'economic' spheres (below, pp. 61–64). In contrast to the other two approaches examined the emphasis is placed on the coercive, class nature of the state from the very beginning; but the state is not presented crudely as an instrument of class rule but as a specific and historically conditioned form of the social relations of exploitation, a discrete form which cannot simply be identified with the economic form, the realm of competition.

Two things follow from this derivation of the state. First, whereas it is implicit in the approaches which derive the necessity of the state from the organizational deficiencies of private capital that the state is in some sense the institutionalization of the 'general interest' of capital, this does not follow from Hirsch's approach. On the contrary, Hirsch quotes Marx (*German Ideology*, MECW vol. 5, pp. 46–7) to the effect that, far from being the institutionalization of the general interest, the state is 'divorced from the real individual and collective interests' (see below, p. 62). The limits to state activity thus pose themselves at a much earlier stage for Hirsch than for the early contributors to the debate. The earlier contributors assume that, within the scope allowed it by the exigencies of capital accumulation, the state can act in the interests of capital in general. For Hirsch the structural relation of state to society makes even this extremely problematic, for he sees the contradictions of capitalist society as being reproduced within the state apparatus, thus making it questionable whether the state can ever act adequately in the interests of capital in general. But if state actions are not to be identified with the interests of capital in general, this breaks the logical link between the laws of motion of capital and the content of state activity. Hirsch is thus the first of our contributors who, without questioning its value, seriously raises the question of the limits of the logical 'state derivation' approach.

Secondly, it nevertheless follows from this derivation of the capitalist state from the relation of capitalist exploitation that, even although the state does not represent an institutionalization of the general interests of capital, its continued existence as a particular form of social relations depends on the reproduction of the capital relation, depends on accumulation. This means that the state's activities are bounded and structured by this pre-condition of its own existence, by the need to ensure (or attempt to ensure) the continued accumulation of capital. Because of its form as an instance separated from the immediate process of production, the state is essentially restricted to *reacting* to the results of the process of production and reproduction; the state's activities and its individual functions (but not its form) thus develop through a process of mediated reaction to the development of the process of accumulation. Although one cannot derive directly the content of state activity (i.e. the particular shape which this reaction takes) from the process of accumulation, the starting point for the analysis of this activity, of the development of the state and its limitations, must be the analysis of the process of accumulation and its contradictory development. It is the contradictions inherent in accumulation (as the capitalist form of class exploitation), contradictions most cogently condensed in Marx's analysis of the tendency of the rate of profit to fall, which constitute for Hirsch the dynamic force behind the development of the process of accumulation and hence the development of the state itself. The tendency of the rate of profit to fall and the counter-tendencies which it calls forth thus emerge as the key to the understanding of the development of the state. It will be clear from a reading of Hirsch's analysis that he sees the tendency of the rate of profit to fall not as an economic law which has some necessary statistical manifestation, but as the expression of a social process of class struggle which imposes upon capitalism the necessity of constantly reorganizing its own relations of production, a process of reorganization which Hirsch relates to the mobilization of the counter-tendencies to the fall of the rate of profit:

> The mobilization of counter-tendencies means in practice the reorganization of an historical complex of general social conditions of production and relations of exploitation in a process which can proceed only in a crisis-ridden manner. Thus the real course of the necessarily crisis-ridden process of accumulation and development of capitalist society decisively depends on whether and in what manner the necessary reorganization of the conditions of production and relations of exploitation succeeds. (Below, p. 74.)

For a rigorously theorized historical analysis of capitalist economic and political development, it is therefore necessary to focus on this process of constant reorganization by struggle and through crisis of capitalist social relations, economic *and* political.

This approach, which takes as its starting point the antagonistic relation between capital and labour in the process of accumulation, thus provides us with a framework for an historical and materialist analysis of the state. The process of constantly renewed reorganization of social relations inherent in the concept of the tendency of the rate of profit to fall is an historical process which does not start completely afresh each time, but in which each cycle of reorganization is moulded by the ever-intensifying contradictions springing from the previous reorganization. Although the reorganization takes on different shapes in specific conjunctures, the fundamental forms have everywhere been shaped by the contradictions of the process of accumulation. It is thus possible to distinguish different phases of (economic and political) reorganization which take place on a global basis. In this approach, the actual history of the development of state functions and state institutions is therefore not something which has somehow to be added after the logical derivation has been completed, it is already implicit in the 'logical' analysis. In other words, the analysis is not only logical but also historical.[20] As Hirch puts it:

> the investigation of state functions must be based on the conceptual analysis of the historical course of the process of capitalist accumulation; it must be borne in mind, however, that this is not a question of the logical deduction of abstract laws but of the conceptually informed understanding of an historical process . . .. (Below, p. 82.)

This point seems to us of central importance. The purpose of the Marxist critique of political and economic forms is not simply to analyse a given society. It makes little sense to talk of the capitalist 'forms' of social relations at all unless one has other forms in mind, unless one regards these forms as transitory. Implicit in the very concept of 'form' is the idea that it is historically determined and historically developing. It is precisely this critique of capitalist forms as transitory forms which provides the basis of Marxist analysis. As Rosa Luxemburg put it:

> The secret of Marx's theory of value, of his analysis of the problem of money, of his theory of capital, of the theory of the rate of profit and consequently of the entire economic system, is found in the transitory character of capitalist economy . . . .. It is only because Marx looked at capitalism from the socialist's viewpoint, that is, from the historical viewpoint, that he was enabled to decipher the hieroglyphics of capitalist economy. (1899, p. 58.)

Consequently, the categories developed by Marx to criticize the forms of capitalist society were designed not to describe a static society but to conceptualize these forms as expressions of an historical process:

> Marx's logical mode of conceptualizing the economy, as Engels says, is ultimately a historical one, stripped of its historical form and disturbing accidents. It provides therefore — albeit abstractly — a mirror image of the real historical process, 'a corrected mirror image, but corrected according to principles which permit us to grasp the real historical processes so that every moment can be viewed at the developmental point of its full maturity, at the moment of its classical perfection'. (Rosdolsky 1974, p. 65.)

It is therefore surely wrong to draw a clear distinction between form analysis and historical analysis, as do Blanke, Jürgens and Kastendiek. Form analysis is analysis of an historically determined and historically developing form of social relations, and it is hard to see how an adequate form analysis can be anything other than historical.

The problem, however, is not simply to see Marx's categories as simultaneously logical and historical categories, for the difficulty still remains of relating the 'corrected mirror image' to 'the real historical process', of relating capitalist accumulation and its formally derived tendencies to the actual development of class struggle, of understanding class struggle not just in its form but in its interaction of form and content. In this respect it is possible to raise doubts about Hirsch's development of his own analysis. The focal point of Hirsch's article seems to us to lie in his analysis of the mobilization of the counter-tendencies to the falling rate of profit as a necessary (form-determined) economic, political and ideological process of class struggle to restructure the social relations of capitalist production. This struggle (the struggle to maintain or restore the conditions for accumulation) is subject to certain formal constraints and goals which can be

derived logically from the nature of surplus value production. The outcome
of the struggle, however, cannot be derived from its form, but can only be
analysed in terms of the concrete contents of the struggle, the organization
and strength of the various classes and class fractions, the manner in which
the struggle is waged on the economic, political and ideological fronts, etc.
This struggle, the struggle to accumulate, in which capital is confronted continually by its own immanent barriers and seeks to overcome these barriers
while remaining within the framework of its own (restructured) existence,
is surely the core of class struggle in capitalist society. This point, central
to his analysis of the tendency of the rate of profit to fall, tends perhaps
to slip away from Hirsch in the subsequent development of his argument.
The second part of his article is concerned with giving an historical outline
of the principal phases of the reorganization of capitalist social relations and
its relation to the development of state functions. While this outline provides
an invaluable framework within which to analyse the concrete process of
the reorganization of the 'historical complex of general social conditions
of production and relations of exploitation', the emphasis on this reorganization as a process of class struggle tends to become submerged. Operating
on this level of abstraction, there is a tendency to suggest that the development of the state corresponds *grosso modo* to the requirements of capital
accumulation, but that the analysis of the manner in which and extent to
which these requirements express themselves and are (or are not) satisfied
would require a theory of class struggle. There is perhaps a subtle shift from
arguing that accumulation must be seen as a form-determined and crisis-
ridden process of class struggle (and hence that class struggle must be seen
as being focused on and formed by the struggle to accumulate) to suggesting
that the relation between accumulation and state activity must be seen as
being mediated through class struggle. Subtle though the shift may be,
the consequences may be marked: whereas the former emphasis would lead
on to an analysis of the separation and inter-relation of the economic and the
political in the concrete processes of struggle to restructure capital, the
latter emphasis is liable to suggest the need for the analysis of the (political)
'missing link' between the (economic) process of accumulation and the
activity of the state. It seems to us more fruitful to pursue the first course,
the analysis of accumulation *as* class struggle.[21]

In this perspective, Heide Gerstenberger's insistence in her contribution
on the importance of concrete historical research in any analysis of the
development of the state is opportune. This emphasis on the historical analysis of the concrete course of class struggles in particular societies reveals
of course the specificity of the development of particular states and brings
to the fore the problem of the extent to which one can talk of *the* capitalist
state. At the same time, however, the universalizing and socializing effects
of the capitalist mode of production means that a general theory of the
capitalist state is both possible and necessary. The global domination of the

capitalist mode of production means that, in contrast to previous modes of production, there are not just a multiplicity of particular states whose forms reflect and result from the particular history of each society. The generalization of capitalist production relations produces a generalization of the conditions of reproduction of those relations. Furthermore, as Gerstenberger remarks, the increasing domination and extension of the capitalist mode of production produces a convergence in the structure and shape of individual states. However, a general theory of the capitalist state must base itself on the particular forms taken by the accumulation of capital and the actual history of the struggles through which the capitalist mode of production developed and spread on a global scale. Thus, Claudia von Braunmühl stresses in her contribution the importance of relating the economic and the political not just in the context of the nation state but on an international scale. Viewed from this perspective, the very fragmentation of capital into national capitals and of the political organization of international capital into nation states (as well as their relations within the imperialist system) must be established from the actual historical growth of capitalist production and the specific historical conditions which established national capitals and their relations in the world market. As she argues, not only the existence, but also the particular shape and historical development of particular nation states can be understood adequately only through an analysis of the relation between the state, the national capital and the *international* development of the contradictions of capitalist accumulation.

The three last-mentioned contributors to the book (Hirsch, Gerstenberger, Braunmühl) raise in different forms the question of the limits of the form-analysis of the state. To raise the problem of the limit of the approach is, however, quite different from questioning the value of the approach. The aim of the 'state derivation' debate has been to come to an understanding of the state as a particular form of social relations in capitalism and of the impetus to and limitations on state activity arising from that form. We suggested earlier that in Marxist discussion of the state in Britain, there has been an underlying tendency to counterpose the 'logic of capital' to 'class struggle' as alternative starting-points for an analysis of the state. We have argued that to counterpose these two approaches is to create a false polarity: the 'logic of capital' is nothing but the expression of the basic form of class struggle in capitalist society. It is wrong to think that social development can be understood by an analysis of class struggle which is indifferent to the question of form of class struggle: such an analysis cannot do justice to the nature of the constraints and the impetus arising from that form. This indifference to the problem of form seems to us to be the essence of reformism, and this has also been the focal point of our critique of Poulantzas, Miliband and Gramsci, and of the Neo-Ricardians. If an analysis indifferent to form is to be rejected, however, it is equally mistaken to think that the analysis of the state can be reduced to the analysis of its form, to mere 'capital-logic'. It is quite possible that at times — especially in the early contributions to the German debate — too much has been expected of the analysis of form. The problem, however, is to analyse social development not simply in terms of the 'form' of class struggle (for this tends to lead to an over-determinist view of social development), nor simply in terms of its 'content', but to see that social development is determined by a dialectical interaction of form and content:

> According to the dialectical approach which Marx adopted, the 'content' and the 'form' to which it gives birth exist in constant interaction and in constant struggle with one another, from which result, on the one hand, the casting off of the forms, and on the other, the transformation of the contents. (Rosdolsky 1974, pp. 66—7.)

This, then is how we must understand the major theoretical advance made by the German debate. It is not that 'form analysis' represents some 'royal road to science' on which no obstacles to an understanding of the political will henceforth be encountered: if the reader finds the debate at times too formal and too abstract, these criticisms are partly justified. The very major advance of the 'form analysis' approach is not to have solved all the problems of the Marxist theory of the state, but to have established the *essential prerequisite for an understanding of the state based on the dialectic of the form and content of class struggle.* Form analysis alone is not enough, but as long as the problem of form is ignored, an adequate approach to the state is just not possible.

It is very important that the contributors to the 'state derivation' debate should themselves understand the theoretical advance that results from the debate, that a realization of the limits of the approach should not lead to scepticism about its value. As the limitations of form analysis have become clear, there have been signs of disillusionment with the formal 'state derivation' approach in some of the more recent essays.[22] Instead of moving forward by elaborating the actual historical struggles which have mediated and formulated the development of the contradictions of the capital relation, there has been a temptation to short-circuit this process by using the political categories of Marxist political theorists such as Gramsci and Poulantzas. Without wishing to belittle the value of the work of these theorists, it seems to us, however, that their analyses cannot simply be 'grafted on' to the state derivation approach, but would need very careful re-working in the light of the theoretical advances made. As the 'state derivation' debate moves into a new stage in which, partly as a result of political developments within West Germany, partly as a result of the dynamic of the debate itself, more attention is being focused on the analysis of the current political conjuncture, it is important that 'concrete' analyses should be seen not as a departure from the state derivation debate but as a development of that debate, that the content of the class struggles should always be analysed in its relation of dialectical tension to their form.

The aim of this introduction has not been to summarize or do justice to the individual contributions to this book: such a task would in any case have been impossible within the scope of a short introduction. The aim has been rather to situate the debate presented here, to outline some of the issues and problems which have arisen and, above all, to explain why we consider the articles which follow mark a major advance on the arduous road towards a materialist theory of the state.

2

The 'Welfare-State Illusion' and the Contradiction between Wage Labour and Capital

Wolfgang Müller and Christel Neusüss

The political importance of revisionist theories of the state

In the history of the workers' movement, the theoretical evaluation of the relationship between the state and capitalist society has been one of the most important elements of the debates on the correct political strategy and form of organization of the working class. Revolutionary and revisionist positions can be distinguished in these debates by their views of the role of the state in capitalist society.

The conception of the state as a more or less *independent* institution standing outside the contradictions of society has been and still is the assumption behind all revisionist strategy and practice. Revisionist strategy starts with the intention of replacing capitalism with socialism; but it takes the path of legal reforms within existing society, by means of the gradual acquisition of state power by the working class. (Revisionist theoreticians gradually give up the concepts of the workers' movement; thus e.g. instead of referring to the 'working class' they speak of 'democratic forces'.) But this option for a continuous 'revolution from above' (cf. P. Lapinski 1928; here too revolutionary language is used as an empty phrase) has so far in the history of the workers' movement always ended in the quite explicit abandonment of socialism as a political goal. 'That is why people who pronounce themselves in favour of the method of legislative reform *in place of and in contradistinction to* the conquest of political power and social revolution, do not really choose a more tranquil, calmer and slower road to the *same* goal, but a *different* goal. Instead of taking a stand for the establishment of a new society they take a stand for surface modification of the old society.' (Rosa Luxemburg n.d. (1899), p. 74.)

A strategy which raises the bourgeois state to the position of an instrument of social change can only be thought to have a possibility of success if the state is seen as a 'sacred vessel' which can be filled with capitalist or socialist contents according to the historical situation, and if it were the state which produced the forms within which social life is reproduced. On this Marx says that the 'concentration of bourgeois society in the form of the state'[1] means that we must treat 'existing society . . . as the *basis* of the existing state'.[2] That is to say that the bourgeois state is the product of a society of developed commodity production (i.e. a capitalist society) and of the contradictions which arise from this form of production. Hence it is an institution moulded by these contradictions.[3] The revision of this concept of the state in revisionist theories consequently involved their rejection of the conception that the abolition of the capitalist mode of production can be achieved not through the state apparatus but only by the revolutionary working class.[4]

Once the bourgeois state is seen to be the product of developed commodity-production (i.e. capitalist) society, and the strategy of the workers' movement is defined accordingly, it becomes necessary to take the critique of revisionism beyond the narrow criticism of its conception of political institutions. Yet so far this has been the usual level of politically relevant debate with revisionist state theories on the part of the Left in West Germany and West Berlin — the critique of parliamentarism. The discussion on participation in the elections to the Federal Assembly, when the SDS (socialist students' association) had to work out a line on the political function of a socialist party in a bourgeois parliament under conditions of monopoly capitalism, were the occasion for the revival of the critique of bourgeois parliamentarism by Marx, Engels, Pannekoek and others. Together with Agnoli's *Transformation der Demokratie* (1967), their works helped to develop a basis for the view that parliament was not a platform for the class struggle, and certainly not an instrument for the introduction of socialism, as the DKP (German Communist Party) still believes.[5] The current uncertainty on the Left as to the degree of freedom of action of the SPD government and its scope for 'crisis management' demonstrates that the critique of parliament, i.e. the political critique of a political institution, can only be *one* aspect of the critical discussion of revisionism. This criticism, if it is taken seriously, must become a critique of the development of the various functions of the modern state — of its 'instruments' for regulating the 'economy' *and ensuring social* 'consensus' — and of its concrete limits and contradictions. For the definition and criticism of state institutions as the instruments of manipulation of the ruling class, does not enable us to discover the limits of that manipulation. These can only be revealed by an analysis which shows in detail the needs for and the limits to state intervention, arising from the contradictions of the capitalist process of production as a labour-process and a valorization-process.[6]

In this light, Lenin's theory of imperialism, for example, is more relevant than his explanation of the Marxist theory of the state in *State and Revolution* for the evaluation of the bourgeois state and its functions in the capital valorization process. This is because in *State and Revolution* Lenin tends to discuss the state in general, independently of the particular form which it adopts in the various historical phases of the organization of the material reproduction of society. So the distinctions between the feudal and the bourgeois state fade away in the immediate polemic with the Mensheviks and the revisionist German social democrats just before the October revolution. This is the direct result of Lenin's purpose in *State and Revolution* of carrying out a *political* critique of *political* institutions, to demonstrate that the state apparatus must collapse and be smashed by the revolutionary working class. In *State and Revolution* the question is, what should be the political strategy of the working class in a revolutionary situation towards the political institutions of the state apparatus? But if the problem is to determine the freedom of action and the strategic perspectives of a socialist movement which is only at a formative stage, a Marxist theory of the state such as Lenin's *State and Revolution* does not offer much help, since it refers generally to the need to smash the state apparatus, but provides no tools to evaluate the effectiveness and extent of state interventions in the process of capital valorization. (Hence it is also not suitable for the use often made of it as an introduction to 'the' Marxist theory of the state). In order to develop strategies, what we need today above all is to develop criteria as to how far the manipulative possibilities of the state apparatus extend, where they stop, where they produce new contradictions, where they contain in capitalist form elements of a true socialization of production (e.g. in the standardization of the elements of production), etc. We are concerned, therefore, not with the formulation of a general Marxist theory of the state, but with the investigation of the specific functions of the state in safeguarding the process of capital valorization under advanced capitalism, and of the limits of these state functions.

Revisionism is the form in which the class enemy entrenches itself within the workers' movement itself, in which the ideology of the ruling class is propagated as the ruling ideology of the working class. This propagation is naturally not 'by means of a mere idea', but results from actual experiences, which are the common background to both revisionist theories and also the false consciousness of the worker. The development of revisionism in the workers' movement depends crucially on the experience of 'social-welfare' legislation enacted by the bourgeois state, which limits the particular forms of exploitation of the worker in the capitalist enterprise. By establishing a minimum subsistence level (through workmen's protection legislation and social security systems) the material existence of wage-labourers is ensured during the times when they cannot sell their labour-power as a commodity on the market (sickness, old age, unemployment). Such legislation could easily seem to be a limitation on the domination of capital over living labour, especially as its enactment has always been the mediated result of class struggles. In the eyes of the working class, or especially of its organization,[7] the state could thus appear to be an instrument which could be used by 'salami tactics' to achieve political and social power bit by bit (one slice at a time). As Sering correctly puts it: 'There is a tendency for the level of development of this state function (transport, education, welfare) to parallel the strength of reformism, up to a certain point' (Sering 1935, p. 717). Increasing intervention by the state for economic and social policy, the concentration of capital and lengthening periods of prosperity, especially before the First World War and after the second,[8] provide the main basis for that experience, which makes it seem possible for capital to be gradually transformed by means of the state apparatus. This possibility reappears in new guises: before the First World War in Bernstein's theory; during the Weimar republic in the theory of organized capitalism and economic democracy (Hilferding, Naphtali etc.); and at the start of the Federal Republic in the 1949 Munich programme of the DGB (Deutsche Gewerkschaftsbund — trade union federation); again in the theories that characterize the present phase of capitalist development as state monopoly capitalism (e.g. *'Imperialismus Heute'*); and finally in the theory of the welfare-interventionist state as developed by the Frankfurt school (Habermas, Offe *et al.*).

The relationship between the empirical consciousness of workers (and also of students) and revisionist theory consists in the effect that theory has of establishing a foundation for experience and reinforcing it, hence giving it the appearance of inevitability. This has two implications: first, political agitation among the working class must take into account a long tradition of reformism. The critique of reformist ideas is if anything more important for student agitation in the university, since they are more closely tied to the state than are wage-workers. This debate with reformism can only take place by demonstrating in detail the connections between economic relations and political forms, between economic and political struggle. Secondly, this leads to the conclusion that revisionism and false consciousness cannot ultimately be destroyed through theory alone, but that social and class struggles are a necessary part of this process.

Capital as the precondition for the particularization of the state[9]

The form of social production based on the relationship of capital and wage-labour has the particular special quality that under it people cannot envisage *at the outset* the way in which they can sustain themselves. Instead, the contradictory internal tendencies of the capital relation, which are mediated of course through the activity of the agents of capital, lead to consequences which the individual servants of capital themselves do not consciously desire, and against which they as individual capitalists are powerless. It is indeed true that the state exists for the sake of private property and capital, and that it is 'nothing more than the form of organization which the bourgeois are compelled to adopt, both for internal and external purposes, for the mutual guarantee of their property and interests' (*German Ideology*, MECW vol. 5, p. 90).[10] But this itself does not at all mean that the state can be simply *identified* with capital, with this particular form of social production. Rather, the state is characterized precisely by the fact that it is based on the emancipation of property as private property from the original unity of common property, and that *on this basis* it 'has become a particular entity, alongside and outside civil society' (*German Ideology*, MECW vol. 5, p. 90).

It is important to emphasize that it is on this basis that this particularization of the state as an entity 'alongside and outside' bourgeois society occurs, that is to say on the *internally contradictory* basis of capitalist production. The actual *particularization* on the basis of this contradiction then leads to conceptions that are 'inverted', 'mystical', idealist (these terms are continually used by Marx). According to these conceptions, the state is independent from and opposed to society, it is the true *subject* whose object is 'society' (as a whole). Marx criticizes this view in his *Critique of Hegel's Philosophy of Law*. (This essentially already contains, although in abstract form, the critique of the revisionist theory of the state, which although it pays lip-service to the primacy of society, to the antagonism of wage-labour and capital, nevertheless by asserting that the state can regulate the social contradiction, elevates the state to a subject). Readers of *Capital* can easily understand this development of the state as a 'particular entity alongside and outside civil society' by recalling the dialectical development of the value-form, and then the money-form, from the contradiction between value and use-value contained in the commodity. Embodied in the dual character of the product of labour as a commodity, this contradiction can only become apparent if it is expressed by a particular commodity, the money-commodity. The value-form of the commodity, which cannot be expressed in its own use-value-form, becomes expressed by the use-value-form of a particular commodity which thus becomes money. Money now *appears* as an independent thing, and the socio-historic character of value becomes attached to it, either as a natural characteristic of it, or by virtue of a supposed common *agreement* between people. The same 'fetishism' can be seen in the form of the state. According to the bourgeois conception, either the state has always existed since man is 'by nature a creature of the state', or else the state is indispensible for social (i.e. bourgeois) life, or again it was established consciously by social contract.[11] The fact that it is the particularization of a specific mode of production (capitalism) is turned on its head. This reification and autonomization of the state is a necessary illusion resulting from the bourgeois mode of production just as much as are the forms of money, capital, wage-labour, profit, factors of production or revenues. These illusions are forced upon the agents of production by the particular mechanism of this form of production, and it is these which really determine their activity.

It is for this reason that the state is not the '*real* collective capitalist', but the 'ideal', 'fictitious collective capitalist'.[12] Capital's interest in maintaining the basis of its existence can only develop *subsequently*, and in face of a threat to the very foundation of this mode of production. The most important relationship, the one that determines the real behaviour of capital, is the relationship of the individual capital to its source of surplus-value, the workers it exploits (cf. *Grundrisse* p. 419 f). '*What could possibly show better the character of the capitalist mode of production than the necessity that exists for forcing upon it, by Acts of Parliament, the simplest appliances for maintaining cleanliness and health?*' (*Capital* vol. 1, p. 452).[13] The process of thus gradually 'forcing upon it' these requirements, mediated by catastrophes and conflicts, victories and defeats, establishes the 'welfare state', the 'interventionist state', etc., as a particular coercive power in which capital externally confronts itself. This process also first engenders the struggles of different 'interest groups' which consolidate positions in the institutions of the state itself and of the approaches to it; this constitutes the 'formation of the political will' (which is then turned into the object of political science, but as a phenomenon uprooted from its original source). Since any intervention in the immanent compulsion to capital valorization must be forced upon capital as an immanent law by an institution external to itself, this institution must be equipped with supervisory jurisdiction and effective sanctioning powers; in short, a giant and growing bureaucratic apparatus of coercion. The mere existence of this 'state apparatus' again reinforces the illusion that the state is 'autonomous', that it is able to 'intervene' in 'the economy'. But the fact that this apparatus exists does not mean that it really can effectively intervene (quite apart from the systematic establishment of counter-apparatuses for evading or resisting this coercive power — businessmen's associations and lobbies, taxation 'advice' bureaux, etc.).

The particular existence of the state is, therefore, not an obvious matter — not even in a class society. This particular existence of an exclusively political coercive institution, the state, becomes possible and necessary only with the privatization of the sphere of subsistence and maintenance of life, which in pre-capitalist societies was *a priori* a common social matter, and with the development of private as distinct from communal property. As early as his *Critique of Hegel's Philosophy of Law* (1843), Marx described the bourgeois 'mysticism' which turned the 'actual relation of family and civil society to the state' upside-down, so that 'the condition is postulated as the conditioned, the determinant as the determined, the producing factor as the product of its product' (MECW vol. 5, pp. 8−9).[14] 'It is obvious that the political constitution as such is brought into being only where the private spheres [property, contract, marriage, civil society] have won an independent existence. Where trade and landed property are not free and have not yet become independent, the political constitution too does not yet exist. . . . In the Middle Ages there were serfs, feudal estates, merchant and trade guilds, corporations of scholars, etc.: that is to say, in the Middle Ages property, trade, society, man are *political*; the material content of the state is given by its form; every private sphere has a political character, or is a political sphere. . . . In the Middle Ages the life of the nation and the life of the state are identical' (MECW vol. 5, pp. 31−2). These comments by Marx on the Middle Ages apply also to every pre-bourgeois social formation, as he subsequently indicates with reference to

the city-states of antiquity and later repeats in the preparatory writings for
Capital.[15] In the old 'communal' system, that of the 'clan', the 'commonwealth' or the 'commune', the state did not exist as 'a *particular* reality alongside the real life of the people', but rather the 'political' organization, e.g.
membership of a tribe, was the pre-condition and guarantee of the appropriation of the objective conditions of life through labour.

For such pre-capitalist communities, catastrophes occur either as actual
natural calamities, or through clashes with other communities, but not as
natural catastrophes of society as is the case in the inverted world of capital.
Hence, it is to express a necessary consequence contained in capital that Marx
in *Capital*, after developing the category of absolute surplus value, immediately
turns to the description of the catastrophes which the production of surplus
value entails for living labour, and from this derives the particularization of
the state in the factory legislation. So long as the purpose of labour is the production of use-values, the subsistence of social individuals, there is no need
for a particular regulatory and coercive organization which seeks to prevent
individuals and society from destroying themselves through an excess of work.
Only with capitalist commodity production is this connection broken and the
problem of the self-destruction of society created. The concentration of
bourgeois society in the form of the state, that is to say its concentration in
an institution which appears as external to itself, which appears to float above
it as a 'particular existence', is necessary because only in this way can the
existence of (capitalist) society be assured at all. Since the direct aim of production is not social subsistence but surplus-value production, and since the
process of production is therefore driven on by laws which are concealed from
the conscious will of individuals and are implemented behind their backs
although by means of their own actions, there is a real need for such a particular social institution which confronts productive society. This *ex post facto*
and makeshift supervision by the state of the natural pattern of the social
production process is necessary for the maintenance of surplus-value production, which is the particular form of appropriation of the surplus-labour of
one class by another class. Therefore this supervision aims to maintain the
class character of this society; it is one of the functions which the state must
take over in this class society. (The function of *direct* oppression will not be
dealt with in this context, since this is the very aspect which is not the *primary*
element typifying this particular form of society. The misunderstanding of
this basic point often leads to a false perspective on the nature and organization
of the revolutionary upheaval; see Part V [not reproduced here].)

'Social policy' (i.e. state activity intervening *ex post facto* in society and
seeking to resolve its 'social problems') thus has the characteristics, down to
its smallest details, of a process of paternalistic supervision, control or 'welfare' of the producer. (This is felt by every worker who has to wait in the

queue to see the medical official, the bureaucrat who certifies him as fit to work, who repairs his labour-power as quickly as possible). Hence, however much state social policy offers individual producers a certain security in the event of their partial or total inability to work, social policy can never provide a conscious and planned care for the maintenance, renewal and improvement of the social working capacity of the collective worker, the associated producers themselves. In a communist society such *planned care* would necessarily be part of the collective social production process; it would be a *public* responsibility of society and of its members, as would the rest of social subsistence, and not the object of the abstract bureaucratic activity of a particular *political* organization.[16]

3

Some Problems of State Interventionism: The 'Particularization' of the State in Bourgeois Society

Elmar Altvater

The state under capitalism is the instrument of the domination of capital over the class of wage-labourers. This assertion is not only a fact of political experience in the history of the various capitalist countries, which has been repeatedly demonstrated in the past and continues to be today; it can also be systematically derived by analysis. However, to carry through this derivation we would need to begin from the starting-point of the conditions of the capitalist process of reproduction and to investigate the political expression of the relation of classes in bourgeois society, in which the function of the state must be determined. This process of derivation will not, however, be carried out in this essay, since we are directing ourselves only to one aspect of the state's actions, namely its actions upon the many individual capitals. Here the decisive question is, what is the process by which a society made up of many individual capitals is actually put together, and what role in this is allotted to the state.

At the level of 'capital in general' which was analysed by Marx[1] the real existence of capital as total social capital is presupposed. Total social capital is the combination as a whole in the sense of the real average existence of the many individual capitals, whose subjective actions, according to the conditions at any given time, result in the creation of average conditions as the conditions of total social capital. The 'laws of motion' of the capitalist mode of production thus always refer to the total social capital, never to the many individual capitals, which nevertheless by their actions are the unconscious means by which capitalist regularity is brought about. For it is not total social capital which carries out transactions but the many individual capitals; but through their transactions the individual capitals produce the conditions of existence of total social capital: average conditions of exploitation, equivalent rates of surplus-value, average rates of profit. At the conceptual level of 'capital in general' it is the average conditions and their regular movements that are analysed; that is, the transactions of individual capitals are of interest not as such, but in the results they produce.[2] It is, indeed, also at the conceptual level of capital in general that we see revealed the *form* in which the general laws (as tendencies) of the capitalist mode of production are constituted, out of and in counteraction to the transactions of the many individual capitals. This form is competition, in which the immanent constraining laws of the capitalist mode of production establish their validity. Competition, however, is not mere form which can contain any content *indifferently*, but is precisely the form of implementation of the immanent laws of capital. It is therefore not a mere instrument, indifferent to content, but a real and comprehensible necessary moment of the establishment of capital as total social capital. The average conditions and movements of real total social capital are the real basis of the conceptual abstraction 'capital in general'.[3]

In the realm of competition capital can only become total social capital to the extent that the individual capitals *really* relate to each other. But this they can only do to the extent that they act capitalistically, that is, as surplus-value-producing capitals. However, not all social functions can be carried out in this sense capitalistically, whether because the production of certain (material) conditions of production yields no profit, or because the level of generality of many regulations under prevailing concrete conditions is too great for them to be performed by individual capitals with their different particular interests. Hence it follows necessarily from the capitalist form of production both that the individual capitals constitute through competition total social capital, *and* also that capitalist society cannot be constituted *only* through the form of competition. The reason for this lies in capital itself, since the specific form of social relations — the exchange of commodities and the production of capital — only permits certain relations to occur provided their production is profitable; or on the other hand requires them to be produced on a scale and under conditions which threaten the existence of the whole of society (e.g. the destruction of the natural resources of a society, 'the environment' as a topical example). Therefore, capital cannot itself produce through the actions of the many individual capitals the inherent social nature of its existence; it requires at its base a special institution which is not subject to its limitations as capital, one whose transactions are not determined by the necessity of producing surplus-value, one which is *in this sense* a special institution 'alongside and outside bourgeois society',[4] and one which at the same time provides, on the undisputed basis of capital itself, the immanent necessities that capital neglects. Consequently, bourgeois society produces in the state a specific form which expresses the average interest of capital.[5] The state cannot be grasped therefore merely as a political instrument, nor as an institution set up by capital, but only as a special form of establishment of the social existence of capital alongside and outside competition, as an essential moment in the *social reproduction process* of capital.[6]

To say that the state expresses the average interest of capital does not mean that it does so in an uncontradictory manner. For the concept of the average existence of capital does not suspend the actions and existence of the many individual capitals, which, as such, stand in antagonism to each other. These antagonisms are not suspended by competition; nor are they attributable to competition or to the 'anarchy of the market', in which they appear; nor can the state eliminate them. In this sense the state is therefore never a real material total capitalist, but always only an *ideal or fictitious total capitalist.*[7] This is the content of the category of the 'particularization of the state', of the 'doubling' of bourgeois society into society and state. From this we can now draw an important conclusion: the state does not replace competition, but rather runs alongside it; and as regards the *law of value*, which conceptually expresses the immanent laws implemented by competition, this does not mean its replacement or even its suspension but rather its corresponding *modification*. So the establishment of a society fragmented into individual interests is only made historically possible by the fact that the state secures the foundations for its existence. For instance, the state maintains the class of wage-labourers as an object for exploitation by capital, or produces general conditions of production, or maintains legal relations, all of which capital constantly tends to destroy due to the pressure created by competition for the maximum valorization of capital (e.g. the lengthening of the working day and increasing intensiveness of work and as a reply to them Factory Acts, etc); or on the other hand there are foundations for its own existence which capital cannot itself produce, since the conditions of production imply a necessity for non-capitalist production (which is so for a large part of the general material conditions of production). Thus the state takes on functions for the preservation of capitalist society. It is able to do so precisely because, as a special institution alongside and outside bourgeois society it is not subjected to the necessities of the production of surplus-value, as is any individual capital, however large it may be. The *adequate form* of the state in capitalism is therefore its particular existence as against the individual capitals, and not that of a 'tool of the monopolies'. (It only becomes this in a mediated sense.)

What then are these functions which the state assumes inside capitalist society, due to the impossibility of their being performed by individual capitals? There are essentially four areas in which the state is primarily active, namely: 1. the provision of general material conditions of production ('infrastructure'); 2. establishing and guaranteeing general legal relations, through which the relationships of legal subjects in capitalist society are performed; 3. the regulation of the conflict between wage-labour and capital and if necessary the political repression of the working class, not only by means of law but also by the police and army; 4. safeguarding the existence and expansion of total national capital on the capitalist world market. While all these functions may be called general characteristics of the bourgeois state, they nevertheless develop on the *historical* basis of the accumulation of capital.[8]

4

Some Comments on Sybille von Flatow and Freerk Huisken's Essay 'On the Problem of the Derivation of the Bourgeois State'

Helmut Reichelt

Editors' introduction

Criticism of Flatow and Huisken is a recurring theme in most of the contributions to this book and, although their long essay is not included in the selection, the main points of Flatow and Huisken's argument and the significance of its critique is brought out in Reichelt's short essay. The distinctive feature of Flatow and Huisken's essay is their emphasis on the *surface* of bourgeois society as the basis for the derivation of the state form. Basing themselves on the statement by Marx and Engels in *The German Ideology* that 'out of [the] contradiction between the particular and the common interests, the common interest assumes an independent form as the state' (MECW vol. 5, p. 46), they argue that this common or general interest which finds its institutionalized expression in the state must be derived from an analysis of the surface of capitalist society. To derive this general interest from simple commodity production (as 'Projekt Klassenanalyse' do) is to confuse the real and formal equality of simple commodity production with the merely superficial or formal equality into which it degenerates under capitalism. In capitalism, equality and the general interest in which it finds expression exist only on the surface of society: 'the whole of bourgeois society . . . falls apart into the surface processes of exchange on the one hand and, on the other, the processes "in the depths" which constantly produce . . . unfreedom and inequality' (p. 99). It is from the surface of society, the realm of 'freedom, equality, property and Bentham' (cf. *Capital* vol. 1, p. 172) that the state must be derived.

Carrying on from where Marx left off at the end of vol. 3 of *Capital*, Flatow and Huisken argue on the basis of the trinity formula ('capital − profit; land − ground rent; labour − wages' (*Capital* vol. 3, p. 814)) that all members of society appear on the surface as owners of a source of revenue and have therefore a threefold interest in common: in the maintenance of the source of revenue, in the highest possible revenue from their source and in a continuous flow of revenue. All have thus a common interest as property owners: 'Simply as private property owners, as representatives of the general interest in the maintenance of the conditions of private property — whatever its substance — the private property owners on the surface constitute that sphere of real appearance of equality, freedom and independence which conceals in itself the *possibility* of the development of the bourgeois state' (p. 107). In relation to the state, the threefold interest of the property owners become a common interest in the protection of property, assured economic growth and the crisis-free functioning of the economy. Once the *possibility* of the state has been thus established, its *necessity* is derived from the inability of the competing private property owners to realize the common interest.

Having thus derived the form of the state from its most general function (administration of the general interest) — rather than from a catalogue of functions which it in fact fulfils — Flatow and Huisken go on to consider the derivation of state functions, being enabled by their derivation of the state form to rephrase the question of state functions as: what makes particular concrete demands arising from society acquire the status of a 'general interest' and be implemented through the state? It is not, they argue, a question of quantity or of the strength of the lobby behind the demand, but of the relevance of the demand to the overcoming of the barriers to capital accumulation. From this follows, *inter alia*, that there is no need for a general derivation of specific state functions (since what constitutes itself as state function can be analysed only in relation to the process of accumulation and its barriers). Flatow and Huisken conclude their argument by looking at the specific example of education in this context.

Reichelt focuses his critique of Flatow and Huisken on their use of the categories of 'surface' and 'general interest', and on the a-historical implications of such an approach. His essay raises important questions of method, and in some respects foreshadows the following essay by Hirsch.

* * *

The two authors develop the argument in their essay in a very strange way: after they have discussed problems of derivation for more than fifty pages, they finally conclude that there is 'no longer any methodological constraint to come to a *general* derivation of specific state activities in our context' (p. 136). Once it is established that the bourgeois state in its specific form of separation from bourgeois society is to be interpreted as administrator of the general interest, and once it is further explained what these general interests are, then research can turn to the real problem and trace the course of the process of capitalist accumulation, in which the barriers to self-valorization present themselves as the real point of departure for the derivation of *individual* state functions; the necessity of surmounting the barriers to the valorization of total capital, appearing each time in a different shape, leads to a new state function which must develop in this specific form. What Flatow and Huisken are concerned with, therefore, is the 'general derivation of specific state activities', or in other words, the derivation of the bourgeois state 'by reasoning which goes beyond all its particular concrete functions'.

But what is this attempt based on, if it finally emerges that the subject itself does not impose 'a methodological constraint to come to a general derivation'? What leads the authors to construct a model in which the problem of the particular state functions and their special content is not raised, but in which the generality of these particular functions is itself made the object of a form-genetic deduction? Raising for discussion a construction which finally (in view of the surmounting of the barriers to the valorization of capital, a surmounting [Aufhebung] which is imposed by the compulsion of capital to valorize and which constitutes itself as state functions) proves superfluous — a construction in which a constitutive function for the genesis of the bourgeois state form is attributed to ideology, or more precisely, to surface conscious-ness — can only avoid being superfluous if this false consciousness concerning the bourgeois state has a central role to play in the framework of a discussion of strategy. However, such a discussion is nowhere to be found in Flatow and Huisken's essay.

Let us recall their argument. Against dogmatic groups they argue that the totality of state functions cannot be explained at all as simply as is commonly done. In order to uphold the thesis of the pure class state, the state is reduced to the three traditional functions: army, police and judiciary — other functions in the areas of social policy, labour law or education policy are simply dis-missed as deception and mystification. This concept of the state must neces-sarily fail in any altercation with bourgeois theory, which sees the state as an essentially neutral instance concerned with the general welfare — an inter-pretation which, according to Flatow and Huisken, cannot be seen as deception in the sense of early bourgeois conceptions of ideology but has a material basis. They refer to the recent widespread discussion, which 'on the one hand tries to come to grips with phenomena such as the social and infra-structural intervention of the state and with the objective roots of the 'welfare state illusion' [Sozialstaatsillusion] of reformist and revisionist origin, and on the other hand tries to derive as a characteristic of the bourgeois state the conceptions of freedom and equality contained above all in the concept of democracy' (p. 85). All that cannot be grasped adequately with a concept which reduces the state to the abstract determination, 'class state'.

Flatow and Huisken see a first step towards a more subtle approach in the argument of Wolfgang Müller and Christel Neusüss, who — basing themselves on the *German Ideology* — explicitly describe the character of class neutrality of the bourgeois state as appearance and relate this appearance of class neutrality to the form of the bourgeois state, that is to the form of the political state, distinct from bourgeois society and standing above it. For all that, even Müller and Neusüss do not carry their argument far enough: they do not explain the constitution of the bourgeois state, the genesis of this particularization, the form of the separation of the state; they merely show how particular measures are carried out through the — already constituted — state and are added as a new function to others already existing.

Flatow and Huisken's peculiar narrowing down of the problem is already clear at this stage. It may well be that Müller and Neusüss merely simulate a derivation by basing themselves on analogies; but implicitly Müller and Neusüss distinguish between derivation of the form as the 'real basis of this appearance', i.e. the derivation of that instance to which this appearance is to be attached, and the origin within this separated state of new functions which first bring out this appearance. In other words: with the form itself, the appearance as such is not yet posited. But it is precisely this that Flatow and Huisken do not want to recognize. Their aim is to construct a theoretical structure which will found the class character of the state not in individual functions but in the form of particularization as such. Since — so they argue — all state functions are to be located within this 'particularization' and thus display no qualitative difference as far as this is concerned, no criteria are to be found here for founding the class character of the state. The Marxist critique of formal law, which shows itself to be class law by its very form once the sphere of simple circulation is deciphered by the dialectical presentation of categories as the sphere of appearance, is universalized in its theoretical structure and extended to the whole state problematic. That becomes clear in their discussion of another position, that of the 'Projekt Klassenanalyse'. The latter approach offers the possibility of bringing together all problems discussed so far in a single theoretical construction; the instrumental character of the state, the form of particularization and the appearance of class neutrality can all be derived by a single line of argument. It is characteristic of the approach of Flatow and Huisken that they do not discuss at all the relation between the anticipating abstract-logical discussion of the relation between economics and politics and the subsequent interpretation of Marx's political writings in 'Projekt Klassenanalyse's' treatment of the topic: they do not discuss, for example, how far such categories as 'doubling', general interest, etc., are meaningfully concretized in the exposition or simply thrown in as verbal affirmations. Instead they concentrate on failings in the abstract construction, which Flatow and Huisken see in the fact that the form of particularization is located on a different methodical level from the representation of the two central functions of the state, and that the derivation of these two state functions (the state as guarantor and administrator of the general conditions of production and as instrument of the ruling class) is not mediated with the derivation of the form of particularization. Moreover, they fail to attribute to the deluding appearance of circulation sufficient force to keep the working class under rein. Basically, Flatow and Huisken accept the construction in which false consciousness at the surface of the process of reproduction plays a constitutive role for the direct linking of the form of the particularization of the state with the appearance of class neutrality; but Flatow and Huisken think that they have to bring in something weightier on the side of the workers to be able to explain the 'stability of relations'. The factual consensus can only be explained, they argue, on the basis of positive, determinable interests which are common to both workers and capital and which find their expression in the form of the state itself, with state activity representing the administration of these common interests. The emphasis on the genesis of the form of the bourgeois state which underlies the discussion of the various essays and the insistence on a general derivation of the form as such not based on particular functions reveals itself on closer inspection as expressing the assumption of a unity which is supposed to be based on more than the ideological force of delusion – namely on a generality of interest. Flatow and Huisken are in basic agreement with the duality of appearance and essence used by 'Projekt Klassenanalyse' to found the character of neutrality of the state; but they try to give the appearance more body as the surface interests of the workers, as the workers' mode of existence as defined exclusively in bourgeois categories, a mode of existence which is later seen to be the form of the realization of the interests of total capital. Thus they write on p. 130, for example: 'Through the historically attested, distinct and partly changing interest of the two big groups of private proprietors there appears the boundless tendency of capital to valorize itself. More precisely, behind the interest articulated by the workers in the maintenance and the continuous use of the property labour power stands the interest of total capital in the continuous productive consumption of labour power.'

In view of such declarations, it is hardly a coincidence that they use a model-like and unhistorical method which in its exclusion of all history is the equal of any bourgeois model-building, but which in its attempt to be 'above history' is painfully contemporary and precisely in this reveals itself to be eminently historic. There are long passages where one cannot avoid the impression that this model is merely an abstract description, using Marxist categories, of present-day capitalism in the Federal Republic. A few years ago such a construction would hardly have been conceivable – for lack of ideological basis. The worker is presented quite unashamedly as a 'member of society' and a unity of society thus surreptitiously presupposed by the terms used, a unity which – if it exists at all – is of recent date. It would never have occurred to a liberal theorist of the stamp of Locke or Kant to count the worker as part of bourgeois society – he simply stood outside it, and no attempt was made to conceal the fact. Thus the identification without more ado of the subject of private law, of the abstract 'personality', with the owner of private property – an identification which is to be found in Hegel's *Philosophy of Right*, but which there is attributable to the unavoidable world-historical limits on knowledge and to this extent has its historical justification – is seen as the product of necessarily false consciousness. Moreover, citizenship of the state is abstractly attributed by Flatow and Huisken to every

worker without even a word being said about the historical process that led to
this. But the most striking thing of all is that a central category of the whole
bourgeois-democratic tradition, a category which is still used in his radical-
democratic phase by the young Marx still caught in Feuerbachian thinking,
but which is used only in an emancipatory context, namely the category of
the 'general interest', is systematically deprived of its emancipatory dimension
and used as an analytical category which serves only to provide an interpretation of that which can be institutionalized in the bourgeois state as the
expression of a supra-individual interest. Much the same can be said for the
category of 'doubling' ('Verdoppelung'). Neither in the 'Circular No. 3' of the
Erlangen group nor in the 'Projekt Klassenanalyse', nor in Flatow and
Huisken's essay is any mention at all made of the radical-democratic image of
human liberation connected with this category: significantly, the category is
used only by analogy with the categorical representation of the value and
money theory and the meaning developed there — significantly because the
orientation towards that particular structure of derivation presupposes that —
just as in the value theory — the unity, the general, is identified as positive.
The dialectical representation of particularization, the theoretical portrayal of
the removal of the general to a particular existence standing 'alongside and
outside' the particular commodities, postulates in advance that the two
moments, the general and the particular, exist in immediate unity. The rest
of the construction is built up according to the same pattern, fulfilling always
two essential requirements: first, a general interest must be identified which
unites all who take part in the process of reproduction, and second the
dimension of false consciousness must be sealed as tightly as possible against
the possible insight that the pursuit by the workers of their own interests is
already the realization of the interests of capital. The constellation of categories described by Marx as the surface of the reproduction process seem to
Flatow and Huisken best able to satisfy these requirements: in competition,
so Marx says repeatedly in *Capital*, everything appears in reverse, the real
relations are recognizable only in distorted and mystified shape; the way in
which the whole process appears to the practical capitalist and to the worker
is not identical with its real shape. The 'trinity formula' at the end of the third
volume, which in Flatow and Huisken's eyes closes the systematic analysis of
the three volumes, opens the way — according to them — to an analysis which
satisfies the second requirement mentioned above. In an 'excursus on method'
it is therefore explained that an exact derivation of the form of the bourgeois
state must always bear in mind that — in like manner to Marx's treatment in
Capital of credit, which, although it is often mentioned beforehand, has its
logical place only at a later stage of the total analysis — the state too can be
derived with logical correctness only at a certain stage of the development of
the concept of capital: 'It is not enough either to name the general preconditions for the existence of the state which are implicit in the development of
the concept of capital, or to try to constitute the state as the sum of its

factual activities: rather, the methodical point of departure must be found
from which the state becomes necessary in its real existence, from which — to
take an expression used by Marx in a different context — the "inner tendency"
comes forward as "external necessity" in the course of the systematic development of the argument' (p. 94). Thus, with the help of an argument by Marx
which refers exclusively to the relation between the laws of capital and their
realization through the competition of individual capitals, and which is not
to be understood as though, at every stage of the systematic analysis, the
analysis of this 'inner nature' of capital necessarily drives, on the basis of some
internal dynamic, towards the development of 'external necessity' (cf.
Grundrisse, p. 414) — with the help of this quotation the 'methodological soil'
is prepared for the subsequent derivation of the form of the state which uses
to some extent the same concepts, and at the same time the correctness of
their own procedure is suggested: for after all it should appear logically necessary that this derivation of the form of the state should take as its starting
point the end of the third volume of *Capital*.

As a result of the discussions of the Erlangen theory group, Flatow and
Huisken think that they can interpret this conceptual determination of false
consciousness without more ado as the attitude of the worker as a private
property owner, putting him on the same qualitative footing as the capitalist
and thus allowing one for the first time to impute identical interests to them —
but also raising doubts about the two authors' grasp of the Marxist method.
Characteristic in this respect are the reinterpretation of Marx's arguments and
a degree of uncertainty in their conceptualization. Thus, basing themselves
directly on value theory and hence on a method which traces the form determinations of social objectivity, they postulate an 'equality' (*Gleichgelten*) of
all those taking part in the reproduction process: but this 'equality' of private
property owners is developed in a form which suppresses the specific dialectic
of the sphere of simple circulation and above all its dimension as a critique of
ideology. Even at the risk of my being accused of 'Marx-scholasticism', it
must be said that Marx did not characterize either money or the commodity,
and certainly not capital, as a thing and the worker or capitalist as keeper or
bearer of this thing (cf. p. 95). But such a misunderstanding is quite logical in
the context of Flatow and Huisken's interpretation. Their presentation of the
dialectic of form and content with regard to the exchange relation is only
possible because they once again fall into the trap of actual reification. Thus,
a capitalist exchanges his money capital for the capital of another capitalist; in
this case they see the equality of exchange as being maintained not only
formally but also in content, because capital is exchanged for capital. 'The
property of both is qualitatively the same, is capital' (p. 98), capital is thus
merely a thing. Capital, in my understanding of Marx, circulates in the shape
of a constant change of form, its existence is process, it *is* the unity of its
forms, it *is* the constant change between the form of generality and the form
of particularity, of money and of commodity, and the problem of political

economy is precisely to explain increase in this constant change of form
which value, the equivalent, goes through. Marx speaks with good reason of a
purely formal distinction, namely the distinction between the form of generality and the form of particularity — the content, use-value, is outside the
economic form because it immediately coincides with it. The distinction
between content and form becomes (economically) significant only when the
exchange between capital and labour is considered. Yet Flatow and Huisken's
interpretation of precisely this act is incomprehensible (or at least compre-
hends the above interpretation only by negative implication) in so far as
equality is now said to be maintained 'merely formally'. How far real equivalents are exchanged in this case (and the term 'exchange' is identical with the
change of equivalents and can only refer to this — it hardly seems possible to
me that one could interpret on the basis of Marx's work an exchange of
capital for capital as being qualitatively equal), how far exploitation is accomplished through the form of the real exchange of equivalents: to explain this
and thereby to portray the real exchange of equivalents as appearance is one
of the focal points of Marxist theory. Equally unclear is Flatow and Huisken's
interpretation of the processes going on 'below the surface' 'in the property
and appropriation relations of production and reproduction' — as though
property were not identical with the right of appropriating surplus value without equivalent, although mediated by the exchange of equivalents. Flatow
and Huisken's concept of property, like their concept of capital, refers to a
mere thing. However they may picture to themselves the appropriation going
on 'beneath the surface', the course of logical presentation in *Capital* is, in
their view, to be interpreted as meaning that at the end of the third volume
the contradiction between 'property and non-property' (which, according to
their own conceptions should not exist, since the worker is also a property
owner) is 'logically subsumed' in the fetishized forms of the surface, which no
longer show any trace of this contradiction.

The inadequacy of these considerations also helps to explain those parts of
their article in which Flatow and Huisken come out against the anchoring of
bourgeois conceptions of freedom and equality in the sphere of simple circulation. Their understanding of this sphere is in line with their reified conception
of property and capital. 'Under the conditions of simple commodity circulation', they write on p. 97, 'freedom and equality referred to the formal act of
circulation and also to its pre-conditions of content (property relation, intention, form of appropriation); when the separation of property from labour
represents the basis of the mode of production and posits the characteristic
contradiction between property and non-property, neither the concept of
freedom nor that of equality can be retained in their comprehensive sense,
embracing form and content of simple commodity circulation'. Obviously
Flatow and Huisken think of simple commodity circulation as the idyll of
petty commodity producers; the conception of freedom and equality is seen
as arising not just from the act of circulation but also from equal conditions

of production — thus free cultivation of the fields, property (understood in fetishized categories) of about equal size, moderate and approximately equal fortunes of the artisans, etc. — so that one could appropriate the products of the work of one's fellow only by giving in return the products of one's own work. If this image is at the basis of their analysis (and the passage quoted allows of no other interpretation), then Flatow and Huisken are reproducing in classical form the ideology which Marx criticized unsparingly with the dialectic of appearance and essence, on which the authors claim to base themselves. In logical form they make the same mistake as bourgeois theory makes when it is unable to understand the determinate forms peculiar to the sphere of circulation as being just such forms, and instead fill them with sensuous content. We need only refer to the many theories of the 'natural condition', that paradise of free and equal persons which has never existed and which even in bourgeois theory is seen through as being merely hypothetical. But Flatow and Huisken reproduce this hypothesis in all seriousness in a time in which, God knows, it has lost all world-historical substance.

Once the division into classes comes into being, then (according to Flatow and Huisken) the conception of freedom and equality can only be based on the intrinsically false consciousness of the private property owner who mistakenly sees himself as a proud bourgeois subject, and who, by reason of the distorting force of the fetishized forms of the surface, shares identical general interests on a wide range of issues with all other property owners. The false consciousness on the surface is, in the view of the two authors, so hermetically sealed in its conceptual structure against every possible insight into real relations that the worker must mistakenly understand himself as a property owner and therefore act in the pursuit of his — bourgeois — interests as the unconscious executor of total capitalist interests. In his delusion the worker relates to his labour power in the same way as the capitalist relates to his capital (understood as a thing), which throws off income in the same form (money form). The interests which he articulates are likewise indistinguishable from those to which the capitalist gives expression: the complete *homo oeconomicus*, he has an interest in the maintenance of this source of revenue, an interest in as high a revenue as possible and in the continuous flow of the same. Everyone knows that he can acquire this revenue only through the use of his particular material source of income; he can employ it, however, and thus acquire income, only when he tries at the same time to protect the general pre-conditions within which he reproduces himself. Thus, independent of the material nature of their source of income, all private property owners have a general interest in securing the conditions which make possible the realization of the three interests based on the three particular sources of income. Their unity is the abstractly uniting interest in securing the pre-conditions which determine the relation of income source and income in its three component parts. To this extent they distinguish between themselves as being interested in the general welfare and as citizens pursuing particular interests which relate to their particular source of income: 'Private property owners thus exist in a twofold manner: as private property owners with particular interests and as representatives of general interests. To this doubling corresponds the doubling into private property owners and citizen, or, referring to private property owners as a whole, the doubling of society into society and state' (p. 119). Whereas 'doubling' for the young Marx was the shaking off of the particular bourgeois reality and the constitution of the abstract existence as citizen (*citoyen*), as member of the state, seen as the emancipation (though still in limited, abstract-political form) of humanity from nature-like pre-history, this better half of the 'double man' is concentrated in Flatow-Huisken's essay on — believe it or not — the protection of private property (as general interest in the maintenance of the source of revenue), guaranteed economic growth (as general interest in the pre-conditions for the largest possible creation of new value to be divided up and distributed) and the 'crisis-free functioning of the economy' (p. 117) as pre-condition for the continuous flow of revenue.

The rest of the argument can be anticipated: the doubling into society and state results from the unmediated unity of unity and plurality, of generality and particularity; the possibility — as Flatow and Huisken put it — of the separation of bourgeois state from bourgeois society rests on the unity, the general interests; the necessity of the real doubling, of the real sundering, rests on the fact that their own unity as such, i.e. their general interest *as* general interest, can neither be recognized nor attained by the private property owners, whose eyes are fixed on the particularity of their own interests. There must therefore be an instance which recognizes and realizes the contents of the general interest and presents itself in particular shape as administrator of the general. The unity of private property owners presents itself in particular form — as state.

This 'general derivation' (as Flatow and Huisken call it), which presents the state in a reasoning process which glides over all its actual functions, then contains also the answer to the question posed at the beginning: how the state in the form of its particularization (and not only in its individual, particular state functions) can be both class state and class-neutral state at the same time. The mediation of both aspects is possible on the basis of the inherently distorting function of objective forms of appearance on the surface of the total process, which not only has the effect of making the mode of existence of empirical living subjects appear to those subjects themselves exclusively as the mode of existence of private property owners, but in addition leads the workers, acting with this consciousness, to pursue real (particular and general) interests as private property owners. The state is, then, also their state as long as they do not recognize that their own interests as private property owners are identical with the interests of total capital. Once they gain some insight into the function of their false consciousness, the mirage is destroyed, they recognize their — supposedly — own state as the state of capital which secures the general conditions of the reproduction of capital and thus accumulation. An instrument of the ruling class — the aspect emphasized both by the dogmatic groups and by theories of state monopoly capitalism — is precisely what the state is *not* in this form of separation (in which it can, after all, turn also against the class of capital owners), but only in times of class struggle, when the class of genuine property owners acts in union with the state to beat back the attacks of the proletariat on all levels. What can have led Flatow and Huisken to construct a model in which an actually existing consensus and stability (attained by whatever means) are presented as the outcome and expression of a general interest which has always united all private property owners? What was it that brought Flatow and Huisken not only to define as an ever-present 'general interest' the obvious fact that there will certainly be conflict if the efforts to secure 'steady growth' and a 'crisis-free functioning of the economy' are not crowned with success, but also to reinterpret this fact ontologically as a general interest which is specific also to the workers as private property owners and which 'has always lain hidden in the economic relations'? The whole undertaking gives one the impression that a specific interpretation of a quite specific process going on at the moment is being generalized with the help of Marxist categories. Flatow and Huisken see that the plight of education has to be related to the structure of the process of capital expansion in the present constellation; the state-controlled reform of education is an attempt to overcome by administrative means a barrier to the process of accumulation and valorization; this barrier manifests itself in part in the fact that many people are wrongly or insufficiently qualified and demand more education and equality of opportunity. Flatow and Huisken explain all this as follows: the total process permeates the conscious actions of the participants. The fact that people want to see equality of opportunity, better education, etc., realized as a right guaranteed by the constitution shows that not only do they not recognize that these demands raised by them at a particular time are the expression of a barrier to the process of valorization, but that moreover they are making demands which are to be understood as being exclusively in the interest of a long-term stabilization of capital as a whole. On this basis, the authors then develop a model which — as the examples which they feel justified in drawing from the first volume of *Capital* show — can claim validity for the whole history of bourgeois society.

We have no wish to deny that Flatow and Huisken's essay brings together for the first time the various aspects of Marxist state theory in a unified construction, which certainly advances the discussion. It must be questioned, however, whether a methodologically legitimate critique has to lead to a construction in which the problem of explaining political stability is thrown together, without mediation, with the derivation of state functions; this improper combination is the central weakness of the essay. They criticize Altvater's procedure for subsuming the various state functions and state activities under a preconceived system of categories, and in such a way that both the system of categories and the ordering of the various state functions in this framework are contradictory (cf. p. 124). In contrast, Flatow and Huisken insist that the state functions must be developed in their genesis and in their inner, materially founded inter-relation; for this purpose, the barriers to the process of the valorization implicitly and explicitly named in Marx's presentation of the 'general concept of capital' seem to act as signposts indicating the way to a systematic portrayal of the genesis of state functions. It is an attempt, in other words, to understand Marx's concept of capital in its logic of presentation as a guideline for the writing of real history — an attempt which in the development of state functions moves on a plane of methodical reflection corresponding to the plane on which Marx moved in his critique of political economy. This attempt is, of course, not to be considered without striving to give information in methodically appropriate form about the particular shape in which the functions, determined by the process of valorization as a whole, must consolidate, i.e. appear as state functions. The state, so the authors argued against Altvater, must not be brought in as a stopgap or a fact of experience, it must be presented positively in its immanent necessity. But why must this be done in the framework of a 'general derivation' which discusses only the essence of the bourgeois state, developing the form of the state in a derivation which glides over the individual functions? Would it not have been sufficient to discuss the basic concept of the form discussion, the contradictory unity of particular and general, in relation to each individual function in its specific shape as state function? Without demonstrating in an abstract-general manner the general in all these functions — namely that they are state functions or, in Flatow and Huisken's words, that it is a question of the general interests being administered in a specific form — the same result could be reached if it were shown that, on the basis of a duality of particular and common interests, a separate, institutional particularization of state functions must take place. However such an undertaking might appear in detail, it would not in any case be burdened with questionable analytical ballast and metaphysical implications, which result from the aim of deriving the bourgeois state forms in abstract general manner and, it seems to me, from the never explicitly declared interest in explaining political stability.

A careful reading of the essay also reveals that the authors hardly pursue to its conclusion their approach, which they declare towards the end to be 'superfluous'. They leave unexplained the methodological status of the concept of 'general interest'. Direct reference to Marx's formulations, which are primarily to be found in the *Grundrisse* in the explanation of the character masks acting in simple circulation and the conceptions which arise there, suggests that the aim is to extend Marx's method of portraying social objectivity; yet, in contrast, Flatow and Huisken use the concept exclusively as an all-embracing concept, which, using the method of logical subsumption, brings together abstractly in the three interests mentioned (maintenance of the source of revenue, the highest possible revenue and a continuous flow) all con-

ceivable and historically-developing actions for securing bourgeois reproduction. Leaving aside the fact that it is presumptuous to imagine an 'as yet un-
discovered' interest of the worker in 'steady growth and a crisis-free functioning of the economy', which the worker is unable to distinguish consciously
from his particular interest, and which, on the other hand, is supposed to
appear in the formal structure of its implementation as 'his state', it should
follow logically from such an approach that the abstract content of this
general interest should autonomize itself as a particular, institutional consolidation distinct from the immediate process of reproduction. That is of course
unthinkable, but as a hypothetical construction it closes the conceptual gap
in Flatow and Huisken's approach: of the form of the state they can only
assert that it is the necessary form of the administration of general interests;
they can only begin to fulfil their promises concretely when it is a question of
definite interest which is tautologically subsumable under one of the three
general interests. In the process, the two authors let drop some revealing
formulations, such as on p. 131, where they speak of a 'more or less general
interest on the surface', so that the concept of the general interest is no longer
taken seriously analytically, but merely ascribed an (ideology-) critical dimension. In the transition to the investigation of the barriers resulting from the
process of the valorization of capital and of the transcending (*Aufhebung*) of
these barriers (an overcoming which develops into state functions), it becomes
clear what is involved in this concept of general interest: it is ideology. 'At
this point, it becomes clear that the concept of democracy based on quantitative determinations is incompatible with the necessity — which often ignores
just these quantitative majority relations — for the bourgeois state to implement interests which would find no majority among the people' (p. 134). In
other words, there are no general interests, but only particular interests which
are declared to be general. It is thus implicitly admitted that the postulated
unity of the general interest was only invented in order to derive the form of
the state in an abstract and over-arching manner — the form of a state of which
it is said at the same time that its institutional frame is to be understood as a
particular form of the overcoming of the barriers to the valorization of capital
as a whole; moreover, it is not clear, in their view, whether the politically
mediated overcoming of ever new barriers to valorization, a process which
presents itself as the accumulation of state functions, leads to an instance
characterized by contradictions, in which the individual functions hamper and
paralyse one another in their effects. Only if the underlying history of the
valorization of capital as a whole is brought into the discussion (capital always
being structured by the opposition between wage labour and capital), does it
seem possible to understand these functions, which are not unequivocally
referable to definite class interests, as being nevertheless not class-neutral in
their formal structure; only on this basis can one try to grasp that, on the
contrary, precisely in this their form as (even mutually contradictory) state
functions, their unity lies in their class character.

But that is precisely what Flatow and Huisken's concept of the general interest does not achieve, since it serves, in a construction developed purely on the level of affirmation, to anchor the class character of every state function in the dimension of the worker who misconceives himself as bourgeois. Indeed, this concept disastrously impedes an adequate understanding of historical processes. It is in the nature of the construction that the possibility of discussing definite measures (e.g. of social policy) as the outcome of strategic considerations is *a priori* excluded; such measures must instead be attributed to the general interest of the worker in private property, which, in its determinate articulation, is to be understood as the expression of a barrier to the expansion of capital, a barrier deeply felt by the workers. If, on the other hand, 'bourgeois democracy [is supposed to be] the form most adequate to the capitalist state for the implementation of interests and the exercise of politics, because it espouses most purely the principle of equality', then the resistance of the bourgeoisie to universal suffrage can clearly only have been based on a misunderstanding of its own state, which was interpreted by the bourgeoisie as its state, as a class state, and sealed against proletarian influence only because it (the bourgeoisie) happened by chance to have articulated and asserted its general interests first and the proletariat had not yet made its contribution to 'supporting the state'.

5

The State Apparatus and Social Reproduction: Elements of a Theory of the Bourgeois State

Joachim Hirsch

The general concept of the Bourgeois State

Modern theories about the interventionist state — whether they come from economists or from students of political and administrative science — are concerned with the specific forms and techniques of the administrative management by the state of the process of social reproduction. The basic assumption of these theories is that there is an 'autonomous' political apparatus which, even though bound by certain external social constraints, is nevertheless *subject* to the dictates of the political decision-making process. The main interest of these theorists is in the investigation of forms of administrative organization and techniques which might increase the capacity of the supposedly autonomous 'political system' to control the process of social reproduction, in order to make this process more or less manageable politically.[1] However, the failure of these scientific attempts at policy advice to produce results — at least as far as this ultimate goal of controlling society is concerned — suggests that there may be a fundamental failing in the theory itself. This weakness, which is shared even by more critical approaches which point out the 'disruption potential' of unbalanced structures of social influence and power and of prohibitive external constraints, has its basis in the peculiarly naive and superficial understanding which bourgeois theorists of the state have of their object. To them the state appears to be a rationally constructed (and therefore just as easily transformable) organizational means for achieving the general interest and the goals of the community. They make no mention of the fact that the state as it exists today is an historical product, an historically determined form of the organization of domination, which, being historical, has its foundation in the manner of social production and reproduction which characterizes the bourgeois relation of production and in the resulting class relations. This means, however, that one cannot make statements about the way in which the state apparatus functions and about the conditions and possibilities of the political management of the system, before one has worked out consistently from the analysis of the basic laws of the social reproduction process what are the conditions for the constitution of the social form of the bourgeois state and the resulting determinants of its functions. The failure to define the social character of the state apparatus — which, however, can be understood only on the basis of an historical-materialist theory of the state — leads to the illusion as to the power of the state characteristic of bourgeois political theory, and the latter's practical failings as well as its explicitly ideological function.

Eugene Pashukanis formulated the crucial question for the evaluation of the bourgeois state and its mode of functioning briefly and precisely: 'Why does the dominance of a class not continue to be that which it is — that is to say, the subordination in fact of one part of the population to another part? Why does it take on the form of official state domination? Or, which is the same thing, why is not the mechanism of state constraint created as the private mechanism of the dominating class? Why is it disassociated from the dominant class — taking the form of an impersonal mechanism of public authority isolated from society?' (Pashukanis, p. 185). This question of what distinguishes the bourgeois state from all previous forms of the exercise of power and domination, is a question of the specific social *form* of the state and not of the particular content of its activity. The 'functions of the state' cannot be discussed so long as there is a lack of clarity about the character and the conditions for the constitution of the specifically bourgeois form of political domination. Max Weber correctly pointed out that the 'state' cannot be defined from the content of its activity and that there was hardly a function 'which had not been taken in hand at some time by some political association, and, on the other hand, also no function of which one can say that it has ever and always been exclusively performed by those associations which one designates as political or today as states' (Weber (1964), p. 1042; cf. Weber 1954, p. 339).

We must however proceed from the observation that 'legal relations as well as forms of state are to be grasped neither from themselves nor from the so-called general development of the human mind, but rather have their roots in the material conditions of life' (Marx, *Preface to Critique of Political Economy*, MESW vol. 1, p. 503). 'The material conditions of life', however, means modes of production, the social conditions under which individuals produce and enter into relations with one another. The starting point of an analysis of the bougeois state must therefore be the examination of the 'anatomy of bourgeois society', that is, an analysis of the specifically capitalist mode of social labour, the appropriation of the surplus product and the resulting laws of reproduction of the whole social formation, which objectively give rise to the particular political form.[2] This analysis and its underlying categories cannot be developed here in detail and so we shall confine ourselves to a brief outline of that which is in any case better explained by Marx.

Bourgeois society is generally characterized by private production and exchange based on the division of labour and private property. The dominant form of commodity production implies the two-fold nature of social labour as creator of abstract value and concrete useful objects. That is, the specifically bourgeois form of socialization is determined by the private labours which are carried on independently of one another, and the social bond which necessarily establishes itself behind the backs of the producers 'is expressed in *exchange value* by means of which alone each individual's own activity or his product becomes an activity and a product for him . . . .. The social character of activity, as well as the social form of the product and the share of individuals in production here appear as something alien and objective, confronting the individuals not as their relation to one another, but as their subordination to relations which subsist independently of them and which arise out of collisions between mutually different individuals . . . their mutual interconnection . . . appears as something alien to them, autonomous, as a thing' (*Grundrisse* p. 156–7). The concept of capital as abstract self-expanding value is however necessarily contained in this two-fold character of labour. Just as the dialectical development of the concept of capital must start from the doubling of commodities into commodities and money, so historically the establishment of capitalist relations of production (primitive accumulation, free wage-labour) is the condition for the full development and generalization of commodity production. The employment of a concept of 'commodity producing society' which disregards the existence of capital, is therefore an inadmissible abstraction both logically and historically. Rather the antagonism of wage-labour and capital, exploitation and surplus value is contained in the fully developed concept of commodity-producing society: the exchange of equivalent commodities merely mediates – as 'necessary appearance' on the surface of society – the production and appropriation of surplus value, the exploitation of living labour power and the valorization of capital.

As distinct from all previous forms of social production and reproduction, capitalist society is therefore characterized by the fact that 'the labour-process figures but as a means towards the self-expansion of capital', and that 'reproduction figures but as a means of reproducing as capital, i.e. as self-expanding value – the value advanced' (*Capital* vol. 1, p. 531). This however presupposes 'the free disposal on the part of the labourer of his own capacities and on the part of the owner of money or commodities, of the values that belong to him' (*Capital* vol. 1, p. 547). The capitalist who normally buys labour power at its value and uses it in the production process, by this means obtains the value of his means of production and in addition appropriates for himself surplus value. The production of surplus value represents the specific use-value of living labour for capital.

It is crucial for our analysis *that this relationship has to reproduce itself permanently on the basis of the historically established capitalist mode of production.* 'But that which at first was a starting-point, becomes by the mere continuity of the process, by simple reproduction, the peculiar result, constantly renewed and perpetuated, of capitalist production. On the one hand, the process of production incessantly converts material wealth into capital, into means of creating more wealth and enjoyment for the capitalists. On the other hand, the labourer, on quitting the process, is what he was on entering it: a source of wealth but devoid of all means of making that wealth his own. Since his own labour has already been alienated and since by the sale of his labour-power it has been appropriated by the capitalist and incorporated with capital, it must, during the process, be *realized* in a product that does not belong to him. Since the process of production is also the process by which the capitalist consumes labour-power, the product of the labourer is *incessantly* converted, not only into commodities but into capital, into value that sucks up the value-creating power, into means of subsistence that buy the person of the labourer, into the means of production that command the producers. The labourer therefore constantly produces material, objective wealth, but in the form of capital, of an alien power that dominates and exploits him; the capitalist constantly produces labour-power, but in the form of a subjective source of wealth, separated from the objects in and by which it can alone be realized; in short he produces the labourer, but as a wage-labourer. This incessant reproduction, this perpetuation of the labourer, is the *sine qua non* of capitalist production' (*Capital* vol. 1, pp. 535—6).

As this process continues and surplus value is constantly converted back into capital, 'it is evident that the laws of appropriation or of private property, laws that are based on the production and circulation of commodities, become by their own inner and inexorable dialectic changed into their very opposite. The exchange of equivalents, the original operation with which we started has now become turned round in such a way that there is only an apparent exchange. This is owing to the fact, first, that the capital which is exchanged for labour-power is itself but a portion of the product of others' labour appropriated without an equivalent; and secondly, that this capital must not only be replaced by its producer, but replaced together with an added surplus. The relation of exchange subsisting between the capitalist and labourer becomes a mere semblance appertaining to the process of circulation, a mere form, foreign to the real nature of the transaction and only mystifying it. The ever-repeated purchase and sale of labour-power is now the mere form; what really takes place is this — the capitalist again and again appropriates, without equivalent, a portion of the previously materialized labour of others and exchanges it for a greater quantity of living labour' (*Capital* vol. 1, p. 547).

Based on the necessary semblance of the exchange of equivalents the capitalist form of society therefore constantly reproduces itself through the blind operation of the law of value. The social bond and the distribution of social labour is established through the laws of commodity production and commodity exchange. The production process, governed by the law of value operating behind the backs of the producers, simultaneously reproduces as a process of valorization its own social preconditions without initially requiring any additional external, conscious, i.e. 'political' intervention. 'It is not just the objective conditions of the process of production that appear as its result. The same thing is true also of its *specific social* character. The social relations and therefore the social position of the agents of production in relation to each other, i.e. the *relations of production*, are themselves produced: they are also the constantly renewed result of the process' (*Results of the Immediate Process of Production*, p. 1065). Concrete class relations and their transformation, the manner in which the labour of society is distributed, the development of the productive forces, in short: the basic social relations are always the historical product of objective laws which assert themselves through the actions of individuals. These laws have a determining effect for as long as the essential structural features of the capitalist form of society remain intact. This means that concrete social structures, the mutual relation of classes and the dominant form of the division of labour are essentially incapable of being subjected to conscious, planned — in this sense political — influence and transformation. The basic structures and laws of development of bourgeois societies are not capable of being 'regulated' politically. The conscious organization of social relations would require the abolition of the capital relation.

If, therefore, we assume that bourgeois society necessarily reproduces its structurally determining characteristics through the operation of objective laws which assert themselves behind the backs of individuals, then the social conditions for the constitution of the form of the bourgeois state can now be more clearly defined by logical derivation. In capitalist society the appropriation of surplus value and the preservation of the social structure and its cohesion do not depend on direct relations of force or dependence, nor do they depend directly on the power and repressive force of ideology. Instead, they rely on the blind operation of the hidden laws of reproduction. But because the process of social reproduction and the appropriation of the surplus product by the ruling class is mediated through the unimpeded circulation of commodities based on the principle of equal exchange and through the free disposal by the wage labourer of his own labour power and by the capitalist of the surplus value which he has appropriated and accumulated, the abolition of all barriers which stand in the way (i.e. of the direct relations of force between the owners of the means of production and of private relations of dependence and restraints ('feudalism') in the sphere of commodity circulation) is an essential element in the establishment of the capitalist form of society. The manner in which the social bond is established, in which social labour is distributed and the surplus product appropriated necessarily requires that the direct producers be deprived of control over the physical means of force and that the latter be localized in a social instance raised above the economic reproduction process: the creation of formal bourgeois freedom and equality and the establishment of a state monopoly of force.[3] Bourgeois class rule is essentially and fundamentally characterized by the fact that the ruling class must concede to the force which secures its domination an existence formally separated from it. 'As the relationship of exploitation is made formally effectual as a relationship of two "independent" and "equal" commodity owners, . . . so political class authority may take the form of public authority . . .. The principle of competition — which is dominant in the bourgeois capitalist world . . . provides no possibility of associating political authority with an individual enterprise.' (Pashukanis, p. 186).

The historical emergence of a central state apparatus with its (initially merely *de facto*) monopoly of force means the suppression of these multifarious 'feudal' restraints and relations of dependence which permeate society. It therefore implies the possibility of the formation of a territorially homogeneous market and the *centralization* of force necessary for reproduction under capitalist conditions in an instance which is raised up above society (which reproduces itself on the basis of its immanent laws) and formally separated from the producers who enter into reciprocal commercial relations with one another. But the creation of a territorially united and circumscribed market area in which capital can circulate freely also requires the *concentration* of force for the purpose of its effective external use: the protection of the bourgeoisie and its rule against forcible external interference and the creation of an apparatus of force as a means of asserting its common interests externally on the 'world market'.[4] 'Constraint as the command of one person addressed to another and confirmed by force, contradicts the basic condition precedent to the intercourse between owners of commodities. In a society of commodity owners and within the limits of the act of exchange, the function of constraint can therefore not come out as a social function, since it is not abstract and impersonal. For a commodity producing society, the subordination to man as such — to man as a specific individual — means subordination to arbitrary caprice, since for that society it coincides with the subordination of one commodity owner to another' (Pashukanis, pp. 187–8). The process of the centralization of force therefore implies at the same time its abstraction from the concrete relations of production — its transformation into 'extra-economic' political force (cf. Preuss 1973, p. 73).

For this very reason, however, the 'particularization' of the bourgeois state as an apparatus of force can *not* be understood as the institutionalization of a 'general will', but means rather the *separation* of the political apparatus of bourgeois society from real individual and common interests: 'This fixation of social activity, this consolidation of what we ourselves produce into a material power above us, growing out of our control, thwarting our expectations, bringing to nought our calculations, is one of the chief factors in historical development up till now [and] out of this very contradiction between the particular and the common interests, the common interest assumes an independent form as the *state, which is divorced from the real individual and collective interests*' (*German Ideology*, MECW vol. 5, pp. 46–7, my emphasis — J.H.). Since the individuals 'are neither subsumed under a natural community, nor on the other hand do they, as conscious members of the community, subsume the community under themselves, it must confront them as independent subjects as an equally independent, external, accidental material thing. This is precisely the condition for their existing as independent private persons in a social context' (*Grundrisse*, German edn, p. 909).

Of course, one would need to examine in detail the historical process by which the bourgeois class gained hold of the state apparatus in appropriate form, how, through long struggles, it remoulded the outdated feudal and feudal-absolutist apparatus of domination for its own ends. In our analysis, however, we are assuming that bourgeois society has been constituted and capital relations fully established, so this process will not be examined more closely. We shall therefore not be discussing the phase of historical develop-ment in which capital, still undeveloped, did not totally determine the law of motion of social reproduction, and in which the bourgeoisie still weak, both politically and economically, needed for the maintenance of its position an alliance with non-capitalist classes and power groups and was therefore com-pelled to turn antagonisms within these groups — for instance between absolute monarchs and estates, between town and country — to its own advantage. Such an analysis of the historical constitution of the bourgeois state would also have to trace in detail the process — likewise omitted here — of the shaping of the specific elements of its form: the establishment of the formal non-disposal by the immediate possessor of state power of the means of production, the consequent maintenance of the state apparatus from deductions from revenue ('fiscal state'), the separation of the spheres of 'private' and 'public' law, the autonomization of the state apparatus as an abstract person *vis-à-vis* the concrete person of the monarch, the emergence of a professional civil service and of professional politicans and with this the formal non-identity of administrative position and class membership, and finally the development of the system of parliamentary representation as the mediating sphere between the state apparatus as an apparatus of force and bourgeois society.[5]

Our argument is that a theory of the bourgeois state must be developed from the analysis of the basic structure of capitalist society in its entirety and that in so doing it is first of all a matter of defining the bourgeois state as the expression of a specific historical form of class rule and not simply as the bearer of particular social functions. The attempt to derive from the develop-ment of the concept of capital analysed by Marx in *Capital*, those social functions objectively necessary for reproduction which can only be performed collectively outside the sphere of individual capitals, is undoubtedly an im-portant component of a materialist theory of the state and one which on the whole has yet to be developed.[6] But such an approach can only found the objective necessity of the state and not the state itself and its concrete mode of functioning. Because of its specific level of abstraction, the mode of repre-sentation in *Capital* cannot be used without further mediation for the development of the concept of the state.

In the determination of the form of the bourgeois state as an autonomous apparatus raised above the reproduction process, its social functions are contained only abstractly and generally. At the same time, however, the character of the capitalist reproduction process also turns out to be the basis of the contradictions contained in the form itself. The function of the bourgeois state can never be more than the creation of the 'external' conditions for the social reproduction process which regulates itself on the basis of the law of value. The social process of production and reproduction cannot be the direct object of state activity; on the contrary, it is the latter which is determined by the laws and the development of the reproduction process. Thus, the state apparatus does safeguard the general rules of commodity and monetary intercourse (which is brought forth by the circulation of commodities mediating the processes of production and exploitation); but it neither creates money nor does it bring into existence the rules of bourgeois legal relations and their foundation, private property. It only codifies the norms characteristic of commodity and monetary relations (the legal protection of private property, commercial laws, the minting of coins, the issue of bank-notes). In this way it ensures the clarity, stability and the calculability of legal relations and relations of exchange and – fundamental to all these – it is able as the apparatus of force to enforce compliance with these norms against the attacks and infringements of individuals. From the capitalist reproduction process as total process of capital circulation, however, there results – at first only as possibility and as general necessity – quite a different category of state activity: the production process as labour process producing concrete use values is, under capitalist conditions, bound by the chains of private production mediated by exchange and determined by valorization. The inherent impossibility of the conscious organization by society of production based on the division of labour *gives rise* to dislocations and frictions in reproduction and to the separation of 'particular' and 'general' conditions of production, i.e. conditions of production which cannot be produced singly by individual capitals. Just as the capitalist process of reproduction initially generates the category of the 'general material conditions of production', so it produces in the bourgeois state as an apparatus removed from the process of the competitive valorization of individual capitals and equipped with specific means of force (and therefore also with material powers) the authority which is capable of creating for individual capitals the prerequisites of production ('the infrastructure') which these capitals cannot establish of their own accord because of their limited profit interest.[7] This same relationship applies to the regulatory and subsidizing intervention of the state in the circulation process as well as to state intervention which safeguards the capital reproduction process beyond the national boundaries. Finally, from the character of the capitalist process of reproduction as a process of exploitation which continually reproduces the existing class structure results the compulsion to use concealed or overt physical force against the proletariat to safeguard bourgeois rule whenever and wherever the proletariat attacks the foundations of its exploitation — foundations which are rooted in capitalist property relations and in the relations of production.

The contradictions of the capitalist process of reproduction in which the bourgeois state apparatus has its source and continuing basis, give rise to the apparent inconsistencies in its mode of appearance and activity. As the authority guaranteeing the rules of equal exchange and of commodity circulation, and autonomous from the social process of reproduction and the social classes, it acquires — a particular form of the mystification of capital — the appearance of class neutrality free from force, which however can and must be transformed into an overt use of force, both internally and externally, if at any time the foundations of the reproduction and self-expansion of capital and of exploitation are threatened. The bourgeois state's appearance of 'generality', which is determined by its form, is continually shattered by the compulsion (also based on its form) to intervene directly and with force. Freedom, equality and the rule of law therefore only represent one side of bourgeois rule, which is based in the last analysis on the direct physical use of force. Likewise, the rule of general laws (which reflect the conditions of commodity circulation) turns out to be constantly breached by executive measures which become necessary in certain situations to guarantee the general material conditions of production and reproduction and to suppress the working class. Thus the violence of the bourgeois state is always characterized by simultaneous abstract generality and concreteness specific to a situation. Safeguarding the rules which express the blind operation of economic relations of force goes hand in hand with the direct exercise of the means of force and power of the state for the specific and particular purposes of ensuring the reproduction and self-expansion of capital and the domination of the bourgeoisie.

Finally, it is implicit in the form of the 'particularization' of the bourgeois state that the state apparatus necessarily and at any time can and must clash not only with the working class or sections of it, but also with the interests of individual capitals and groups of capitals — interests determined by the requirements of valorization.

But this means that — just as the bourgeois state does not originate historically as a result of the conscious activity of a society or class in pursuit of its 'general will' but rather as the result of often contradictory and short-sighted class struggles and conflicts — its specific functional mechanisms also evolve in the context of conflicting interests and social conflicts. That is: the concrete activities and measures of the state come into being not as the result of the abstract logic of a given social structure or of an objectively given historical process of development but only under the pressure of political movements and interests which, acting on this basis, actually succeed in pressing home their demands. The state's 'particularization' has continually to re-establish itself afresh and maintain itself in this process of conflict and collision of interests. Not least of the consequences of this is the imperfection, incompleteness and inconsistency of state activity, but also at the same time the relative contingency of the political process, a contingency which cannot be derived from the general determinations of the capital relation.

To sum up: from the determination of the form of the bourgeois state the possibility and the general necessity of its general functions can be derived — the *possibility* in so far as the state as a force separated from bourgeois society is functionally in a position to guarantee the general and external conditions of reproduction which cannot be created by private capitals and to intervene with force 'against the encroachments as well of the workers as of individual capitalists' (Engels, *Anti-Dühring*, p. 382).[8] This possibility implies at the same time the impossibility of interfering with the foundations of the capitalist reproduction process, namely: private property and the availability of free wage labour. The general *necessity* of state intervention results from the fact that the capitalist process of reproduction structurally presupposes social functions which cannot be fulfilled by individual capitals. The general condition of the possibility for the state to guarantee the 'general and external conditions' of the capitalist process of production, i.e. to mediate necessity and possibility, ultimately lies in the fact that the bourgeois state as an instance raised above the direct production process can only maintain its form if the capital reproduction process is guaranteed and its own material basis thus secured. This will necessarily manifest itself as the specifically political and bureaucratic interest of the direct holders of state power and their agents in the safeguarding of capital reproduction and capital relations. This is why the bourgeois state must function as a class state even when the ruling class or a section of it does not exert direct influence over it.

Beyond these general determinations, nothing more can be said on this level of analysis about the functions of the bourgeois state.[9] To that extent, the general 'derivation of form' cannot go beyond trivialities. To go beyond this would require an analysis of the concrete historical development of the capitalist reproduction process and of the changing conditions of capital valorization and class relations. It would be wrong, however, to reduce this to a matter of crass empiricism and historiography. On the contrary, it is necessary to develop a theoretical and conceptual framework for the analysis of the process of capitalist development. In other words, an analysis of the concrete mode of appearance of the bourgeois state and its changing functions is only possible on the basis of a theory of the capitalist process of accumulation and crisis. Only such a theory can supply the categories which define how empirical history is to be written and interpreted. Like the analysis of the form of the state, such a theory must start from the dual character of labour and the consequent determination of the capitalist process of production as the contradictory unity of labour process and process of valorization. The expanded reproduction of capital involves not only the tendency for the capital relation to be universalized, the generalization of the production of exchange-values, the subsumption of ever more spheres of social production under capital and with that the determining imposition of capitalist class relations, but also the permanent transformation and technological revolutionization of the labour process and its material basis — the progressive development of the productive forces to the point where they must burst the bounds of the capital relation. The capitalist mode of production is 'a technologically and otherwise *specific mode of production — capitalist production —* which transforms the nature of the labour process and its actual conditions' (*Results of the Immediate Process of Production*, pp. 1034–5).

The compulsion to produce relative surplus-value and thereby to transform constantly the technological basis of the labour process, to create large machinery and establish fixed capital as the adequate form of capital is posited by the capital relation itself. Driven on by capital, the development of class relations and of the productive forces, of the material shape of the labour process and hence the socialization of production, fundamentally alters the political structure of bourgeois society, imposes specific, technologically determined changes in the form of individual capitals (limited companies, monopolies) and thereby alters the conditions for the operation of the law of value which is mediated through the circulation of money and commodities. This leads to a situation where 'with the increasing socialization of production it is precisely the material side which increasingly gains in significance and this necessarily (because capital with its narrow orientation towards surplus-value is indifferent to the use-value side of production) leads to disruptions in the reproduction process, which require the intervention of the state' (Läpple 1973, p. 60). The capital accumulation process and the change in the technological basis of production embodied in it gives rise continuously to material barriers to the process of valorization — barriers which cannot be overcome by privately producing capitals alone. An analysis of the capitalist accumulation process must above all explain how the capitalist production process, on the strength of its inherent laws and through the technological transformation of the labour process and the development of the productive forces, itself produces the barriers to the valorization of capital which manifest themselves through crisis, and the way in which the capitalist crisis itself becomes the necessary vehicle for the actual implementation of state interventions to safeguard reproduction.

The capitalist process of accumulation and crisis

The capitalist process of reproduction is of necessity reproduction on an expanded scale — a process of accumulation. The permanent re-conversion of surplus-value into capital is imposed on the individual capitalist as an external coercive law through competition. 'It compels him to keep constantly extending his capital, in order to preserve it, but extend it he cannot, except by means of progressive accumulation' (*Capital* vol. 1, p. 555). What decisively determines the process of accumulation and, according to Marx, constitutes the essential point of analysis, are the transformations in the composition of capital, which inevitably come about in the course of the accumulation process and with the development of the productive forces advanced through this process — that is, the transformations in the relation of objectified and living labour in the production process, the results of which culminate in the *tendency of the rate of profit to fall*. For Marx this 'law of the tendency of the rate of profit to fall' is 'in every respect the most important law of modern political economy and the most essential for understanding the most difficult relations. It is the expression of the tendency, inherent in capital itself, towards the progressive development of the productive forces' (*Grundrisse*, p. 748).

The necessity for the changes in the value composition of capital which bring about the tendency for the rate of profit to fall, *can be derived from the fundamental class contradictions of the capitalist mode of production*: 'Once given the general basis of the capitalist system, then, in the course of accumulation, a point is reached at which the development of the productivity of social labour becomes the most powerful lever of accumulation' (*Capital* vol. 1, p. 582), i.e. at which the technical transformations of the labour process and the development of the productive forces appear as the pre-condition for further accumulation. The technical revolutionization of the process of production becomes a necessary instrument in capital's conflict with wage labour mediated through the expansion and self-assertion of individual capitals in competition. 'Growth of capital involves growth of its variable constituent or of the part invested in labour-power. A part of the surplus-value turned into additional capital must always be re-transformed into variable capital or additional labour-fund. If we suppose that, all other circumstances remaining the same, the composition of capital also remains constant (i.e. that a definite mass of means of production constantly needs the same mass of labour-power to set it in motion), then the demand for labour and the subsistence-fund of the labourers clearly increase in the same proportion as the capital, and the more rapidly, the more rapidly the capital increases. Since capital produces yearly a surplus-value, of which one part is yearly added to the original capital; since this increment itself grows yearly along with the augmentation of the capital already functioning; since lastly, under special stimulus to enrichment, such as the opening of new markets, or of new spheres for the outlay of capital in consequence of newly developed social wants, etc., the scale of accumulation may be suddenly extended, merely by a change in the division of the surplus-value or surplus-product into capital and revenue, the requirements of accumulating capital may exceed the increase of labour power or of the number of labourers; the demand for labourers may exceed the supply, and, therefore, wages may rise' (*Capital* vol. 1, p. 575).[10] By the very mechanism of its own accumulation, capital is therefore forced to introduce into the production process technical changes which continually set living labour free and make it superfluous.

The mechanism of its self-valorization therefore compels capital constantly to detach itself from its basis, living human labour-power. It can only utilize the productive force of labour by developing this productive force, and this means intensification of the division of labour and the subjection of living labour-power to the system of machinery. Under developed capital relations the process of production ceases to be 'a labour process in the sense of a process dominated by labour as its governing unity. Labour appears, rather, merely as a conscious organ, scattered among the individual living workers at numerous points of the mechanical system; subsumed under the total process of the machinery itself — as itself only a link of the system, whose unity exists not in the living workers, but rather in the living (active) machinery . . .' (*Grundrisse*, p. 693). 'The development of the means of labour into machinery is not an accidental moment of capital, but is rather the historical reshaping of the traditional, inherited means of labour into a form adequate to capital. The accumulation of knowledge and of skill, of the general productive forces of the social brain, is thus absorbed into capital, as opposed to labour, and hence appears as an attribute of capital, and more specifically of *fixed capital*, in so far as it enters into the production process as a means of production proper. *Machinery* appears, then, as the most adequate form of *fixed capital*, and fixed capital, in so far as capital's relations with itself are concerned, appears as *the most adequate form of capital as such*. . . . The full development of capital, therefore, takes place — or capital has posited the mode of production corresponding to it — only when the means of labour has not only taken the economic form of *fixed capital*, but has also been suspended in its immediate form, and when *fixed capital* appears as a machine within the production process, opposite labour; and the entire production process appears as not subsumed under the direct skilfulness of the worker, but rather as the technological application of science.' (*Grundrisse*, p. 699).

With the establishment of its mode of production and the constant expansion of its sphere (the world market), capital carries through the progressive division of social labour and the enormous extension of machinery as the embodiment of the social productive forces of society confronting the individual worker. To the individual capitalist searching for additional profit in the struggle for survival, this movement appears as a continual pressure to reduce wages (which, to him, represent a deduction from the capital advanced) through rationalization, i.e. through the replacement of living labour by machinery. The very concept of capital, therefore, posits the need for thorough-going transformations of the technology of production (the different phases of the 'industrial revolution'). Because it is inherent in the capitalist form of exploitation that objectified labour stands opposed, in growing quantity and in constantly changing form, to living labour, sucks it up and again repels it, science and technology appear as the necessary supplement to capital in its struggle with labour.

The process of progressive accumulation and the associated development of the productive forces do in fact come up against a boundary line drawn by the changing composition of capital. The increasing productive force of labour means that the individual worker sets in motion ever increasing masses of the means of production and raw materials, etc.; the technical composition of capital — the relation between the mass of the means of production and labour-power $\left(\dfrac{MP}{L}\right)$ — changes. Therefore, all other things being equal, the value-composition of capital $\left(\dfrac{c}{v}\right)$ must also change — if not proportionally, at least in the same direction. Marx calls 'the value-composition of capital, in so far as it is determined by its technical composition and mirrors the changes of the latter, the *organic composition* of capital' (*Capital* vol. 1, p. 574).

Given a constant rate of surplus-value $\left(\dfrac{s}{v}\right)$ the rate of profit (which refers to total capital) $\left(\dfrac{s}{c+v}\right)$ must drop if the organic composition increases. If the rate of profit falls to a point at which the mass of profit produced is too small to enable newly produced surplus-value still to be profitably accumulated (at which point there is a relative overproduction of capital), the process of accumulation must break down. In this tendency for the rate of profit to fall lies the absolute necessity of that which is contained only as possibility in the circulation of money: the manifest crisis of capitalism.

The accumulation process of capital as a process of exploitation contains the constant feature of open or latent class struggle and must therefore be analysed basically as a social process of crisis. The open outbreak of economic crises can therefore not be looked upon as 'a deviation' from 'the normal course' of accumulation. Rather, it signifies the sharpening and manifestation of a fundamental contradiction propelled by the accumulation of capital. It can be deduced from the law of the tendency for the rate of profit to fall that this contradiction cannot remain dormant but that the latent crisis of capital must repeatedly be transformed through the disruption of the accumulation process into open crisis. Then at the latest, however, the objective sharpening of class contradictions makes itself openly felt: the ability of living labour to maintain a capital value which constantly swells as accumulation proceeds and the productive power of labour develops and thus to produce a growing mass of use values is at the same time the basis of its own permanent overproduction, of masses of workers being continually replaced and displaced, of the production of an industrial reserve army. With the growth of capital (of total capital) its variable constituent increases too, but in constantly decreasing proportion. Therefore, with the development of the capitalist mode of production, an ever greater amount of capital is required to employ the same or an increasing number of workers. In this way the reserve army, present but latent in a period of rapid accumulation, comes openly to the fore only when the accumulation process slackens and stagnates. It is thus only with the slackening or with the breakdown of the accumulation process that the contradiction of the development of the productive forces under capitalist conditions is manifested and the intensifying class antagonism comes into view. Progressive accumulation or 'steady growth' therefore constitutes a decisive and at the same time an increasingly unattainable prerequisite for the latency of class conflict.

If the 'progressive tendency of the general rate of profit to fall is, therefore, just *an expression peculiar to the capitalist mode of production* of the progressive development of the social productivity of labour' (*Capital* vol. 3, p. 213), this shows that the capitalist mode of production finds its own limits in the development of the productive forces which it itself brings about. 'The contradiction of the capitalist mode of production, however, lies precisely in its tendency towards an absolute development of the productive forces, which continually come into conflict with the specific conditions of production in which capital moves and alone can move' (*Capital* vol. 3, p. 257). 'The real barrier of capitalist production is capital itself' (*Capital* vol. 3, p. 250).

After this general presentation of capitalism's tendency towards crisis and collapse, which results from the implications of the law of value itself, there now remains the real problem of the investigation — the question why this collapse has not yet occurred, i.e. what concrete developments have modified and modify the operation of this general law.[11] This is a decisive question for the determination of the functions of the state. Therefore it is necessary to go more closely into the *character of the capitalist mechanism of crisis*.

A fundamental determination of the capitalist mechanism of crisis lies in the fact that — mediated through the actions of individual capitals in competition and through class conflicts — '. . . the same influences which produce a tendency in the general rate of profit to fall, also call forth counter-effects, which hamper, retard and partly paralyse this fall' (*Capital*, vol. 3, p. 233). The principal basis of these counter-effects is, on the one hand, the fact that growth in the productive power of labour itself cannot leave the value composition of capital and the rate of surplus-value unaffected and, on the other hand, the possibility of concentrating increasing masses of surplus-value in the industrial centres of accumulation. Marx only began to describe these 'counteracting influences' in the 14th chapter of *Capital* vol. 3 — and indeed it is not possible to do more: not the law itself but rather the 'counteracting tendencies' and their mode of operation can be determined from the concrete development of the accumulation process; they change their mode of appearance and their significance according to the phase of capitalist development.

If one starts from the basic underlying value relation — leaving aside for the moment an historical analysis deduced from the capitalist system's mechanism of crisis and class struggle — the 'counteracting influences' must be differentiated and systematized as follows.[12]

The most important counter-tendency, itself based on the technological transformations of the labour process which determine the law, results from the associated increase in the productivity of labour. This produces a tendency

for the cheapening of the elements of constant capital and an increased economy in their use, consequently curbing the rise of the organic composition.
Technological progress also provides the basis for the form of 'economizing'
in the use of constant capital resulting from an increase in the rate of turnover (the shortening of the production and circulation time resulting for
instance from the development of techniques of organization, planning and
management, or the improvement of means of communication). On the other
hand, the increase in the productivity of labour can lead to a relative cheapening of the means of consumption of the worker and thus to a fall in the value
of the commodity labour-power. Providing that labour time remains the same,
the relation between necessary labour and surplus-labour shifts in favour of
the latter: the rate of (relative) surplus-value increases and, all other things
being equal, so does the rate of profit. This means that in the accumulation
process the organic composition of capital will not change to the same extent
as the technical composition and that the rate of exploitation, based on the
production of relative surplus-value necessarily increases. The fact that the
same causes which bring about the law of the tendency for the rate of profit
to fall — the technological transformation of the labour process — also gener-
ate consequences which weaken its effect means that it is enormously difficult
to assess quantitatively, let alone predict, the extent and the speed of the
change in the rate of profit. The force with which the law actually asserts
itself also depends very much on the quality of the technical changes (referred
to in bourgeois economics as 'labour-' or 'capital-saving' innovations). It is
already clear from this that the validity of the law of the tendency for the
rate of profit to fall does not exclude a temporary increase in the average rate
of profit — which of course does not detract from its effect in the long term.

On a different level, there are those factors which influence the tempo of
technological development and thus the changes in the technical composition:
the possibility of accumulation on an unchanged technological basis and the
subsumption of social spheres of production with lower organic composition
under the *reproduction process* of capital. Both are linked to the existence of
a relative surplus population and are increasingly restricted by the progressive
subjection of the world to capitalism. In yet another context, there are those
factors which lead to the destruction and devaluation of capitals already
accumulated: by war, in a cyclical crisis or by new inventions. Finally, the
rate of profit is, of course, influenced by measures which lead to an increase
in the absolute rate of surplus-value: lengthening of labour time, intensification
of labour and the forcing down of wages below the value of labour-power.

We can thus distinguish two groups of influences, one of which is directly
based on the technological changes in the labour process, whilst the other
'counteracting influences' supervene in an external or only mediated form.
Significant for a theory of accumulation but without influence on the development of the average rate of profit are, on the other hand, all those processes
which lead to an unequal distribution of profit between capitals. Essential

here are above all the factors which lead to a concentration of profit masses in the industrial centres of accumulation. These include the reduction of the share of the non-industrial parts of the bourgeoisie in total surplus-value (decrease in ground rent, elimination of commercial profit and what Keynes called the 'euthanasia of the *rentier*'); equally, but in fact increasingly difficult to realize with the development of the crisis-ridden nature of capitalism: the decrease of unproductive groups of the population living on deductions from revenue — the liberal professions, state employees, the military. Of decisive importance in advanced capitalism are, finally, the non-equalization (or splitting) of the rates of profit resulting from the development of (international) monopolies, the formation of share capital and the taking over by the state of unprofitable spheres of production, and also the continuous transfer of value flowing through unequal exchange on the world market within the imperialist system from the dependent countries to the advanced industrial metropoles.

Such a systematization of the counteracting tendencies does not yet tell us much about their actual effect. This can be clarified only by an examination of the concrete development of the process of accumulation, the competition of individual capitals and crisis, through which the laws analysed by value theory actually assert themselves in their contradictory form. At this stage only a few general statements can be made. As the rate of accumulation cannot diminish proportionally with the fall in the rate of profit, but must, as accumulation of competing individual capitals (and on pain of an open outburst of class conflict), advance progressively with the impetus of the capital already accumulated, a crisis erupts when the amount of produced surplus-value appropriated by individual capitals is no longer sufficient to maintain the necessary rate of accumulation, and hence the existing mass of surplus-value can no longer be profitably capitalized. The 'over-accumulation of capital is always at the *endpoint* of a period of accumulation wherein the expansion of production parallels the expansion of capital. When existing conditions of exploitation [i.e. the value relation of dead and living labour, rate of surplus value, etc. — J.H.] preclude a further profitable capital expansion, crisis sets in' (Mattick 1959, p. 32). The relatively decreasing mass of surplus-value consequently appears as the over-production of capital. This means 'that accumulation has reached a point where the profits associated with it are no longer large enough to justify [for the average individual capital — J.H.] further expansion. There is no incentive to invest and because there is no new, or no substantial new investment of capital, the demand for all commodities declines' (Mattick 1959, p. 43). 'Overproduction of capital is never anything more than overproduction of means of production — of means of labour and necessities of life — which may serve as a capital, i.e. may serve to exploit labour at a given degree of exploitation; a fall in the intensity of exploitation below a certain point, however, calls forth disturbances and stoppages in the capitalist production process, crises, and destruction of capital' (*Capital* vol. 3, pp. 255–6). 'The resulting general lack of demand appears as the overproduction of commodities, and this apparent overproduction suggests the realization problem as the cause of crisis' (Mattick 1959, p. 43).[13]

Existing disproportionalities, unevenness of the economic structure and circulation problems which remain concealed in a period of smooth accumulation emerge into the open in the crisis and are violently pushed aside through the crisis. They are of course not to be grasped as the cause of the general crisis but as a reinforcing and possibly triggering element.

The *function* of the crisis does not, however, consist only in abolishing existing disproportionalities in the production mechanism. It is at the same time, and above all, a vehicle for the mobilization of the counter-tendencies to the fall in the rate of profit (for example through increased rationalization or through the intensification of imperialist exploitation). 'At any given time the actual borders of capital expansion are determined by general social conditions, which include the level of technology, the size of the already accumulated capital, the availability of wage-labour, the possible degree of exploitation, the extent of the market, political relations, recognized natural resources, and so forth. It is not the market alone but the whole social situation in all its ramifications which allows for, or sets limits to, the accumulation of capital' (Mattick 1969, p. 74).[14]

Since these general social conditions of production do not automatically adapt to capital accumulation, the crisis breaks out into the open when the process of accumulation comes up against their limits. In the crisis these limits are in fact re-defined and the general conditions of production are reorganized. The necessity to reorganize fundamentally the conditions of production and the relations of exploitation whenever they no longer correspond to the level of accumulation attained, but also their relative rigidity and independence from the direct process of production at each level reached, explain among other things the periodic nature of the crises. The various cycles of the crisis appear as an imitation in miniature of the long-term trend of capital accumulation as 'an interrupted tendency to collapse'.[15] Thus, it is clear that the 'counter-tendencies' to the fall in the rate of profit should not be understood as the sum of isolated factors but are rather the expression of a *social complex of conditions of production*, and assert themselves in an increasingly crisis-ridden manner and in any case not merely in the normal course of the accumulation process and in the expanded reproduction of capital relations by capital itself. The mobilization of counter-tendencies means in practice the reorganization of an historical complex of general social conditions of production and relations of exploitation in a process which can proceed only in a crisis-ridden manner.[16] Thus the real course of the necessarily crisis-ridden process of accumulation and development of capitalist society decisively depends on whether and in what manner the necessary reorganization of the conditions of production and relations of exploitation succeeds. This is essentially affected by the actions of the competing individual capitals and by the outcome of class conflict on an international scale. Therefore the course of capitalist development is not determined mechanically or by some kind of law of nature. Within the framework of its general laws, capitalist development is determined rather by the actions of the acting subjects and classes, the resulting concrete conditions of crisis and their political consequences.[17]

It is now possible to say something about the logical character of the law of the tendency for the rate of profit to fall and its relation to empirical reality. The law denotes the objective reference point (grasped in value categories) of capital strategies and class conflicts, which can appear on the 'surface of society' and in the consciousness of the production agents only in mediated and inverted form and the results of which do not leave any *direct* imprint on the level of empirical measurements (composition of capital, wage ratio, profits).[18] In so far as capital in its struggle for rate and mass of profit is forced to mobilize 'counteracting forces' in the form of increased exploitation, so as to be able to continue to exist, the law of the tendency for the rate of profit to fall denotes the objective basis of actual class struggles.[19] Only the formulation of the value-theoretical context comprised in the law allows one to define the actions of fighting classes as strategies so long as their social context remains hidden (or partially hidden) from the actors acting under the domination of the law of value. It depends on the success of these strategies and on the result of the struggles whether the tendency of the rate of profit to fall becomes empirically visible or not. The same laws (the existence of which can remain hidden for long periods by the effectiveness of 'counter-tendencies') manifest themselves with the development of an open crisis.[20] The law of the tendency for the rate of profit to fall expresses the objective framework of reference within which class conflicts take their historical course; the 'counteracting influences' denote the results and conditions of these conflicts, which assume the form of complex social relations. In other words: the law of the tendency for the rate of profit to fall cannot by itself explain the empirical course of development of capitalist societies; the former is the formulation of the latter's contradictory motive forces which manifest themselves — always modified by a great variety of empirical conditions and historical peculiarities — and are expressed in class struggles, capital strategies and in the course taken by crises.

The historical process of development of capitalist society is therefore to be understood as the progressive development of the productive forces advanced by the accumulation of capital — a development which continually comes into conflict with the narrow basis of capitalist relations of production (cf. *Capital* vol. 3, p. 241). This contradiction manifests itself in a fundamental tendency towards crisis and collapse — which can only be counterbalanced by the permanent reorganization through crisis of social conditions of production and relations of exploitation. The barriers set by capital in the course of its self-valorization through the necessary transformation of the technological basis of the labour process, the development of the productive forces and socialization, can only be temporarily broken through by the reorganization (through crisis and mediated by political and economic struggles) of complex social relations and conditions of production. The historical concretization of state functions is essentially to be determined from the context of crises so defined and from the political movement to which the crisis gives rise. What 'the guarantee of the general and external conditions of the process of production' means in concrete terms essentially depends on the crisis-ridden course of the reproduction process; it is achieved politically by means of the political actions of social groups and classes, actions which proceed from the changes in class relations and the relations of exploitation.

Before we go on to derive the way in which the state apparatus functions from the context of the reproduction and crisis of the capitalist system it is important to have a more precise understanding of the concept of the 're-organization of the conditions of production'. It is a question of analytically distinct (if also closely related) changes in the whole economic basis, the implementation of which can be objectively determined as a strategy of capital for the organization of complex 'counter-effects'. The historically determining features are above all: first the changes in the form of capital itself — monopolies, the transformation of property relations and relations of control (joint stock companies), the extension of the credit system; second *the expansion of capital on the world market*, the export of capital and the formation of an imperialist world system; third the forced development of the productive forces and the *acceleration of scientific-technical progress*.

1. The cyclical course of the capitalist process of accumulation is coupled with a progressive concentration and centralization of capital. Some capitals are destroyed and disappear in the crisis, others lose their independence and are absorbed by larger capitals (cf. *Capital* vol. 1, p. 585). This process is itself an essential element in the periodical reorganization of the general conditions of valorization, in so far as it reduces the total value of capital and eliminates less productive individual capitals. The tendency towards monopoly is not simply a mere consequence of the crisis but is at the same time one of its essential functions as the mechanism for reorganizing the structure of capital. This is true especially in so far as with the progressive development of the productive forces, increasingly only the larger individual capitals are still in a position to implement the technical changes in the production process necessary for reproduction (for instance the transition to mechanized and automated mass-production) and their economic pre-conditions (for example the control of large markets and the extension of comprehensive sales organizations).[21] Decisive prerequisites and levers of a progressive centralization of capital are the extension of the *credit system* and the formation of joint stock companies (cf. *Capital* vol. 1, p. 588; vol. 3, pp. 435–6). As '. . . the abolition of capital as private property within the framework of capitalist production itself' (*Capital* vol. 3, p. 427), and as '. . . control . . . over the capital and property of others, and thereby over the labour of others' (*Capital* vol. 3,

p. 429), they allow the productive forces to develop beyond the limit set by the direct private ownership of the means of production. Given the objectively increasing socialization of production, they create an area in which capital can act as social capital within the private capitalist relations of production. Augmentation of the productivity of labour leading to a cheapening of the elements of constant capital and an increase in relative surplus-value, rationalization in the use of the means of production and raw materials as well as the augmentation of the rate of turnover of capital are, with the progressive development of the productive forces, increasingly dependent on the emergence of powerful individual capitals based on the joint stock company and the credit system, and on the consequent concentration of enormous masses of value and surplus-value under one direction. This effect is strengthened by the centralization of surplus-value as a result of the abolition of the free competitive market. Monopolistic market structures enable the monopolies and cartels to sell their products above the price of production and thus to an increasing extent internationally — they are able to increase their rate of profit to the disadvantage of other capitals. But if progressive monopolization thus appears as a *condition* for the maintenance of capitalist accumulation in the decisive centres of the development of the productive forces, at the same time the permanent non-equalization of the rate of profit associated with it and the partial failure of the mechanism of market regulation intensify the *contradictions*, which express themselves in the disturbance of the balanced process of reproduction of the whole system on the basis of the law of value and in the permanent expansion of structural disproportionalities, and the crisis-ridden effect of which is augmented by the extension of the 'credit superstructure' (cf. *Capital*, vol. 3, p. 441).

2. Because the ultimate cause of the capitalist crisis mechanism lies in the contradiction between the progressive development of the productive forces and the narrow basis of the relations of production, there is an absolute tendency for capital constantly to extend the market and the external field of production, and to create a world market.[22] The slackening of production on a given basis of production must be overcome by incorporating ever new spheres and peoples into the capitalist mode of production (i.e. the possibility of accumulation on an unchanged technological basis) or by creating relative surplus-value — which again is necessarily linked to the expansion of the division of labour, the awakening of new needs and the development of new branches of production internationally. 'On the other side, the production of relative surplus-value, i.e. production of surplus value based on the increase and development of the productive forces, requires the production of new consumption; requires that the consuming circle within circulation expands as did the productive circle previously. First quantitive expansion of existing consumption; second: creation of new needs by propagating existing ones in a wide circle; third: production of *new* needs and discovery and the creation of new use values. . . . Hence the exploration of all of nature in order

to discover new, useful quantities in things; universal exchange of the products of all alien climates and lands; new (artificial) preparation of natural objects, by which they are given new use values' (*Grundrisse*, pp. 408–9). In other words, as accumulation progresses there are clearly defined limits to the successful reorganization of the conditions of valorization in a restricted national framework. The tendency for the rate of profit to fall must lead to the extension of the sphere of capital beyond national boundaries. The progressive extension of the market and the export of capital are therefore the direct results of falling rates of profit and of a relatively too small mass of surplus-value. 'Capitalism is in crisis not because of an abundance of surplus-value but because it cannot raise the surplus-value short of reorganizing the world capital structure' (Mattick 1959, p. 48).[23] The progressive capitalization of the world and the creation of the world market as the product and pre-condition for the reorganization of the conditions of production mean at the same time the intensification of competition, increasing pressure towards monopolization, the generalization of crises and the increased aggressiveness of advanced capitalist countries in the struggle for control of areas of cheap raw-material production markets and spheres of investment.[24] If, on the one hand, the capitalization of the world is an absolute necessity for the permanent reorganization of the conditions of production, the increase in the productive power of labour and the (absolute or relative) increase of surplus value, at the same time its incomplete achievement and the resulting unevenness in worldwide economic development are the foundation of a permanent and one-sided transfer of masses of value between the developed countries themselves but mainly from the backward countries to the imperialist metropoles. This 'unequal exchange' is intensified by the existence of international monopolies and cartels (for example cartels which purchase raw materials). It is based on the coexistence of differences in the organic composition of capital and the productivity of labour with the international equalization of the rate of profit so that the less developed country gives 'more objectified labour in kind than it receives', the more developed country taking back 'more labour in exchange for less labour' than the undeveloped.[25] If therefore the losses and profits of the exchange of goods offset one another within a country, this is not necessarily the case in foreign trade. 'Here the law of value undergoes essential modification' (*TSV* vol. 3, p. 105). The permanent transfers of value to the industrial capitalist metropolitan countries (which appear in the trade figures as a 'worsening' of the 'terms of trade' for the backward countries) are furthered by the differences in the value of labour power, by the possibility in undeveloped countries of depressing wages below this value and thereby physically wrecking the labour force in order finally to transfer steadily the extra profits made in this way by capital invested there to the capitalist centres. As economic development in the advanced capitalist countries becomes increasingly crisis-ridden, the exploitation of the dependent countries (which mostly produce raw materials or primary products) on the basis of unequal exchange, and the imperialist concentration and centralization of masses of surplus-value become a decisive condition for the successful compensation of the general tendency towards crisis and collapse, and for the maintenance of the process of accumulation in the centres. In contradiction to the tendency for a progressive capitalization of the world and a generalization of the capital relation, a development towards a continuous augmentation of existing differences in development and economic imbalances emerges. In accordance with the logic and laws of the process of accumulation, the concentration of the metropoles on technically advanced production is given greater impulsion precisely by the transfer of value from the dependent countries. The result is that an extraordinary intensification of the imperialist 'division of labour', which at the same time increases the real economic dependence of the metropoles on the less developed countries: certain raw materials, textiles, foodstuffs and primitive finished products *can* be obtained only from these countries if the rate of profit is not to fall more sharply. Thus the metropolitan countries are compelled on pain of ruin to accelerate the development of production technology and at the same time to control effectively these countries and their relations of exchange. Developed imperialism differs from the older colonialism essentially in that the imperialist countries are no longer primarily concerned with the organization of direct pillage but rather with safeguarding existing spheres of investment, sources of raw material and above all unequal exchange relations. With the advance of the accumulation process and the results of the reorganization of the conditions of production *in* the metropoles, there emerges an increased dependence of the metropoles in general on the Third World and consequently a latent generalization of class struggle.

3. The tendency towards the progressive development of science and technology posited by the concept of capital is therefore imposed — on the individual capitals — with increasing pressure as the imperialist world market expands and the competition on the world market intensifies (cf. *Grundrisse*, pp. 540–2). The reorganization of the structure of capital by the progressive revolutionization of production and the multiplication of use values on the basis of the systematic application of science only asserts itself in an historically determining manner with the complete establishment of the world market and the associated universalization of the mechanism of capitalist crisis. As a means of achieving the technological reorganization of the labour process, the intensification of exploitation through the augmentation of relative surplus value and the imperialist exploitation of dependent countries, the development of science and technology represents an increasingly important counteracting influence to the tendency towards crisis and collapse in the developed capitalist countries. In detail the cheapening of the element of constant capital, the reduction in the value of the commodity labour-power and the relative increase in surplus labour time, the acceleration in the rate of turnover of capital, the intensification of labour and the imperialist system of the

concentration and centralization of surplus-value in the metropoles constitute the complex of 'counter-tendencies' directly associated with the development of science and technology. The acceleration of scientific and technological progress forced by developed capitalism's tendency to crisis signifies an increase in the pace of the development of the productive forces and rapidly advances the socialization of production. The result of this is that the external, material conditions of production and reproduction which have to be produced by the state acquire increasing significance for the maintenance of the accumulation process.

With the progress of science and technology, however, the immanent contradictions of the capitalist development of the productive forces are also intensified. First, there is a contradiction in the peculiar character of scientific findings, which once produced can in principle be applied at will and do not wear out, i.e. they give rise to no reproduction costs and therefore in the strict sense they are not commodities and do not possess value (cf. *Capital* vol. 1, p. 104). This means that definite limits are set to the production of scientific results on the basis of capitalist commodity production. These limits show themselves concretely in the fact that individual capitals are increasingly unable to produce and to realize (from the point of view of production technique) the mass of scientific and technological knowledge necessary to stabilize the system as a whole, and indeed are the less able to do so the greater the required mass becomes and the less it is possible to fall back on knowledge gained outside capitalist commodity production as a 'free productive force' (cf. *Capital* vol. 1, pp. 365, 569; *Grundrisse*, pp. 699, 765). Second, the tendency towards the destruction of the natural basis of production and the natural foundations of civilization, which had been at the disposal of capital in earlier phases of its development (likewise) as 'free productive force', grows stronger with the progressive revolutionization of production techniques. Thus the advance of the process of accumulation gives rise to a growing number of negative 'external effects' which are not neutralized by the self-reproduction process of capital. Capital not only inadequately produces its general material conditions of production but it also continuously destroys them ('destruction of the environment'). This is the way, third, in which the fundamental contradiction of the capitalist development of the productive forces concretizes itself. Form and content of this development depend on the conditions of the increasingly difficult and to ever greater extent monopolistic valorization of capital: science becomes the power of capital, an alien power confronting the worker, an instrument of exploitation and class struggle (cf. *Grundrisse*, p. 694; *Capital* vol. 1, pp. 410 f., 597 ff.). The discrepancy between the monopolistically determined form of the development of productive forces, social needs and the reproduction requirements of the system as a whole must therefore steadily increase with the progress of the process of accumulation. Fourth and finally: apart from this, a limit is set to the effect of the technical progress as a counter-tendency to the fall in the rate of profit by the fact that an increase in the productive power of labour cannot raise relative surplus-value in the same proportion. 'Thus the more developed already capital is, the more surplus labour it has created, the more terribly must it develop the productive force in order to realize itself in only smaller proportion, i.e. to add surplus value' (*Grundrisse*, p. 340). Magnified by the restrictions which are imposed on the progress of science and technology on the basis of the competition of individual capitals, technical progress loses its power as a stabilizing counter-effect with the progressive development of the productive forces and the further capitalization of the world. The application of science to production which becomes, as the capitalist process of accumulation and crisis advances, the historically determinant form in which the counter-tendencies to the fall in the rate of profit are realized, magnifies at the same time the inherent contradictions of this mode of production and progressively creates its absolute barrier.

The historical development of state functions

Following what has been said so far, the investigation of the state must proceed from the analysis of the operation of the law of value in its pure form, without disturbing accessory circumstances and historical peculiarities. But, following the method of ascending from the abstract to the concrete, this approach has to be developed further to extend to the forms which 'the various forms of capital . . . assume on the surface of society, in the action of different capitals upon one another, in competition, and in the ordinary consciousness of the agents of production themselves' (*Capital* vol. 3, p. 25). Only the systematic derivation of these movements on the 'surface' (changes in the form of capital (monopoly) the establishment or non-establishment of an average rate of profit, the movement of prices, class differentiations, the existence of only partly capitalist countries, movements of the world market and so on) from the 'central structure' of the capital relation, allows us to analyse concretely the functions and the modes of functioning of the state apparatus. The logical and at the same time historical concretization of the movements of capital and the way in which they shape class struggles and competition must thus be the starting point for any investigation of political processes if it is not to relapse into the failing of mechanical economic determinism or abstract generalization.[26] In the third volume of *Capital* Marx himself began to carry the analysis further from the level of 'capital in general' to the 'concrete forms of capital', even if he did not pursue this to the end (cf. Rosdolsky 1968, pp. 24 ff.). At any rate, it seems to us that the necessary logical connection between the investigation of 'capital in general' and the movements which appear on the surface of society, the conscious actions of social subjects and thus of political processes, is to be seen in the analysis of the 'law of the tendency of the rate of profit to fall' in the third volume of *Capital*.[27]

In historical perspective it can be seen that the state apparatus, which was of decisive importance (at least under feudal absolutist conditions) as midwife and support in the emergence of capitalist society, was 'pushed back' in the period of the accomplishment and full development of capital, tendentially (though by no means absolutely) being reduced to the function of guaranteeing capital relations and the general external conditions of production; and finally, as the contradictions of capitalist production have sharpened, it has acquired an ever more determining significance as apparatus of force at home and abroad and as 'economic' power (i.e. directly involved in the process of reproduction). From this point of view it can be seen that the liberal phase of bourgeois society with its comparatively — though this varies from country to country — weakly developed state bureaucracy and relatively well-functioning parliament was no more than an episode (which, moreover, because of particular historical conditions, was hardly of formative significance in Germany).

The development towards the modern interventionist state is to be understood as the development of a form peculiar to the capitalist system within which the contradiction between the growing socialization of production and private appropriation can temporarily move.[28] Therefore, the investigation of state functions must be based on the categorical analysis of the historical course of the process of capitalist reproduction and accumulation; it must be borne in mind, however, that this is not a question of the logical deduction of abstract laws but of the conceptually informed understanding of an historical process, in which the objective tendencies determined by the law of value and the capital relation assert themselves through the mediation of concrete political movements and processes, class struggles and conflicts between individual capitals and groups of capitals on a national and on an international level. The theoretical investigation of the state cannot be limited to the conceptual development of the law of value and the analysis of 'capital in general' but must embrace the whole of the social, political and national conditions of the production of the social formation, conditions which are subject to certain historical processes of transformation.[29]

This means that the attempt to systematize concrete functions of the state cannot proceed abstractly from the apparently objective logic of economic structures or developmental processes but must focus on the development of class relations and class struggles mediated by the transformations in the economic base, and the resulting conditions for securing the political domination of the bourgeoisie. The concrete content of the functions potentially falling to the bourgeois state apparatus on the basis of its specific social form determination is essentially determined according to the conditions (which are changed by the development of the social basis of capitalism) for the maintenance of the capitalist form of exploitation and the securing of bourgeois domination. The contradictory character of the capital relation has never allowed the protection of bourgeois domination to rest merely on the state guarantee of the circulation of commodities (which mediates the process of exploitation and its foundations) — the guarantee of private property and of the adherence to the rules of exchange, the enforcement of uniform, formal rules of competition, etc. Instead, it has always required concrete interventions by the state apparatus in the material pre-conditions of the production process and the conflicts between classes to keep the process of economic reproduction in motion and the class struggle latent. However, the nature of these interventions necessarily changes as the economic and social basis is modified by the process of the accumulation of capital, the technological revolutionization of the labour process and the course of capitalist crises. In this general process, there are three moments, resulting from the process of capitalist accumulation and crisis, which are of importance for the development of the state's functions: *the imposition of the capitalist class structure,* determined by the extension and universalization of the capital relation and thus the strengthening of the proletariat as a class, but also at the same time the immediate material dependence of what is now the overwhelming majority of the population on the course of the process of accumulation; *the centralization and monopolization of capital with the formation of the imperialist world market,* driven forward by the course of capitalist crises and the technological transformation of the labour process; and finally of the *growing significance of technological revolutionizations of the labour process and process of circulation* as a basis for introducing 'counter-tendencies' to the falling rate of profit and as a cause of increasing state interventions to establish and secure the 'general' material conditions for the process of production and reproduction of capital.

It seems to us that this is the frame of reference within which the development of the concrete activities of the state must be interpreted. However, a strict 'derivation' of the functions of the state is still not possible in an investigation which remains at the analytical level of 'capital in general'. At this stage, only the objective material foundations of the concrete development of the activities of the state can be indicated, without claiming thereby to define these activities as 'necessary' in their particular historical form. A derivation of state functions which aims to avoid the mistake of taking, without more ado, empirical history to be an objective necessity, for which there could have been no alternatives, needs to be supplemented by a conceptually informed analysis of the movements of competition and of the development of class struggles — since concrete state functions come into being only through the mediation of competition and class struggle. In itself the derivation of objective determinants of the functions of the state apparatus from the laws of the reproduction of capital tells us nothing decisive about whether and in what form certain state activities result from those determinants. In addition we need to know how the objective determinants are transformed into concrete actions of competition and class struggle. Therefore an analysis at the present level of abstraction has also only very limited prognostic value. For a strict 'derivation' of the functions of the state from the movements of the class struggle and competition, we would need however an adequate theory of these processes on the 'surface' of society: a theory which we do not yet have. We shall content ourselves, therefore, with a presentation of the empirical complexes of functions which result from the laws of the process of social reproduction, and which can be determined as being 'objectively necessary' in their character and their general structure, but not, however, in their concrete form of appearance.

1. The increasing political and economic strength of the working class, which grows with the progressive extension of the capital relation, is the essential foundation for the extension of 'welfare state' intervention. The introduction of measures of social security (protection of employment, accident, illness and old age insurance, social assistance, etc.) is indeed a direct consequence of changes in the labour process (increasing physical and mental exhaustion of labour power) and the dissolution of traditional forms for reproducing and maintaining labour power (semi-agrarian family structures and modes of production, private charity). Likewise, with the increasing application of technology to production and the growth of fixed capital, it becomes increasingly important for capital that the state as general social instance 'in its fractional parts undertakes for Mr Capitalist the business of keeping his virtual instrument of labour . . . intact as reserve for later use' (*Grundrisse*, pp. 609—10) (unemployment benefit, industrial retraining, etc.). Nevertheless these elements of a welfare state — even if they are in the objective interest of capital and although they are essentially forms for redistributing income within the working class in the framework of state control of part of the wages fund — have to be fought for by the working class and their organizations against the resistance of the bourgeoisie. Historically, the gradual and partial successes of the working class in safeguarding and improving their conditions of labour and reproduction with the help of the state apparatus and within the framework of bourgeois society have shown themselves to be at the same time an essential moment in social pacification and in keeping class struggles latent. However, the possibility of safeguarding the political domination of the bourgeoisie by means of 'welfare state' concessions to the working class depends on the undisturbed progress of capital accumulation. A decline in the rate of profit and a slackening of accumulation narrow firstly and decisively the material basis of the 'welfare state' and lead increasingly — this is illustrated in exemplary fashion by German fascism in the 1930s — to the use of open violence as a means of waging class conflict. With the increasingly thorough structuring of society by capital, the 'undisturbed' accumulation of capital or 'continuous economic growth' comes to be the precondition — in the long run impossible to satisfy — for the relative latency

of the terrorist use of force and for the maintenance of the peaceful, civilized, formally legal and democratic form of appearance of bourgeois rule.

2. Thus — not least because of the 'competition between the systems' (i.e. with the socialist countries which have come into being since the Russian October revolution) and its effects on the internal political situation of the capitalist states — the 'normal course of accumulation' has become an important condition for safeguarding the parliamentary-democratic form of bourgeois rule, based as it is on welfare state and reform ideologies. But precisely this normal course of accumulation is increasingly endangered (through crisis) by the disruptions and tendencies to stagnation resulting from the tendency of the rate of profit to fall, and by the frictions and disturbances of the reproduction process which are associated with the progressive monopolization of capital.[30] It is essentially the crises of reproduction — growing more intense with the advance of the process of accumulation and the concomitant technological transformation of the labour process — which give rise to modern state interventionism in this political context. The origin and extension of interventionist regulation functions can therefore not simply be explained by the objective logic of the development of the accumulation process, they must be understood in relation to the changing conditions for safeguarding bourgeois rule, conditions which change with the historical development of capitalism and its class structure. With the increasing monopolization of capital, the 'general conditions of production' to be established by the state become more and more the particular conditions of production of monopolies and groups of monopolies, thus bringing more sharply to the fore the fundamentally contradictory character of the 'particularization' of the state *vis-à-vis* capital.

Under the conditions of an intensifying monopolistic and imperialist competition on the world market, a change is undergone by those state *functions which relate to guaranteeing the interests of the bourgeoisie 'against the outside world'*. The external protection of a network of reproduction taking place within 'national' bounds is no longer limited to the classical alternative (depending on relative economic development) of free trade or protection and the military conquest and domination of colonial spheres of influence. Rather, with the growing universalization of the capital relation, the resulting imperialist structure of the world market and increasing international centralization of capital, the state becomes the direct instrument and object of the monopolistic competitive struggle (cf. Hilferding 1968; Lenin, *Imperialism*). There results not only a heterogeneous collection of activities of the state apparatus in foreign policy and commerce, but at the same time the development of competition on the world market proves to be the decisive determinant of economic regulatory measures altogether. Externally, 'political power [becomes] decisive in the competitive economic struggle, and for finance capital, the power position of the state becomes a direct profit interest' (Hilferding 1968, p. 450) — but of course it must be borne in mind that 'finance capital' is itself not a homogeneous group and that the interests of the monopolies (determined by competition) must come into constant conflict with the necessary requirements for the reproduction of capital as a whole. The consequences are manifold and often mutually contradictory foreign economic policies which show a regional and sectoral bias; the continuing and possibly growing relevance of military force in securing vital and profitable sources of raw materials, exchange relations and spheres of investment; and a contradictory policy of integration which shows particularly clearly that the state apparatus, in a thoroughly ambivalent manner not only 'modifies'[31] but at the same time also 'executes' the law of value, and indeed is compelled, when the accumulation of capital has reached an advanced stage, to pursue by all methods the extension of the spheres of circulation and investment and the securing of cheap sources of raw materials, in order to safeguard the rate of profit.[32]

A decisive aspect of the reproduction of capital under monopoly conditions is that the *law of value* as a mechanism for regulating the distribution of social labour and imposing the proportionality of the various spheres of production operates — without being transcended — in a very much more frictional and contradictory manner than under the conditions of competitive capitalism.[33] In this process, the state apparatus has the contradictory function of supporting (or at least not hindering) the monopolistic centralization of surplus value necessary for the maintenance of the accumulation process whilst at the same time maintaining the equilibrium disturbed precisely by this centralization by means of direct or indirect interventions in the process of circulation and valorization. In this way state intervention becomes a moment in the operation of the law of value. The equalization of the rates of profit, checked by monopolization and disproportionate technical development on both a national and a world-market level, compels the state apparatus to intervene with subsidies in favour of individual capitals by influencing the conditions of valorization by means of duties, currency or taxation, or via direct redistribution of revenue. Since the increase in fixed capital has a tendency to make it more difficult for capital to apply itself flexibly to the investment spheres with the highest profit rate, there arises a growing pressure for state 'aids to adaptation' right down to the nationalization or quasi-nationalization of unprofitable production.

As the development of the productive forces progresses, the maintenance of the process of accumulation demands, on the one hand, forms and individual capitals of an order of magnitude which capital, to some extent, is no longer able to bring forth itself directly in its reproduction process, and which can therefore be realized only through the intervention of the state apparatus. On the other hand, this very process creates the necessity for 'counteracting' state interventions to guarantee a relative equilibrium in the process of reproduction as a whole. State promotion of the formation of monopolies, 'the favouring of concentration' and 'the mobilization of capital'[34] in favour of large capitals are the counterpart of measures for redistributing revenue, which aim to make partial compensation for the monopolistic non-equalization of profit rates. Thus the redistribution of revenue, mediated by the state, directly supports the accumulation of capital in the expanding 'growth industries', but at the same time is used to subsidize the growing number of structurally and sectorally backward areas (mining, agriculture, crafts, etc.) — not least to retain the loyalty of the bourgeois middle classes employed in them. Both lead to the consolidation of an extensive state or state-controlled finance and credit apparatus, which in its turn has as its precondition a largely centralized banking system and the foundation of large-scale 'capital depots' (insurance or investment funds). The particular significance of the state apparatus is that as an authority raised above individual capitals and at the same time vested with the coercive power to collect taxes and create deficit credit it is in a position to undertake financial measures stabilizing the system or favouring powerful groups of capitals even against the resistance of individual capitals and independently of the immediate conditions of their valorization process. Here it must be noted that the growing centralization and redistribution of revenue is not only reflected in state expenditure but similarly realized by means of differential taxation and inflationary deficit credit financing.

These structurally determined interventions by the state in the process of capital valorization are overlaid by controlling and regulatory functions in connection with the cyclical movement of the reproduction process. With the growth of monopolization, technological change in the process of production, the increase of fixed capital and the partial suspension of the regulating mechanism of the market, there is a direct possibility that, if the conjunctural cycle is left to itself, a general crisis of overproduction will occur on a scale which would endanger the system. Since the world economic crisis of 1929 at the latest, this has led to a strengthening and extension of the state's instruments for regulating the sphere of circulation. The objective demand, arising from the development of the productive forces, for the social planning and direction of production, thus receives as its response in capitalist conditions specific forms of 'global management of the economy', which on the whole are applied as attempts at a contradictory coordination of complex system variables in the sphere of circulation. By 'global management' is meant all measures which by way of cyclical equalization of the general conditions of valorization aim to mitigate the conjunctural cycle (monetary and fiscal conjunctural policies with the aim of a relative dissociation of private investments and mass consumption, state guarantees against risk, export subsidies, etc.). In addition, it is necessary on the one hand to perfect the state's 'range of instruments' for implementing conjunctural policies (instruments for regulating the credit system, adapting budgetary law and technique to the requirements of economic management, etc.); on the other hand, it requires the setting up of an apparatus for economic analysis and forecasting as an 'early warning system' (institutes for research into economic cycles, councils of experts).

Since even perfect analyses and prognoses can only confirm the fundamentally crisis-ridden character of the economic process and this cannot be abolished by manipulating the sphere of circulation, further concrete interventions in the conditions of capital valorization are imperative.[35] '*State incomes policy*' and the *extension of 'state consumption'* are of decisive significance in this respect.

A central aspect of the conjunctural and structural regulatory activity of the state is to be seen in the fact that it essentially means redistribution of revenue in favour of capital or individual groups of capitals and thus has an immediate influence on the development of income structures. There is, however, something to be said for the view that the success of a policy of cyclical regulation and the application of the instruments of money and credit policy essentially depends on whether the government succeeds in exerting pressure on the development of wages. State *incomes policy* is not least a consequence of the fact that the progressive monopolization and organization of capital is opposed by a collectively organized working class: by the construction of strong and comprehensive trade union apparatuses the 'conditions of competition' of wage labour are intrinsically tendentially improved. The relative inflexibility of wage rates, guaranteed by collective bargains with respect to the cyclical fluctuations of the accumulation process and the relatively limited possibilities in a strongly integrated world market of compensating for the cyclical fluctuations in profit by inflationary price increases, leads to a constant increase in the strength of the state's influence on wage negotiations. In reality, as practised for instance in the Federal Republic of Germany in the context of the 'concerted action' and with the more or less official provision of 'wage guidelines' (leaving aside slogans such as 'stability', 'social symmetry' and similar terms serving as a propagandistic smokescreen), the aim of 'incomes policy' is, with the cooperation of integrated trade union apparatuses, to prevent the wage earners from realizing their cyclical opportunities on the market, in order gradually to lower the rate of increase of real wages, if not to bring about real cuts in wages.[36] Recent experience has shown that what is at issue is not the 'stabilization of planning data', i.e. the long-term calculability of wage movements for the employer (as the Council of Experts still maintained recently), but a direct increase in profits at the expense of the wage earners. This explains the prominent position which 'incomes policy' has in the meantime attained in the range of instruments of conjunctural policy.[37]

First, therefore, state conjunctural policy means administrative (and administratively supported) influence on the movement of wages, with the aim of relatively or absolutely reducing the real income of the masses. The 'instruments' used stretch from concerned explanations and moral appeals, through the resort to appropriate 'expertise', open threats (with the loss of jobs or increased taxation as a punishment) to the formal abolition of collective bargaining (wage freeze) (not as yet directly practised in the Federal Republic). The 'welfare state' alternative to the cyclical creation of a reserve army depressing wages is the pressure, created with the decisive help of the state apparatus, on workers to forego wage claims 'of their own free will' — the result being a continual relative or absolute deterioration in their material condition.

The second essential element in state regulation of the course of the conjuncture is the 'anti-cyclical' character of state expenditure. Apart from incomes policy, the expansion or restriction of state or state-financed purchases of commodities represents — at least in theory — an important means of countering a declining 'inclination to invest', i.e. decreasing profit expectations on the part of capitalists, to whom the tendency for the rate of profit to fall must inevitably appear as a problem of realization, i.e. as a shortfall in demand. Although meanwhile state fiscal policy (in the form of planned 'deficit spending', anti-cyclical finance planning and 'contingency budgets') has been declared to be the real focal point of economic 'global management', its actual effectiveness is still unclear. Since the state apparatus, if it wishes to raise the profits of private capitals, cannot appear as their competitor (by buying up and distributing mass consumption goods, for example), there remain as the object of state demand essentially only the so-called 'infrastructure investments' and the purchase of non-reproductive goods, i.e. the administratively mediated destruction of values by armaments and similar production. Both have at least this in common — they are hardly subject to cyclical (i.e. short term) variation and are therefore of only limited value for the intended goal.[38] The only certain point is that a permanently increasing state expenditure fund for subsidies, 'the mobilization of capital' and the purchase of commodities, with revenue as its source of finance, is, in an extremely regressive system of taxation (i.e. one which imposes relatively heavier taxes on the lower income classes), a central element of an increasingly unequal distribution of incomes and of a tendency towards a relative deterioration in the living conditions of the working class.[39] The growing compulsion (with the increase in monopolization) to regulate cyclically and 'balance' structurally the reproduction process of capital by means of state intervention has the basic effect — whether it be achieved through a successful 'incomes policy' or through the various forms of state redistribution of revenue to the benefit of capital — of lowering the real income of the working class, and increasingly so as growing frictions in the process of reproduction necessarily increase the scope of state intervention.

Thus, the mechanism of state interventionist regulation of the reproduction of capital (in the sense of securing bourgeois domination) proves to be thoroughly contradictory: not only because state structural policy and 'global management' do not do away with the laws of the capitalist reproduction process and therefore cannot attain their ends at all fully, but also because they bear in themselves the moment of an intensification of social conflicts.[40] The expanding system of state redistribution of revenue for the purpose of guaranteeing and equalizing profits on capital, but also for the purpose of

pacifying the wage labourers by means of welfare-state measures, generates in
its turn the opposition of disfavoured capitals and hence conflicts between
capitals (for instance, monopolies versus non-monopolized capitals) and between monopolies (e.g. 'old' versus 'new' monopoly industries); and at the
same time capital as a whole puts up a permanent resistance to an expansion
of the state's 'share' in the social product (and of course especially of the so-
called 'social budget') because this must tend to restrict the margins for private
accumulation. In this way, the principal consequence of the state's regulation
of the reproduction process and of the compulsion imposed upon the state
apparatus to expand its funds for subsidy and regulation, is that the contradictions of the process of capitalist reproduction reproduce themselves in
intensified form on the political level in conflicts over tax rates and tax quotas
and over the extent or allocation of state expenditure — with the struggle of
the working class to maintain and improve the material conditions of its
reproduction being of necessity increasingly directed against the state. These
conflicts must increase all the more as the process of capital accumulation
slows down and comes to a standstill. Consequently, the state's guarantee of
the general conditions of the reproduction of capital cannot be confined
either to the protection of the general rules of the circulation of commodities
or to international strategies of competition and expansion, or to global
measures for 'managing' circulation and redistributing revenue. Rather, as a
result of the basic laws governing the process of capitalist accumulation and
crisis, the state apparatus increasingly comes under pressure to pursue a 'policy
of growth' which would ensure a continuous process of accumulation, in
order to secure social reproduction within the framework of the existing
relations of production. This means that the material conditions of production and the development of the productive forces of society become a central
area of the functions of the bourgeois state which at the same time must thereby reveal ever more clearly the limits of its possibilities, limits determined by
its form.

3. The basis of the increasing significance of state '*infrastructural* policy'
is the real growth in the socialization of production, impelled by the process
of the accumulation of capital, through the transformation of the technological basis of the labour process and the development of the productive
forces. The revolutionization of the technology of production and the consequent tendency for the rate of profit to fall unceasingly impose the necessity
of further technological changes in the process of production and circulation
in order to increase labour productivity (raising the rate of relative surplus
value) and the turnover of capital, changes which are forced upon capitals
under the conditions of intensifying competition on the world market, while
they (the individual capitals) are only to a limited extent in a position to
create and themselves organize the material preconditions for these changes.
The historic dynamic of the capitalist process of accumulation, condensed in
the law of the tendency of the rate of profit to fall, thus implies progressively

increasing pressure for technological innovation, which propels forward through crisis the contradictions between the social form of production and private appropriation of the product.

The separation of 'general external' and 'particular' material conditions of production is intrinsic only to the capitalist mode of production, resting as it does on the division of labour, private production and the exchange of commodities. No individual capital in the process of production based on the division of labour produces in sufficient scope the substantive conditions of its individual production process; rather, with the advance in the social division of labour, these are increasingly created outside its sphere. (This becomes clear, for example, in the setting up of a distinct means-of-production industry (machine construction) which supplies other industries with the required instruments of production.) What is essential is that a part of the material conditions of production required by individual capitals is constantly produced by other capitals and furnished by them — mediated through the exchange between capitals on the market. Capital itself thus always produces a considerable part of the 'material conditions of production' of individual capitals. However, there are always certain material conditions of production which, because — and in so far as — they do not appear to be profitable (or sufficiently so) from the point of view of the valorization of private capital, have to be furnished by an instance standing outside the direct process of the valorization of capital, the state apparatus. The capitalist unity of labour process and process of valorization necessarily creates a category of material conditions of production which fall outside the process of surplus value production and exchange between capitals and must be provided from outside the sphere of capital.

From this it follows that the creation of *'general' material conditions of production* is indeed a basic component of the functions of the bourgeois state, but that 'it cannot be concluded from the fact that . . . conditions of production are common to a larger or smaller part of social production, that they must therefore be created communally' (Läpple 1973, p. 111). Basically, the creation of the general material conditions of production too is regulated by the law of value. From the structural features of bourgeois-capitalist society, one can thus derive the general necessity (and the abstract possibility contained in the form determination of the state) of the provision from outside the individual capital of the general material conditions of production, but one cannot determine in the same way what, concretely, must become the object of state 'infrastructural provision' at any historical point of time, nor whether the state apparatus will supply the need.[41] Obviously it depends on the penetration and development of capital at the time, the development of the power of individual capitals (limited company), on the stage reached in the development of the productive forces and on the conditions of valorization which change in the process of accumulation, what becomes the object of the 'general, material conditions of production' to be created by the state apparatus — and this determination can be completely reversed, depending on the development of the factors mentioned.[42] From this follows indeed 'the senselessness of trying to define infrastructure enumeratively and conclusively . . .. What is to be counted as part of the infrastructure *at any given time* is subject precisely to change'. What 'holds the infrastructure together' is not its 'scope', but its — functionally determined — 'production institution: the state, or, put negatively, the fact that they are not produced by capital' (Ronge-Schmieg 1973, p. 271). All attempts to define 'infrastructure' undertaken within the framework of bourgeois infrastructure theory end up in this tautology.

On this level, therefore, one can do no more than enumerate phenomenologically the usual characteristics of the material conditions of production which have to be furnished by the state: their establishment requires capital outlays of a magnitude which cannot be realized by individual capitals but presupposes the state-organized provision of finance; their establishment or their management is insufficiently (or not at all) profitable (e.g. because of extremely long capital turnover times) or too risky; exclusiveness of use for the individual capital ('principle of exclusion') cannot be guaranteed — either because the product because of its specific use-value structure cannot enter into commodity circulation (qualification of labour power, research results), or because the organization of the value return would hinder the whole process of reproduction excessively (e.g. road tolls).[43,44] In all cases, finally, it is necessary that the relevant precondition of production is 'general' in so far as its *absence* represents a considerable hindrance to the process of production and reproduction, with the result that its establishment is forced on the state apparatus, if need be by crisis.

Consequently, Altvater's view, that 'material peculiarities are not of decisive importance' (Altvater 1973b, p. 177) in deciding whether the state apparatus assumes responsibility for the establishment of material conditions of production, is scarcely tenable. On the contrary: it is precisely the changes in the material peculiarities of production resulting from the technological transformation of the labour process, which lead historically to a change and to a tendency for the 'general conditions of production' established by the state to expand. It does make a difference whether energy is provided by steam engines fuelled by coal or by central electricity generating stations, or if technological processes of development are systematically developed in large research centres rather than 'empirically' within the immediate production process. It is the historic tendency of capital to posit fixed capital as the form adequate to itself, 'to release production ever more clearly from its natural basis and to transfer the conditions of production (particular and general) into the general context of social production mediated through exchange value' (Läpple 1973, p. 170). This means growing division of labour and socialization of production, the compulsion to produce material conditions of production socially to a greater extent, the exhaustion of the possibility of

having recourse to natural 'free productive forces' lying outside capitalist production and reproduced by nature (necessity of systematic research in the
natural sciences and qualification of labour power, exhaustion or unadapt-
ability of traditional sources of raw materials, etc.); but it also means the
progressive destruction of the basic natural conditions of the process of production and reproduction as a 'negative', 'external' effect of the technology
of production, driven forward anarchically by the valorization interests of
individual capitals — an effect to be compensated by state intervention.

The increasing importance — increasing with the socialization of production — of the general material conditions of the process of production and
reproduction which have to be produced or restored socially (since because
of their specific technological peculiarities and the character of their use value
they can not — or only to a limited extent or in an inefficient manner — be
produced even by highly monopolized individual capitals) forms the basis,
under the effect of the law of the tendency of the rate of profit to fall, of a
qualitative and quantitative expansion in the process of capital's historical
development of the 'infrastructural services' to be furnished by the state. The
decline in the rate of profit leads more and more individual capitals to with-
draw from the production of 'general material conditions of production' for
other capitals when it becomes insufficiently profitable or brings losses for
individual capitals, forcing the state apparatus to take under its direction
(nationalization or quasi-nationalization) these areas of production for the
purpose of safeguarding the reproduction process as a whole. At the same
time the state apparatus is under growing pressure, imposed upon it through
the intensifying competition on the world market, to take measures to
mobilize 'counter-tendencies' to the fall in the rate of profit in order to safeguard the continuous accumulation of capital, i.e. to carry out a 'growth
policy' which will reorganize the general social conditions of production.
Under capitalist conditions, this can only mean: creation of general *external*,
principally material conditions of production oriented to the labour process
and valorization process of individual capitals, conditions of production which
are the basis and precondition of technological changes in the labour process
which increase the productivity of labour and the speed of circulation of
capital.[45] State 'growth policy' is thus of necessity primarily 'infrastructural
policy'. Consequently, in a report written for the Federal Government,
Schröder defines as the central features of such a policy, apart from the promotion of concentration and support for the expansion of capital on the
world market (monetary and integration policies), above all infrastructural
'activities': education, expansion of information services, research, health,
transport, the building of towns and the provision of energy — the promotion
of building in towns being seen in particular under the aspect of a reorganization of the collapsing inner-city transport, and expansion of the health service
meaning essentially maintenance of living labour power for capital: 'Put very
plainly, it is a question of preventing by health care measures losses of labour

whether temporary (through illness) or permanent (through death). We do not know to what extent the relevant medical expenditure is "economic", i.e. is "compensated for" by the reduction in labour time lost, but we suppose that the "economic" nature of preventive medicine is constantly on the increase' (Schröder 1971, p. 383). This cynical calculation makes it particularly clear that with the progress of technological development and the intensification of exploitation, even living labour power has become for capital a condition of production to be produced socially, one which can no longer be left to the processes of spontaneous reproduction and anarchic destruction.

Within the context of the material conditions of the production process furnished by the state to safeguard the reproduction of capital, the state-organized and state financed development of science and technology acquires increasing importance as the process of accumulation advances. The accumulation process's inherent tendency to crisis, based on the tendency of the rate of profit to fall, manifests itself to the capitals of the industrial metropoles in an increased pressure to innovate, determined by competition on the world market.[46] At the same time, under the existing conditions of world politics, administratively mediated measures to destroy value — and guarantee the profits of armaments concerns — are linked to the continuous advance of armaments technology and the associated 'moral obsolescence' of arms and instruments of war. That is to say, the imperialist arms dynamic produces technological innovations as the basis of production processes which, because of their non-reproductive character, must tend to intensify the general crisis of accumulation and thus for their part exert pressure on the 'civil technological' innovations in the reproductive sector.[47] Of decisive importance here is the fact that in the production of technologically advanced products and in the introduction of new methods of production, capitals can rely less on general experience and existing social knowledge the more the development of the productive forces advances, and that these have to be produced socially to an increasing extent.

But this comes up against the immanent barriers of the capitalist mode of production in two ways: first, knowledge and technologies which cannot be monopolized, and therefore cannot be used for the expansion of private capital, tend to be produced in insufficient quantity by capital itself;[48] second, the necessary organizational and financial resources come with the advance of technical development to surpass to some degree even the capacity of large concerns (in nuclear energy or in space travel, for example). Not only does the capital requirement for the realization of comprehensive research and development increase, but the profit risk for the individual capital rises considerably as the 'moral obsolescence' of fixed capital accelerates. Thus, the systematic generation of science and technology — relatively separated from the conditions of competition and valorization of individual capitals — becomes an important area of the functions of the state administration in guaranteeing 'the general external conditions of the reproduction process', i.e. a stage in the development of the productive forces has been reached at which the socialization of production must tend to break through even the limits of the private monopoly. It becomes indispensable if the rate of innovation necessary for accumulation is to be guaranteed by means of the state apparatus, to construct and enlarge a comprehensive system of general production of science, technology and qualifications, and to ensure directly through state subsidies the technological development of expanding monopolies.[49] Private individual capitals increasingly find themselves in a situation in which the surplus value which has accrued to them is no longer sufficient to achieve the reorganization of the technological conditions of production necessary to support the process of accumulation.

This leads to specifically new forms of state 'capital mobilization' in the sphere of technology, in which process of course the particular form and scope of state intervention is determined by the relative size and the conditions of competition of the capitals concerned on the world market scale. In any case, it is characteristic that state subsidies in the area of the expanding monopolies ('growth industries', in particular the electro-technical industry, air and space industries) have increased considerably in recent years in comparison with the declining sectors (mining, agriculture). To some extent opposed to this tendency, there is an increasing necessity, as the capitalistically impelled 'scientification' of production advances, administratively to dampen the effect of the continuous destruction of the natural bases of social production and civilization. State mobilization of social resources for capital thus goes hand in hand with administrative compensation for the destruction of natural resources by capital (protection of the environment, city clearance, town and country planning). The special feature of this development is to be seen in the fact that the provision of research results and technology concepts no longer has the character of a 'general' condition of production relatively unspecific to the individual capitals, as may be the case with the building of roads or the running of railways. Rather, especially in the area of a so-called 'applied' research and development, the state-organized labour processes have to be tailored directly to suit the structure of production technology in the highly concentrated monopolies of the 'science-based industries'. With the advancing monopolization of capital, research and technology policy presents itself in part as the state guarantee of conditions of production which in the form of their provision are indeed 'general' and 'external', but which in practice and in their concrete content must be directed to the needs of specific capitals or specific capital groups. The development of the productive forces has reached a stage where, under the given relations of production, the state apparatus is brought in as an instance for the organization of social labour and the mobilization of value masses for capital, directly into the process (propelled forward by the individual capitals) of the revolutionizing of the technique of production.

That has effects on the detailed organizational structure and mode of functioning of the state apparatus. This development leads first to the extension of 'state-monopoly' forms of organization beyond the narrow sphere of the so-called 'military-industrial complex'. The state apparatus not only furnishes the general scientific potential necessary for reproduction (basic research, scientific qualification of labour power), but also finances technological developments in individual industries and supports particular forms of 'intermediate production', i.e. the production outside the immediate organizational sphere of the individual capitals interested of 'formulae' important for production technology in the sphere of 'big science' and 'big technology'. This appears to be relevant above all where scientific-technical developments of an overlapping nature are being advanced at the seams of existing spheres of production or monopoly groups, or where the requisite scale of the project surpasses the capacity of individual capital groups, or indeed makes 'international cooperation' partially necessary.[50]

The significance of the state as an 'organizational power' grows with the sharpening of competition on the world market and the intensification of imperialist relations of exploitation on an international scale. In this process, the extent and scope of the development of state-monopoly forms of organization are to a certain extent dependent on the particular strength and competitive position of the monopolies on the world market. So, for example, considerable technological backwardness (conditioned by the relative degree of concentration and similar factors) can lead to the state apparatus vigorously promoting technological developments when they are of fundamental importance for the reproduction of total capital, even without being subjected to pressure from the monopolies concerned, and possibly even against the opposition of some monopoly groups.[51] Conversely, individual monopolies can compel the state to take measures to promote technology which are in their special valorization interest, determined by competition on the world market, but which stand opposed to the reproduction requirements of the particular 'national' total capital. State technology policy can therefore not be interpreted as the smooth reaction to the objective requirements of reproduction; it is rather moulded in a particular way by the conflict between the partial interests of monopolies and the general reproduction demands of capital as a whole.[52]

In this a relation is expressed which fundamentally determines the way in which the bourgeois state functions — even if it takes different shapes as a result of differences in economic development: the activity of the state apparatus and its relation to individual capitals are decisively influenced by the strength of these capitals, their position on the world market and in the world imperialist system. The development of the contradiction between the necessary 'particularization' of the state vis-à-vis capitals and the state-monopoly 'interlacing' of state and monopoly as a result of the impulsion of the progressive socialization of production must be investigated not least from this angle.

With the development of this state-monopoly 'science-technology complex', the state apparatus organizes in the face of intensifying social division of labour forms of 'mediate' production in the science-technology sector, i.e. production outside the individual capitals, but oriented to their production processes — which means that a further area arises in which the distribution of social labour is achieved no longer immediately by the movement of individual capitals determined by competition and mediated through the market, but rather in a manner derived therefrom, with the help of 'the control room of society'. The implications which this has for the concept of 'collective social worker' and for the importance of the categories of 'productive' and 'unproductive' labour would have to be determined more precisely in relation to the class position of those employed in the state science sector.

Conclusion

In conclusion, we summarize some important results of the preceding inquiry and outline hypotheses and questions which seem to us important for further research in the area of state theory and the analysis of state interventionism. That we are moving on this still very provisional plane has its basis in the fact that a comprehensive, stringent and empirically valuable theory of late capitalism (i.e. one which mediates conclusively the general structures and laws with the manifold 'appearances on the surface') has not yet been elaborated. A theory of the bourgeois state which could be used for evaluations of political strategy can only be developed in the framework of such a comprehensive theory of the historic form of society. This does not mean, however, that one cannot develop on a more general and provisional level elements of a theory and analytical approaches which can be worked out further and made more precise in the context of practical inquiries.

The basic point to be retained is that the bourgeois state, by reason of its essential character, cannot act as regulator of the social process of development, but must be understood in the determination of its concrete functions as a reaction to the fundamentally crisis-ridden course of the economic and social process of reproduction. The developing state interventionism represents a *form* in which the contradictions of capital can temporarily move; but the movement of capital remains historically determining. The tendency to extend state interventions qualitatively and quantitatively is an expression of the gradual penetration by the capital relation, the development of the productive forces driven on by capital and the social contradictions which objectively become more acute as the socialization of production increases. These can be condensed in terms of value theory in the law of the tendency of the rate of profit to fall, which also means that this law must be the conceptual point of departure for an analysis of state functions, to be developed out of the concrete course of capital accumulation and class conflicts.

The bourgeois state is in its specific historical shape a social form which

capital must necessarily create for its own reproduction, and, just as necessarily, the state apparatus must assume and maintain an existence formally
separated from the ruling class, the bourgeoisie. This means that concrete
state activities always develop out of, and the social form of the state maintains itself through class conflicts and political struggles mediated through the
basic social context of capitalist crisis. If one fails to develop these moments
of the constitution of the bourgeois state in a strict theoretical context embracing the historically concrete course of the capitalist process of development, one is bound to come to specific short-cuts and false conclusions in
statements about the state, its concrete manner of functioning and its relation
to classes.

In this context, the first problem to explore is the question of the state
apparatus's capacity to 'manage' the economic and social reproduction process — a question standing today at the centre not only of bourgeois state and
administrative science but also of the Marxist theory of the state. For both
theories this question is central: for bourgeois theory because of its interest
in the social-technical mastery and the ideological justification of existing
social relations, for Marxist theory because of the way in which the course of
economic and social crises can actually be modified by state intervention. We
have already criticized the mistaken view of bourgeois theory, which thinks
that it can analyse administrative processes of regulation and 'management'
without concerning itself with the basic social determinations of form and
function, which thus declares the state to be a natural form and its apparatus
to be an historically contingent product. It can be shown, however, that a
certain lack of clarity exists even in the work of those theorists who start
from a basically correct evaluation of the character of the bourgeois state.
Characteristic is, for example, the investigation of Ronge and Schmieg,
Restrictions on Political Planning (1973), which addresses itself above all to
the actual 'success' of state measures in the sphere of infrastructure designed
to secure reproduction. The authors conclude that this policy has failed to a
large extent — at least measured by the standard of the claims that had been
made — but they have to observe at the same time that the capitalist system
has nevertheless not collapsed. The logical conclusion is that there must be
'functional equivalents' for state administrative measures in the infrastructural
sphere, which secure the reproduction of capital even in the case of a relative
deficit or delay of state intervention, or that there exists on the side of the
administration a faulty perception of the conditions of reproduction. Leaving
aside from the discussion here the question of the conclusiveness of the empirical investigation, already in posing the question the authors make the
mistake — and this is decisive here — of adopting a 'restriction-analytical'
approach which overlooks the form determination of the state: the inquiry
starts from the assumption that the reproduction of capital is assured by the
state apparatus as an instance *detached* from the movement of capital, as
though capital had a pivot outside itself, in the absence of which (as a result

of specific 'restrictions') 'functional equivalents' would have to come into play — 'functional equivalents' which cannot initially be defined more closely by theory. State apparatus and capital appear in a mechanical relation of opposition. The fact that the state apparatus is itself a moment of the movement of capital and of the struggle of the classes is overlooked. The fundamental condition of the capitalist process of reproduction as process of exploitation is the production and appropriation of a sufficient mass of surplus value — sufficient in relation to the stage of accumulation reached: this basic condition cannot be affected in its essence by the state apparatus, but only modified by it. In capitalism there is no equivalent to the exploitation of living labour power — state intervention included. The actions of the state apparatus, such as the extension of the functioning infrastructural bases of production, are, as form of movement of the capitalist contradiction, important for the *conditions* — more or less civilized — under which the exploitation is carried out, but they do not replace it. This means that the question of the ability of capital to reproduce itself can basically never be a question of administrative efficiency, but always depends on concrete class relations and the character of class struggles. Inadequate administrative infrastructural provision can always be compensated for by intensified exploitation, and whether this succeeds depends again not on the technical competence of the state apparatus, but on the economic and political strength and militancy of the working class. State measures 'to manage the economy' and their success can only be really evaluated in such a context and not as detached strategies of a political instance, understood finally as being indeed 'autonomous', i.e. as obeying independent laws of motion and as thus subjected to specific capitalist 'restrictions'. This means generally that from an investigation of sectoral areas of state intervention on its own no general conclusions can yet be drawn about the crisis-ridden development of capital and its ability to reproduce itself. The argument made against Ronge and Schmieg is also essentially directed against their postulate that theory has above all to ascertain the 'hard limits' of administrative stabilization policy. Here too the mistake is already in the way that the question is posed: to try to determine with economic data the limits of the ability of the capitalist form of society to reproduce itself, i.e. to try to develop something like a mathematical model of crisis, contains a crude economistic mistake in approach which precisely screens out the decisive basis of capital reproduction. The 'hard limits' of capital reproduction are not to be sought in constellations of economic data but in concrete class struggles, which admittedly are not open to econometric quantification. That is to say that what should be the central point of the analysis is relegated to a rim of data. This does not mean that one could do without empirical, quantifying investigation such as Ronge and Schmieg have undertaken. The manifold interventions of the state and their respective success are indeed important for the development and the course of class struggles and the associated form of securing the political domination of the bourgeoisie. What must be borne in mind, however, — and this is implicitly recognized also by Ronge and Schmieg — is that state regulation of the economic reproduction process is only an (albeit important) form with which capital is temporarily able to break through the self-posited barriers to its valorization, and that the use of the state apparatus as an apparatus of ideological and physical force in the class struggle represents a quite essential 'functional equivalent' thereto.

Another problem often neglected in the context of analyses of state interventionism lies in the fact that the state apparatus in the functional sense (i.e. including parties, integrative mass organizations and ideological apparatuses) but also the actual administration cannot be understood as a closed formation, but represents in reality a heterogeneous conglomerate of only loosely linked part-apparatuses. Under these circumstances and in view of the fact that the development of the modern interventionist state is accompanied by a progressive diversification of the administrative and political apparatuses, to speak of the 'management capacity' of *the* state apparatus is to commit an error from the very beginning. The heterogeneous and increasingly chaotic structure of the bourgeois state apparatus is a precondition for its being able to maintain complex relations to the various classes and class fractions, relations which are the conditions of its ability to function as guarantor of the domination of the bourgeoisie.[53] It must be open to the divergent interests and influences of individual capitals and groups of capitals, which always encounter one another in competition as 'hostile brothers', and in order to secure the political domination of the bourgeoisie and keep class conflict latent, it must maintain links both with the proletariat and with other classes and strata not to be counted as part of the bourgeoisie. The alternative to this would be the absolute political rule of coercion, which — although it is not excluded as an historical possibility of capitalist development — stands in contradiction to the fundamental conditions for the reproduction of capital. The contradictions and conflicts inherent in this social relation cannot be mastered by a unified and closed apparatus; it requires a pluralism of apparatuses whose specific achievement as a cohesive system lies — as shown above — in 'reducing' by means of specific mechanisms of selection the real 'complexity' of class relations, in what is moreover a thoroughly contradictory and conflict-ridden manner, to the objective class interest of the bourgeoisie. The bourgeois state can and must act in a relatively closed and decisive manner whenever its repressive core (police, army, judiciary) — if need be, abolishing or materializing individual part-apparatuses (parties, trade unions, ideological apparatuses) — confronts the proletariat as a physical force of repression and thus expresses the genuinely common class interest of the bourgeoisie. However, when it takes regulating, organizing or subsidizing measures relating to the economic process of reproduction, it necessarily falls apart into a conglomerate of relatively unconnected part-bureaucracies, because it must, in a contradictory manner, relate to and support itself on competing individual capitals having, under the conditions of competition on the world market, extraordinarily different valorization interests, *and* on opposing classes and class fractions — not least because certain measures which secure the reproduction of capital in the long term can regularly be implemented only under the pressure of non-capitalist classes and against the resistance of individual capitals and groups of capitals. Already from this it follows that under capitalist conditions there can be no unified interventionist strategy, let alone consistent political planning, but that state interventionism necessarily consists of a heterogeneous conglomerate of individual bundles of measures (which of course does not exclude relatively strict and even successful partial programming). The programme of unprincipled 'muddling through' is therefore also not to be understood as the peculiarity of a particular political party but is inherent in the system. However, this structure acquires a particular quality through the fact that the system of competing individual capitals has long since taken on an extremely monopolistic shape and decisive monopolies and groups of monopolies — as in the area of science and technology policy — have in practice steadfastly occupied specific *parts* of the state apparatus.[54]

Under these conditions it is in any case impermissible to claim abstractly for the state apparatus as a presupposed whole the function of 'guaranteeing the general external conditions for the reproduction of capital'. It has always had to, and increasingly it must, secure the quite particular profit interests of dominant monopolies and monopoly groups, which brings it into serious difficulties and conflicts in the performance of its function of assuring the minimal conditions for the reproduction of capital as a whole and keeping the class struggle latent.[55] From this double contradiction — having under monopoly conditions to consider the interests of competing individual capitals, and at the same time having to secure the political domination of the bourgeoisie as a class and thus implement measures to guarantee the reproduction of capital as a whole — results the segmented and fragmented organizational structure of the political-administrative apparatus, the constant attempts to develop a coordinating 'system policy' and their regular failure. Under these conditions, the question of the state apparatus's 'capacity to manage' or of the ability of administrative interventions to reach their target can, strictly speaking, relate only to individual parts of the total apparatus or to functional areas of intervention, which also means that even from the point of view of the institutional preconditions, one cannot speak of an assured administrative guarantee of the general external conditions of capital reproduction.

Accordingly, our investigation of science and technology policy in the Federal Republic has shown that, under the conditions of the socialization of production propelled by capital, the development of technology in the relevant sectors shifts to a state monopoly complex characterized by close interweaving between parts of the state administration and industrial concerns; but from this one cannot conclude that there has been a qualitative change in either the planning competence of the administration or in the character of the development of the productive forces. Even in the complete absence of a comprehensive planning of scientific-technical development, there is indeed some more or less stringent and partly even successful sectoral programming, but even under the conditions of advanced state interventionism the *contents* of the development of the productive forces are moulded decisively by the investment and competitive strategies of individual capitals, determined by the world market. State acceptance of responsibility for the general material conditions of production is therefore not politically programmable even in this area, but asserts itself at best anarchically in the conflict of diverging monopoly interests and their transformation into a 'political system' subject to specific imperatives of securing bourgeois domination. It follows too that one cannot proceed on the assumption that the observed growth of state involvement in the science and technology sector represents a linear historical tendency in 'late capitalism'. The objective necessity of this form of state interventionism can indeed be derived from the laws of the reproduction of capital; its realization, however, is decided upon by specific historical relations which are determined by the structure and development of the imperialist world system and the character of the class conflicts that occur.

On this general level of inquiry, however, i.e. without taking into account the concrete class relations, the existing organization of capital, the form of monopoly competition and the movement of capital on the world market, only such general structural determinations are possible. That is to say that without further logical and historical concretization of the analysis, no stringently derived and determined statements can be made about the manner in which and the success with which the state apparatus is in each case drawn into securing the reproduction of capital, and about how the further development of state interventionism is to be foreseen — whether it will be in the direction of a quantitative and qualitative extension of regulating infrastructural measures to 'guarantee growth', or of the forcible suppression of the proletariat, or, more exactly, what combination of both. An analysis of the basic laws of motion of capital accumulation shows, however, that, accepting that the fall in the rate of profit cannot be prevented in the long term and hence that the process of accumulation must tend towards stagnation, the forcible securing of the 'conditions of reproduction' must become more probable. The history of capitalism and the present political tendencies in the more developed capitalist states both lend support to this supposition.

It is inherent in the historical logic of the capitalist process of accumulation that the problem of administrative planning and management comes ever more sharply to the fore. As a result of the technological transformation of the labour process, driven progressively onwards by the accumulation of capital, the material side of the production process, in the form of external material conditions of production to be provided administratively, becomes an increasingly important element in the interventionist activity of the state.[56] As the socialization of production increases objectively, the contradictions contained in the form determination of the bourgeois state appear ever more clearly in this activity: in the necessity for systematic planning of the process of reproduction while at the same time there are structural deficits of information relevant to planning, of organizational structures that would make sense in terms of planning technique, and of indispensable material resources (cf. Ronge and Schmieg 1973). It would, however, be inadequate to see in the absent planning and management capacity of the state apparatus a moment of crisis. While it is true that, as the state apparatus is drawn increasingly into the economic process of reproduction, social contradictions are reproduced to an equally increasing extent within the state apparatus, one can strictly speak of 'political crisis' only when class conflict which is politically relatively latent decisively asserts itself. Thus there remains the important question of how one is to determine the role of the interventionist state apparatus (subject as it is to specific, objective determinants of function) in relation to erupting and developing class struggles.[57]

Of fundamental importance for this relation must be the fact that the state apparatus, in accordance with the logic of its own function, is ever more strongly drawn directly into the increasingly intense economic struggles and is thereby forced to confront the proletariat as a barely disguised apparatus of repression. Assuming the effectiveness of the law of the tendency of the rate of profit to fall, one can indeed envisage a point at which the maintenance of the process of accumulation at the level attained is possible only if there is not only a relative but also an absolute decline in the real income of the masses — produced if need be by inflation. The state apparatus is doubly involved in this process. On the one hand, it is forced to defend the profit of capital as the basis of smooth economic reproduction against the material demands of the proletariat and thus intervenes in wage struggles ever more clearly in favour of capital — with the involvement (by no means free of conflict) of the bureaucratic trade union apparatus. On the other hand, the short- and long-term state interventions to secure the valorization of capital (conjunctural and growth policy in the broad sense) require, just when accumulation is slackening, an increased injection of state revenue in favour of capital, revenue which can be raised, if at all, only by progressive inflation or tax exploitation, in any case only by the reduction, manipulated by the state, of real mass incomes. Even a slight intensification of the economic crisis of capitalism forces the state apparatus to take the side of capital *openly*, while at the same time the permanent, structural and intensifying shortage of state financial resources reduces very considerably the scope for 'welfare state' reforms.[58] That means that, on the one hand, the welfare state's potential for pacification disappears in conditions of tendentially stagnating accumulation, while at the same time it can hardly be concealed any more that even economic struggles for the maintenance of the living conditions of the masses must be directed against both capital and its state.

Thus, on the basis of economic development, even attempts to articulate

and protect collectively minimal and fundamental — i.e. measured by the
stage of development of the productive forces — life interests in the spheres
both of production and reproduction, have the tendency to destroy a basis of
bourgeois domination, namely the illusion of the state's 'neutrality' and
'dedication to the common weal', and to put in question its ability to guarantee
the material and ideological conditions of capital reproduction. To this extent,
the strengthening and simultaneous extension of active struggles for the realization of even limited interests (struggles over wages and conditions of work,
active protection of interests in the sphere of reproduction, democratization
of social institutions) acquire considerable importance in the context of a
strategy, the first aim of which must be to make the class character of the
state a matter of concrete experience. This holds true even (or precisely) if it
should prove possible to stabilize relatively the economic reproduction process under the conditions posited by capital, i.e. if the cyclical collapse is
replaced by 'stagflation' as the new variant of crisis in state interventionist
capitalism.

A necessary consequence of this development is the appearance of specific
conflicts within the state apparatus — perennial strife between the trade union
bureaucracies and their rank and file, quarrels between trade union and
government apparatuses, increasingly bitterly waged struggles between the
wings of the parties (especially in social-democratic parties, by their nature) —
conflicts which reproduce themselves in the different sectors of the administrative apparatus and find their final journalistic expression in constant cabinet
disputes or in the propagandistically puffed up bogey of a head of government
supposedly 'lacking in leadership'. But precisely this makes it clear that 'crises'
within the political apparatus must be interpreted essentially as the consequence of actual class struggles and gain practical significance for scientific
inquiry only in this context.

The *ideological crisis* of bourgeois rule can be adequately understood and
evaluated only on the basis of the economic process of crisis mediated in this
way through the state apparatus.[59] It has an important basis in — to speak
with Offe — the disruption of specific 'selectivity structures' of the political
system directed to systematic 'non-decisions', i.e. in a manifestation of the
class character of the bourgeois state, which of course cannot be explained
without taking into account the laws of the economic process of development.

The compulsion imposed upon the state to provide, on an increasing scale
as the socialization of production increases, decisive material and organizational pre-conditions for the process of social production and reproduction
(which is determined by the movement of capital) is certainly an essential
basis for 'welfare state illusions' of reform. But this tendency is thoroughly
ambivalent politically. When the decline in the rate of profit and the tempo
of accumulation becomes manifest, this must lead to an intensified exploitation of labour power mediated through the state apparatus, while at the same
time potential state resources for 'superfluous' measures of pacification and

reform — 'superfluous', that is, for the immediate profit interests of capitals — are drastically restricted. This is the context in which the 'consequences' of economic growth — decay of the cities, chaotic traffic situation, collapse of the ecological equilibrium, etc. — become politically explosive: not because the 'managing capacity' of the state is too small in a technical sense or indeed restricted by an outdated 'view of the world', but because capital comes up against the self-produced barriers of its valorization, which can be broken through only by an intensification of exploitation and class struggle. The growing involvement of the state apparatus in the process of social reproduction and the associated necessity of developing administrative programmes and calculations directed towards the use value side of production acquire under these conditions a no longer merely latently politicizing effect: the overburdening with reforms of the political apparatus, which the latter must constantly produce itself in order to secure existing relations of domination, rebounds on the state apparatus when substantive reforms prove to be unrealizable and leads also from this perspective to a dismantling of welfare state illusions. This means, however, that now not only do the advancing involutionary tendencies of parliamentarism and the increased imperialist aggressiveness of the metropoles come into open contradiction with the postulated norms of bourgeois democracy — this was however an important basis of the student revolt — but that the class character of the state becomes explicit in a much more direct way which touches the immediate life interests of the masses. It can be seen clearly in the development of the Social-Democratic party (SPD) as party of government that the 'bond between representatives and represented' (Poulantzas) necessarily begins to break down when the managers of the bourgeois state are forced openly and cynically to abandon the fundamental interests of the masses and themselves to enter actively into the struggle against the proletariat. But this means that, at this point at least, a decisive moment in the preservation of the domination of the bourgeoisie, namely the bond of the state apparatus with the working class, is tendentially undermined.

However, the indication of structural and intensifying 'legitimation problems', to which the domination of the bourgeoisie is exposed in view of the laws of economic development, does not yet tell us anything decisive about the manner and the direction in which these problems become politically practical. This is essentially a question of the political organization of the proletariat itself. The decisive 'crisis of the political system' does not come about simply because the ruling class is suffering from a loss of legitimation and the disintegrated state apparatus subject to manifold 'restrictions' has serious 'management problems' to report. These are only *conditions* for a political development in which class struggle is no longer waged only from above: only this would be the real 'political crisis' of the bourgeois state. The process of politicization on which this is based is indeed mediated through the perennial legitimation and functional deficits of the state apparatus, but it acquires its perspective only when it is organized and practically directed against the social relations which are the basis of the bourgeois state and its peculiarly deficitary mode of functioning.[60]

It must be taken into account in this that the moments of disintegration and conflict within the political-administrative apparatus, which come to the fore as the valorization difficulties of capital increase and the class struggle consequently intensifies, are linked to a stronger and more direct emergence of the state apparatus as an apparatus of force and repression. The strong ideological repression in wage disputes exerted above all with the help of the state apparatus, the outlawing and forcible suppression of non-permitted labour struggles, the repressive use of the law relating to foreigners, restrictions on the freedom of demonstration and of opinion and — characteristic of the present stage of political development in the Federal Republic — sharp repression within the 'ideological state apparatuses' (universities, schools, trade unions, parties): all these show this trend of development very clearly. The less the political apparatus is able, on account of economic development, to keep the capitalist class antagonism latent 'reformistically', i.e. by partial measures of compensation and pacification, the more it must — if and so long as the existence of a fascist mass movement does not produce quite different constellations — lop off its increasingly dysfunctional relations to the masses. This is seen in the dissociation of the party apparatuses from their 'rank and file' (increased hierarchization and bureaucratization of the apparatuses, struggle against the so-called 'imperative mandate' and for the 'freedom of conscience' of officials), the organizational removal from power or expulsion now not only of dissenting individuals but of whole sections of the organization, exclusionary 'delineation decisions' *vis-à-vis* the left and prohibitions of left-wing organizations which are already practised or indicated developments in this direction — as also the threatened and in this sense logical re-creation of the 'community of necessity' of the party bureaucracies in the form of a national government or 'grand coalition'. This expresses an increasing inability to secure the domination of the bourgeoisie by integration of the masses, which must finally lead to the stronger emergence of the state as a coercive apparatus.

The question of the possibility of a new fascism is certainly not to be brushed off with the observation that the abolition of bourgeois-democratic forms of intercourse 'would in the last instance bring more problems with it than it would solve and will therefore not come about' (Offe 1972, p. 103). This argument overlooks the fact that capital unfolds its contradictions according to its own logic and has never yet bothered about historical reason, that the barrier to capital is capital itself and the possibility of fascism cannot be discussed in terms of an enlightened class interest, when the class which might have such an interest is nowhere to be seen. However, the question of fascism has to be treated somewhat discriminatingly: one must start from the fact that the perfection of the instruments of manipulation and repression attained in the meantime makes a crude new edition of Hitlerian fascism improbable, and that the openly authoritarian state, which has always represented the logical consequence of the inner contradictions of bourgeois-democratic rule, has historically assumed and will in the future assume very different shapes.

In any case it is to be assumed that the strengthening of the repressive function of the state does not have to mean that its institutional structure changes fundamentally; in accordance with its basic character, the bourgeois state is recognizably and essentially constructed as an apparatus of force. It is much more a question of a process characterized by shifts in relative weight between the repressive, ideological and regulative state apparatuses and specific changes in their social basis.[61] Hence, it will be vital for the theory of the state not to derive the state apparatus always only on a general level as an abstract form, but to come to grips with it as the concrete social organizational nexus which it represents in practice. At least for the variant of materialist state theory current in the Federal Republic, it can be said that it must specifically first de-idealize and demystify its own concept of the state before it can become politically practical. If one starts from the fact that the bourgeois state apparatus appears as a relatively heterogeneous conglomerate of bureaucracies, governing cliques, party apparatuses and bureaucratic mass organizations and that it is fundamentally necessary to recognize the complex functional cohesion in which these state apparatuses relate to one another and to the classes, the present deficits in theory become fairly clear. It is of central importance for the organization of the political struggle that the bourgeois state — without prejudice to its structural class character — stands, through the mediation of its part apparatuses, in a changing relation to the social classes and class fractions, a relation determined by the prevailing economic conditions and the historical class relations. That means that a real materialist theory of the bourgeois state presupposes a discriminating and empirically substantial analysis not only of the process of accumulation and development of capital and of the movements of competition, but also of the concretely developing class structures and their changes. We must clarify — also empirically — what classes and class fractions — individual monopolies and monopoly groups, the different parts of the middle bourgeoisie, the 'new' and 'old' middle classes and the divisions of the proletariat — stand in which relations to the various parts of the state apparatus. In other words: *the class character of the state must be worked out in historical concreteness.* This is a decisive and as yet hardly satisfied pre-condition for evaluating in a strategically meaningful way the political process also, and especially in a time of the growing use of force by the state machinery.

6

On the Current Marxist Discussion on the Analysis of Form and Function of the Bourgeois State

Reflections on the Relationship of Politics to Economics

Bernhard Blanke, Ulrich Jürgens and Hans Kastendiek

Introduction

Introductory note on the publication of this paper

The following study was prepared as a paper for the Congress of the German Association for Political Science (1–4 Oct. 1973) – in particular for the seminar 'Global Control'. The general theme of the congress was 'Politics and economics – what are the possibilities for a political system to act autonomously?'

Both the theme of the seminar and the general one of the congress essentially determined the logical structure of our paper. Our central points of enquiry were:

1. How, on the basis of Marxist theory, is the very separation of 'politics' and 'economics' – evidently taken for granted by bourgeois social scientists – to be understood? On the one hand, how is it to be *criticized* as a *mystification*, an external appearance which presents to the mind (even a scientific mind) as in opposition to each other phenomena which inwardly belong together; and on the other, how can it be *explained* as a *reality* made up of separately organized and self-reproducing social relationships?

2. How, in this dual sense, are the *possibilities and limitations of action* for the state or 'political system' of a capitalist society to be determined?

The fact that these questions pose themselves automatically if one works through both the older and more recent *bourgeois* discussion on the state (cf. Blanke, Jürgens and Kastendiek, 1975), in no way means that our foundation in Marxist theory is a mere formality. On the contrary we believe that a materialist theory of the state must be based on a *critique* of *bourgeois* political theory.

For it can be shown that recent Marxist attempts at a 'derivation of the state' are stamped by handed-down 'theories' of 'the state' unconsciously borrowed without acknowledgement and mostly without reflection — they infiltrate into attempts at a derivation which apparently only embark from the general concept of capital and hope to get by without any cognizance of the abundant mainstream literature on the state. Even then — and indeed precisely then — 'prejudices' creep into the analysis as soon as the concept of the state is used, prejudices whose consequences can only be discovered in details and are difficult to criticize because the authors think that by simply disowning (bourgeois) scientific discussion, they have overcome their quite 'private' notions of state and politics determined by their own history of socialization (parental home, civic education, participation in elections or political actions).

If, on the contrary, one tries to discover the 'principal conditions'[1] of the bourgeois state which appear also in bourgeois theory as central problems, then one finds universally (cf. Blanke, Jürgens and Kastendiek, 1975) a 'bipolar focus' (Oertzen 1974) around which bourgeois thinking about the state has revolved since the classics of political theory: *state authority* (sovereignty, executive, state apparatus, etc.) on the one hand and right or law on the other (laws, legislation and 'parliamentarism', application of the law by the judiciary, etc.).

Of importance for our work was the observation that reflections on state power and law in bourgeois theory (and ideology) are shaped to a considerable extent by the problem of the legitimation of political rule, and that the analysis of the functional interrelation between state power, law and society is distorted precisely by the fact that the separation of politics and economics enters into all these theories as the undiscussed basic assumption. Only with the emergence of the phenomenon commonly referred to as 'state interventionism' does the economy again become a problem (above all as an *external* problem of 'state planning') also for bourgeois state theory, which, however, is unable to explain the functional 'restrictions' or 'interdependencies'.

On the other hand, we have the impression that most Marxist discussion is based on a specific limitation which we shall discuss and criticize extensively in what follows, but the central problem of which we shall indicate here, because it has arisen again and again in the discussion of our paper (in informal, pre-publication discussions).

By 'politics', the complete or perfected bourgeois state is generally always understood — the complete bourgeois state with the resulting forms of interest and power struggles on the basis, above all, of the contradictions peculiar to capital, between the individual capitals on the one hand and between wage labour and capital on the other. The *basic form* of politics, namely the conflict surrounding, and the establishment of, *legal relations*, is simply overlooked in the hasty leap to the fully developed capitalist class society. In this way, the law much too easily acquires in Marxist discussion a purely instrumental character, which can produce practical false conclusions — not only of a reformist tendency but in conceptions which grasp the the law as mere appearance, ideology, mystifying veil (cf. Seifert 1971, pp. 195 ff.). We shall briefly indicate the theoretical mistakes which ought to be refuted by our analysis by looking at a few essential objections that have been raised against our analysis.

Objection 1: That our emphasis on form analysis is unnecessary in so far as it is in any case self-evident that under the conditions of capitalist production relations between people acquire 'forms determined by capital'. Therefore the separation of form analysis and historical analysis is, it is claimed, wrong. 'On the contrary, one should proceed from the fact that the development of specific state *functions* signifies nothing other than the *formation* of the state and should thus be the real object of form analysis.'[2] A similar objection is made, agreeing with us in principle, but referring to the *organizational forms* of the state (Gerstenberger 1975; see p. 148 below).

We were concerned, however, to distinguish that which is understood in normal bourgeois theory also as 'state forms', namely specific organizational structures *of* the bourgeois state, from the state-form. It was first a question of investigating why it is that on the basis of capitalist commodity production certain social relations are *not* shaped and regulated by the general forms of capital reproduction developed by Marx, but assume quite specific forms, such as law and politics. For this purpose it was necessary to distinguish between the historically changing organizational forms (e.g. constitutions, bureaucracies and other types of administration) and those *basic* requirements of the reproduction of capitalist society which manifest themselves in the necessity of extra-economic forms. Only when these have been developed is it possible to discover in the empirical variations in the development of the bourgeois state a general tendency common to *all* capitalist societies and relate it to the historically and regionally varying traditions, types of constitution, types of policy, etc. It is clear to us that our analysis in this direction is not yet finally accomplished, that also in the 'political systems' there are still elements to be analytically elaborated which have a general character (cf. the still important work of Agnoli 1967). We regard our work, however, as a framework for such an analysis. This is especially true for those 'channels' and institutions (cf. Gerstenberger 1975, p. 148 below) in which generally in bourgeois society, demands (functions) of the capitalist process of reproduction which require organization by the extra-economic coercive force assert themselves as *interests* and are brought to a political solution.

Objection 2: That we start from 'simple commodity circulation' in which there is as yet no necessity for an extra-economic force of coercion. There, so it is claimed, (a) the 'identity of labour with property in the result of the labour' is presupposed, and (b) the 'sphere of material laws and individual action' coincide. Only with the emergence of the tendency of capital

to destroy the existence of the wage labourer — and here the struggle for
the normal working day is cited — does there arise a struggle for 'rights'.
Hence, right (or law) and the force which guarantees it have to be developed,
it is maintained, as forms determined by capital.[3] How from 'rights', i.e.
conceptions about legitimate needs, we are to derive the *form* of right or of
law, remains, however, inexplicable because the conception that one must
fight for 'rights' presupposes this form. A similar objection (Stöss 1975)
maintains that law and state can be developed only out of the contradiction
between exchange value and use value, between capital reproduction and the
needs of the workers which are opposed to its tendencies. In our view, these
objections overlook two central points:

1. Even in 'simple commodity circulation', it is not the commodities or
money that act, but people. The argument that these are only the character
masks of economic categories overlooks the particular significance of Marx's
argument: pointing out that the 'actions' of persons are functional relations
of social reproduction tells us as yet nothing about the *form* in which people
are brought to behave functionally. That occurs certainly not only through
law, but also through conventions, forms of consciousness, etc. The essential
form is however the form of law. This is a necessary form because although
the social interrelations in capitalist commodity production assert themselves as reified ('objective') compulsions, their assertion nevertheless requires
individual ('subjective') actions. This still says nothing about the idea that
there is a free scope of action for deviations, corrections, etc., which is a
basic conception of bourgeois thought (especially of a sociology which
builds on the concept of 'social action').

An examination of the *process* of exchange, in which, it has been said,
material laws and individual action coincide, shows how the social nexus,
precisely because it is established only *a posteriori*, requires individual action
in which it both transposes itself and is recognized supra-individually as an
'objective' nexus. The fact that Marx abstracted from this problem in his
analysis of 'simple circulation' in order to destroy the veil of subjectivist
notions (such as still exist today as 'science' in, for example, bourgeois cost-
benefit theory) does not mean that this problem does not exist.

To demand of people that they recognize the *forms* in which the law
of value asserts itself requires, over and above the *sanctioning instance* of
money, particular forms which are tailored to fit people as 'subjective
agents' and in which there are posited at the same time the mystification
of the individual freedom of action, i.e. of will, and the reality of the social
nexus of compulsion. This is the form of law and the extra-economic force
of coercion which guarantees the law.

2. Simple commodity circulation is interpreted in the critique of our
analysis as a phase preceding capital production. Against this it must be
emphasized that the forms of simple circulation which Marx develops in
Capital are *general forms* of *capitalist* production. And the correct opposi-

tion is that between general, 'simple' circulation and the circulation of capital as phases of the circuit of capital, which, however, is accomplished in the forms of simple circulation (commodity, money). The problems which this raises for the analysis of the state are examined more closely in the main body of the article.

Objection 3: That our argument that the extra-economic force of coercion can relate as extra-economic force to the process of capital reproduction only through the medium of the basic forms of law and money overlooks the 'reality of state intervention' (Gerstenberger 1975; see below p. 148).

1. Now, it is hardly ever said which other forms are thinkable. Even if a powerful state apparatus has developed, with the most various relations to the process of reproduction, it is nevertheless a mistake to confuse the organizational forms of state activity or 'methods of intervention' which are not organized in the form of the state but as a 'state enterprise' or association under private law or simply as a private enterprise,[4] with their *effect*, i.e. with the functional relation and the particular form of mediation to the process of capital reproduction.

With such organizational forms or 'methods of intervention', the *mediated* relation to the process of reproduction is overcome only when 'state activities' organize themselves in the material-economic forms of the social process of reproduction and are thus exposed *immediately* to the movement of capital accumulation (but then it is quite irrelevant whether the state, for example, has taken over part of the share capital of Volkswagen; it cannot solve the crisis of the car industry in that way). The fact, however, that there are 'state activities' whose form of mediation *vis-à-vis* the process of reproduction is still unclear to us in detail (e.g. the educational sector or, from a legal perspective, the activity of public law corporations) shows that it is important to analyse individually the increase in functions which require state organization and to discover their particular relation to the process of reproduction. This holds true especially for the question of the 'general conditions of production', which we have not examined closely because in our view they are not relevant for a discussion of the *form* of the state (apart from that, cf. Läpple 1973).

2. The call for detailed analysis and presentation refers also to the distinction between the 'system-limit' and the 'activity-limit' of the bourgeois state which we have made in our article. This distinction has been mistakenly equated by the critics of our article with the 'distinction between' logical and historical analysis. On the one hand we have certainly furthered this misunderstanding by our concentration on form analysis, on the other hand it should be clear that we base the distinction in the difference between *general form analysis* and *particular analysis of the development of state functions* and their specific conditioning by and mediation to the capitalist process of reproduction. Such state functions can be 'general' in the sense

that they express an average constellation of capital accumulation and class struggles existing in all capitalist countries, a constellation which is not already posited by the general concept of capital. We have brought these particular structures — looked at from the angle of the question of the 'autonomy' and 'possibilities of action' of the bourgeois state — together in the concept of the 'limit of activity'. In our view the chasm which exists between the analysis of the 'principal conditions' and the analysis of the 'empirically given circumstances' (*Capital* vol. 3, p. 792) can be overcome only through the analysis of particular, historically given structures which at the same time, as average conditions, are *general* for all capitalist societies at a given stage of development. However, we are all still miles away from a presentation which would have assimilated in its general features the development of capital in the last two hundred years. The problem in the continuation of our analysis is therefore to mediate, in a theoretically more compelling manner than we have so far managed, the system-limit and the limit of activity.

In these preliminary remarks we have dealt only with the essential objections which have been brought to our notice. Apart from that we are presenting the original paper for discussion. We have not been able to discuss publications which have appeared since then (October 1973). It seemed more important to make our work accessible to general and public discussion.

Problems of the recent Marxist discussion on the state:

(a) The separation of politics and economics (state and society) in capitalism seems to be so obvious and self-evident that one wonders what is supposed to be achieved by painstaking and 'subtle' conceptual attempts to derive the *genesis* of these different 'spheres' or 'systems', instead of looking directly at the specific mediations or 'interdependencies' and starting on empirical research.

We think, however — and that is generally agreed among Marxists — that it is indeed necessary to trace the genesis of this separation, for only in such an explanation can one find a basis not only for an external analysis of the relations, but also for an analysis of the specific internal mediations between these 'spheres' or 'systems'.

How can or must such an explanation proceed? In bourgeois state theories (of juristic or sociological origin) one can find essentially two types of explanation — we leave aside the 'normative':

1. An historical-typologizing explanation (e.g. in the work of Weber, Heller, etc.). The separation of 'state' and 'society' (or other social 'spheres') which has become self-evident is retraced historically. The state is then the 'modern' outcome of an historical process, and as such as *result* of development it can be typologically generalized.

2. A functional explanation (already implicit in the work of the authors

mentioned above, but especially in sociological functionalism).[5] One or more functions are reconstructed, which the state (or the political system, or 'politics' as such) fulfils *for* other areas of social systems or in the context of social systems. The state's existence is taken as being explained by this function. Without simplifying, one can identify the 'taking of binding decisions' as the determination of function common to such approaches. This function is assumed to hold for all sorts of human socialization, from the primitive to the industrial society. In content this function coincides with the concept of sovereignty which is central to the historical typologizing explanations.[6]

If Marxist state theory is not to repeat the mistake of 'placing itself on the standpoint of the finished phenomena' (*Capital* vol. 2, p. 220) and taking abstract, ahistorical definitions as the starting point for its explanation, it cannot content itself with noting the existence of an institution or sphere of 'the state': it must found its necessity in determined requirements of capitalist society. These requirements were developed generally by Marx in *Capital* and a 'derivation' of the state must start from there. In all work on the general concept of capital,[7] it is however important to keep the theoretical goal in view: namely, the conceptual reconstruction of the empirical, historical-concrete state in specific bourgeois societies.

The derivation of the state from Marx's general categories of capital is confronted by considerable methodical difficulties. It has not yet been made unambiguously clear by Marxist discussion how the 'logic' of capitalist society theoretically reconstructed by Marx is to be 'applied' to the analysis of historical and concrete forms of appearance, or indeed how the relation between logical and historical analysis is precisely to be determined;[8] nor is it clear from what point or points of 'capital-in-general' the derivation of the bourgeois state should depart.

(b) We have said that we are concerned with the *theoretical* reconstruction of the *empirically* existing bourgeois state. In order to avoid creating the impression that what follows is pure conceptual scholasticism, we shall briefly outline the questions which the recent Marxist state discussion was initially faced with, even before the attempt was made to answer these questions by direct reference to Marx's *Capital*.

The problem of the state was revived mainly in the discussion of certain historical phases of capitalist society, especially of fascism, and of various obvious problems of the labour movement in the evaluation of measures of the bourgeois state (such as measures of social policy or, more generally, of the 'welfare state').[9] Out of these discussions arose essentially two complexes of questions, which refer to the supposedly instrumental character of the state:

1. If one understands the state directly as a committee for the protection of the interests of capital, how are those phases in the history of bourgeois society then to be explained in which 'the state' (apparently) acts indepen-

dently of or against the interests of capital? This debate[10] which developed around the key phrase 'autonomy of the state' has by no means ended. From it results the central question: how is the domination of capital over and in the production process mediated into the 'sphere of politics' and the institution of the state; what is the relation of the bourgeoisie as a class to its state?

2. If the state is understood as an instrument of class domination, how then do we interpret measures which are implemented through or by means of the state *in favour* of the working class? This debate too, carried on around the key phrase of the 'welfare state'[11] is by no means concluded. It could hardly be concluded as nearly all the strategic problems of the labour movement (reformism, revisionism) are involved. The central question which results from this discussion is: how are the actions of the workers (understood as not yet being the 'class for itself') mediated into the 'sphere of politics'; do political victories of the working class (e.g. in elections) change the quality of the state as class state (in whatever way that is understood), so that the bourgeois state can undergo a change in function and become the instrument of social change in favour of the dominated classes?

(c) We do *not* want to answer these questions here, but we think it very important that it should not be forgotten — as it sometimes appears to be in some of the recent theoretical essays — that such empirical problems and political questions (must) determine the Marxist discussion on the state. We also do not wish to draw up a new variant of the Marxist derivation of the state — or to summarize the various answers which have been given to the questions mentioned in order to locate each one within such a theory. Our intention is rather to peg out a framework for a systematic analysis of the bourgeois state.

This analysis must avoid two pitfalls. They are:

1. to allow the category determining our point of departure to serve as an implicit answer to all subsequent questions — that is, no concept of the state may be posed at the outset which then needs only to have its various particular features 'unfolded',

2. to restrict ourselves in the derivation of the state to the general concept of capital as portrayed by Marx and to regard its history and empirical aspect as external to the concept, thereby including them in the analysis as mere modifications.

The 'general concept of the state' and the general concept of capital

The 'general concept' of the bourgeois state

In recent Marxist discussion of the state it has become customary to set out from a 'general concept' of the bourgeois state even where, for reasons of method, such a postulate is expressly rejected.[12] This general concept seems to be defined by the categories which Marx and Engels use in their *Jewish Question*, the *Critique of Hegel's Law of the State* and in the *German Ideology* — all in *the course of their critique of Hegel*. Such categories are: the state as standing both 'alongside and outside' bourgeois society: the 'doubling of society into society and state'; 'the illusory "general" interest as the state'. They all fit under the umbrella concept of 'bourgeois society summed up in the form of the state', the reason for the necessary summing up being seen as the conflict peculiar to bourgeois society between 'interests which are general or communal and those which are particular'. The state is understood as a form *separated* from society in which the general interest is preserved or administered.[13]

(a) Our first criticism is that the category 'separate form', despite its frequent use, is no longer properly understood and thus degenerates into a mere tag; further, that the proof of the 'particularization' is widely confused with a derivation of the state. One example may serve for many:

> In societies based on commodity production and division of labour, we find the most general form category of the bourgeois state in its separation from society undergone during historical development — a separation which is an illusory and contradictory embodiment of social generality, based on a system operating through formal personal independence coinciding with material dependence. (Hirsch 1973, p. 203.)

Even if it is maintained that only the 'most general form determination' of the bourgeois state is in question here, an as yet quite 'empty' determination which has still to be 'concretized'[14] step by step — even so it must be pointed out in criticism that the determinations of the state taken from Marx's 'early writings' relate to a determined and already substantial concept of the state.

In the early writings Marx and Engels develop the state principally in terms of Hegel's concepts — although the implications they draw differ from Hegel's — out of the fragmentation of bourgeois society posited by private property.[15] The concept of state with which we are dealing here is, however, still specifically 'juridical', couched in terms of moral and legal philosophy. The counterposition of general and particular, public and private has been the main substance of classical bourgeois theory of the state immersed in natural law ever since Hobbes and Locke. Whilst this theory understands the bourgeois subject as a 'private property owner' (Locke in particular), he is in no way seen in his economic determination on the basis of capitalist production but rather as the subject of right or law. This concept of private property stands in the total context of the bourgeois classics and characterizes their attempt to found a legitimate rule of domination.[16] The formulations mentioned above such as 'general will' or 'general interest' presuppose this concept of the subject of right and they already imply a certain transcendence of the contradictions between particular and general interests by and in the (legitimate) state.

If therefore the 'particularization' of the state was first established in juridical terms,[17] it becomes apparent that modern attempts must fail which posit new, economically determined categories[18] in the place of the legal subject (the individual, abstract and equal legal person) (Pashukanis, p. 189) and otherwise wish to preserve the earlier determinations of the state. They overlook the course taken by Marx's own critique which progressed from the still general portrayal of private property in the earlier writings to the analysis of the 'anatomy of bourgeois society' and so to the analysis of capital itself. The logical basic category of the early concept of the state, 'private property', was thus (just as 'alienation' and 'doubling') transcended in the analysis of the capitalist mode of production (cf. Reichelt 1970; Bischoff 1973).

We must remember that it is important not only to decipher this juridical concept of the state as such but to reverse the procedure and in a 'second step' (cf. Backhaus 1969) to derive its necessity. However, that can only be done on the basis of the general determinations of the capitalist mode of production.

(b) With the previous attempts to develop the 'state' in terms of Marx's analysis of the anatomy of bourgeois society setting out as they do from the 'general concept of the state' criticized above, the specific content of this 'pre-conceived' concept soon becomes a methodological trap. We have said that the transcending of the contradictions resulting from private property is already contained to a certain extent in the concept. In Hegel in particular, the contradictions to be transcended are presented from the beginning in such a manner as to allow an *a priori* unity to work itself out 'in the Spirit'.[19] Such a 'determination of the essence' also creeps into the Marxist state discussion. In so far as the state is determined *a priori* as the 'general', a general competence of 'the state' to 'administer' 'general interests', to 'regulate' the contradictions, is presupposed.[20] If *all* the functions of 'the state' are thus already contained *in nuce* in its essence, enquiries into the reasons for the functions, but above all into the limitations of the state in capitalist society can no longer be adequately answered. There then remain essentially only two ways out:

Firstly to add another category of 'essential being', that of the *class state* as the 'final' function; or *secondly* to point to historical modifications, empirical peculiarities and political, tactical variations.

The general concept of capital and the analysis of the state

The shortcomings of definitions of the state so far or of the 'general concept of the state' are essentially also the expression of an uncertainty of method and theory in the relationship between the general analysis of capital and the derivation of the state. What follows are our reflections on this question, which in our estimation is still an open one.

(a) We have said above that recent Marxist discussion on the state tries to put the category of form to fruitful use in the analysis of the state. We too see this category as the methodological point of departure for a Marxist analysis of the state, quite independent of the criticism which we have made of the content and use of statements on the 'particularization of the form'.[21]

We believe that the state can be analysed systematically only when every pre-conceived concept of the state has been abandoned, when mere associations and immediately, empirically derived notions of the 'state' (whether as authoritarian or as parliamentary—democratic) do not already infiltrate the initial stages of the enquiry as premises. The 'state' must to some extent be liberated for a theoretical reconstruction. The substance of this reconstruction, the modern state, can thus, in our opinion, not be analysed directly 'at close quarters', at least not if it is understood as a compound institution which formally connects the most disparate functions for and in relation to the process of capitalist reproduction; at least not if the modern state is to be understood in its contradictions and in its evidently limited capacity for action.

Our enquiry is not directed immediately to the 'state' as a concrete, historical structure; we attempt first to show the determinations of the state which can be derived systematically from the general concept of capital. Marx sees this concept as comprising the general laws of motion and interrelations of a form of society which is both historical and thus transient as well as being characterized by the quite definite, necessary relations which make it a capitalist society. These relations, as relations between people, take on determinate forms.

Thus commodity, money, capital, wage labour, but also commodity capital, money capital, profit, interest, wages as the 'price of labour' are essential forms whose emergence makes a society capitalist. The concept 'form' expresses both the basic problem and the essential characteristic of the historical materialist method: the investigation of the connection between the material process of production and reproduction of the life of socialized people and the relations between these people who constitute themselves in this process of material reproduction.

The materialist method consists then of examining the *forms* in which the particular relations between men are expressed and:

1. resolving them into their fixed character, a character alienated from man, apparently materially conditioned and a-historical, and then presenting them as having become historical, grown out of and reproduced by human activity, i.e. as socially and historically determined forms;

2. uncovering their inner connections, thus theoretically reconstructing the entire historical—social formation. Here the point of reference must alway be the *present* conditions in which the forms have reached their furthest point of historical development. The aim of the analysis is not, however, to realize in retrospect the 'course of history' but to present the forms in the

context in which they stand 'logically', that is, in which they reproduce themselves under the conditions of a particular historically concrete form of society.

(b) It must be determined then *whether* the state belongs amongst the essential forms of capitalist society and *how* it is to be developed as such. To answer the first part of the question, we must work out from the determinations of capital in general those conditions which make the genesis of a certain form necessary, a form which exists as the 'state' *alongside* the other forms of capitalist reproduction. The second part of the question concerns the relations existing *between* the different forms including that of the state. This means that the state must be developed not only as standing 'alongside and outside society' but also as a necessary form in the reproduction of the society itself.

We call this procedure *form analysis* for short. Our attempt to outline a conceptual framework for a Marxist analysis of the state follows Marx's presentation of the forms in which the capitalist mode of production generally reproduces itself. On this level of abstraction, however, we can give only the *general points of departure* for the development of 'functions' of the process of reproduction, which must take form in such a way as to stand outside the system of privately organized labour. The question of how this formation takes place in detail, how it is transposed into structure, institution and process of the state, can no longer be answered by form analysis. It would have to be made the subject of historical analysis. Indeed the exact delimitation and mediation of form analysis and historical analysis raises difficult problems. It depends on how one determines the historical character of Marx's concept of capital in general.[22]

Later on we try to come to terms with this difficulty by differentiating conceptually between system limits and activity limits in regard to the way state actions are related to the capitalist economy. Thus we point to steps mediating the analysis of general determinations and that of specific phenomena within an historically concrete totality.[23]

On the question of the point of departure for a derivation of the state based upon the general concept of capital

In criticism of the hypostatization of a 'general concept of the bourgeois state' we pointed out that the economic determinations of private property as capital were not yet developed in it. Our insistence on form analysis could, however, be interpreted as containing the demand that the concept of the state should assimilate all the determinations of developed capital. However, if in what follows we set out from the *commodity* as the 'cell' or primordial form of the bourgeois mode of production, we are not concerned simply to repeat the determinations of capital in order then merely to 'crown' them with the state. (This seems to us to be the procedure of numerous attempts at a derivation of the state.) Rather we shall try to show in these determinations of capital as a form of social relations all those moments to which the analysis (of the development) of the state must relate. Why we begin with the commodity, and which problems can be solved in this way can best be demonstrated by a critique of previous starting points.

1. Some Marxist authors maintain that the possibility for the state to 'administer general interests' can be developed only from the *surface* of capital. On the level of 'simple commodity circulation' there exists as yet no contradiction between 'particular and general interests'. Here, they claim, there exists a real equality (and thus identity of interest) between all subjects of exchange.

To embark from a specific concept of interest, however, distorts this method's perspective on two problems:
(a) 'Simple commodity circulation' is no historical phase existing before or at the outset of the capitalist mode of production. It represents rather the most general surface of this mode and is the most general form of the relation between the people socialized in this mode. It is fully developed only when labour power circulates as a commodity.
(b) As a result, those categories of 'freedom and equality' which are attributed to simple commodity circulation belong inherently to the concept of capital; they already contain the contradiction between formal equality of the commodity owners and their real inequality in the context of production.[24]

2. A second starting-point is the category of crisis: the contradiction between needs and value production, from whose dynamic of conflict there results the necessity of a different form of social organization from the structurally unconscious form mediated through the law of value. This approach to the problem *seems* to have the great advantage of determining the state both as organization of domination and as potential administrator of needs not satisfied by a social production governed by the law of value. However, this leaves two questions unanswered:
(a) The existence of these two fields of scope for action: the violent suppression of unsatisfied needs (i.e. class character) or the organization of the satisfaction of previously unsatisfied needs (i.e. 'welfare state' character) still does not establish the existence of the state as agent. Despite this, this derivation leads to a conception of the state which is based solely on categories of power relations, whereby the state assumes the character of an instrument, which in the last analysis is neutral.
(b) Alongside the general methodological objection that the crisis cannot establish laws or forms, the crisis approach would have to explain why the normal solution to that contradiction, namely competition and the crisis itself, should not suffice to clear up that contradiction. And at this point the argument must seek recourse in the category of class struggle.[25]

3. Other authors hold (without any digression on crisis) that the category of *class struggle* must be the point of departure for any analysis of the bourgeois state, and indeed (following Engels) for any analysis of the 'class state', of which the bourgeois state is seen merely as a particular species. To this, Pashukanis posed the classical question:

Why does the dominance of a class not continue to be that which it is — that is to say, the subordination in fact of one part of the population to another part? Why does it take on the form of official state domination? Or, which is the same thing, why is not the mechanism of state constraint created as the private mechanism of the dominant class? Why is it dissociated from the dominant class — taking the form of an impersonal mechanism of public authority isolated from society? (1951, p. 185.)

The critique of all three approaches leads us to the *social relations of commodity production*, which must be made the point of departure for the analysis of the state:

Freedom and equality of the subjects of exchange cannot remain categories related exclusively to the material relations of the law of value, but must constitute determined characteristics on the side of the acting subjects (Approach 1). The value *form* must therefore find an adequate form on the 'subjective side', a form which makes possible the association of private property owners as subjects, and without their being forced to an exceptional solution of conflicts through a crisis of their relations (Approach 2). The 'separate organization of a public apparatus of coercion must have its basis *also* in the mutual relations of private property owners (in developed form: of capital owners); the state's 'function of domination' must therefore have a dual character (Approach 3).

These arguments lead — as will be shown in the next section — to the category of the *form of law* and to the necessity of a force to guarantee the law, a force which we will call *extra-economic (coercive) force*.[26] By this we mean not so much the organized apparatus (or an instrument) but essentially only a basic function[27] which can be derived on the conceptual level of form analysis. With that we have by no means arrived at 'the state', but at different forms of social relations, namely economic and political relations,[28] which are peculiar to the bourgeois mode of production.

The divergence, the 'separation' of politics and economics which as we pointed out at the beginning seems so obvious and easy to understand, is not an historical act which happens once, but is constantly reproduced. The question is why bourgeois society, the reproduction process of which is apparently regulated in the apparently material (economic) mediation of the law of value, requires an *external* relationship between politics and economics. Since the commonplace (scientific) notion of the relation between politics and economics contains the assumption that only politics has to do with domination, that economics on the other hand has to do with 'material laws', we must look more closely at the *specific connection in this system* between domination and production.

The external relationship and inner mediation of politics and economies

The movement of value and the subject of law

That the fundamental function of the state as a 'concrete structure' is hidden in the form of the commodity has so far occurred only to Marxist theoreticians specializing in *law*. But evidently a pre-determined concept of the state has prevented them from pursuing this thread further.[29] This is what we shall attempt to do.

The movement of value as material-economic nexus represents, as the form of economic societization of the producers, a type of societization free from personal, physical force. The supremacy of this purely material nexus is ensured, however, by *exchange* as the form of societization, by *price* as the 'indicator of sociality' and by *money* as the sanctioning instance.

(Historically, however, it is true that a process necessarily preceded bourgeois society which originally led to the 'depoliticization' of the economy: the abandonment of club-law and of brigandage, and the subjection of the propertyless (i.e. those having become propertyless) to the relations of wage labour. It can be shown that the 'depoliticization' of the economy coincides with the emergence of commodity production and of money relations, and that simultaneously an instance becomes necessary to guarantee this process. Absolutism, understood in this light, is the historical phase marking the transition to the bourgeois mode of production. It is precisely the parallelism between the emergence of the money relation *and* of a separate extra-economic coercive force (seen from the point of view of the bourgeoisie)[30] that justifies the course of our analysis, which is to derive the function arising necessarily from the level of the commodity independently of the specific, concrete historical structure (here that of sovereign principalities).[31]

The material nexus of the movement of value is, however, a *social relation* amongst human beings. It is a feature of the capitalist mode of production that this relation assumes two different, opposing forms: as a relation between things and a relation between people.

The value-relation as a relationship of commodities (things) to each other exists independently of the will of the producing and 'communicating' beings. *Value* is the reified form of the sociality of their labour; in it the worker exists as nothing more than the 'result', than an abstract quantity of reified labour. On the other hand, the realization of value, i.e. the actual act of exchange, presupposes a conscious act of will in the commodity owner. Commodities cannot go to market by themselves, as Marx puts it; the act of exchange presupposes acting people and constitutes a relationship between acting people, albeit only as agents of circulation. Corresponding to the structure of exchange as the comparative commensuration of unequal products of labour (use value) according to an abstract measure (a quantity of gold representing labour time), the exchanging parties relate to each other as different beings with different needs — all of which necessitates the formation on this plane of action of an abstract point of reference making this commensuration possible. This point of reference is man as the subject of exchange. The decisive fact for the form of relationship between the exchanging parties is not the difference of needs (even if this difference constitutes the initial necessity of the exchange); what is decisive is that the parties take on an identical social and formal quality. This social quality is that they have a will which relates to the act of exchange and thus to all other subjects of exchange. This relationship is expressed in the form of a mutual recognition as private property owners (and thus private property as a fundamental human right), and in freedom of contract.

It is in this apparent freedom of the subject of exchange, in its material — economic, just as in its juridical dimension that we find the origin of the social and political theories (as well as of common, everyday notions) based on categories of action. Concepts like the 'interaction' or 'social action' of individuals from whom the functional and structural nexus of society is apparently constructed are in the pejorative sense abstractly general and they accommodate without differentiation every kind of social relationship. We intend instead to pursue further the juridical dimension of 'social action' in order to reach a clarification of the basic categories of politics. Thus we shall continue to use the terminology 'relations of will and of law'.

Relations of will give rise to a system of legal relationships of right, or of law, at the very moment when they are agreed and fixed (*Capital* vol. 1, pp. 88 f; Pashukanis, pp. 163 ff). The individual assumes the form of the *legal subject*, the relationships between individuals become 'relationships expressing will between independent, identical units, i.e. ones between legal subjects'.[32] If the category of contract, a joint act of will founded on mutual recognition, is considered to be the original modus of law, then it is clearly a form that cannot exist without constraint. Contract itself presupposes constraint or the compulsion to perform contracts: *pacta sunt servanda*. What arises, however, is no one-sided disposition over the will of another, but mutual obligation based on common agreement. With the ever-broadening nexus of exchange and thus of legal relations, the rules of exchange must be made more general so as to provide for the equality essential to the conditions by which exchange and its law of equivalent operates. The implementation of the law of value constitutes the implementation of the rule of law.[33]

The form of law, extra-economic constraint and politics

Thus out of the commodity relation as the specific, reified form of the cohesion of social labour, there arises the form of law and of the legal relation as the specific, apparently quite separate form of the relationship between isolated 'individuals'. This provides a starting-point in our conceptual derivation of extra-economic force, the 'legislative function', i.e. the function of formulating the law (not to be confused with the way in which the law comes into existence). Law, however, must be enforced and its 'appropriate enforcement' (Locke), must be guaranteed by the 'executive function'; the guarantee of law as a basic requirement itself generates extra-economic coercion.[34]

Thus out of the commodity form we can derive the function of coercive force (sanction = formulation of law and its execution) but not as yet the state as a concrete structure. The next step in the derivation can only be the *development of certain principles of form which this coercive force must observe if it is to conform adequately to the form of the commodity*. These principles are to be found in the concept of the general law, the *norm* as embodying the impersonal, general, public quality of the law.[35] As the specific form of commodity production separates human, social relations into material relations and relations of legal persons, so the cohesion of society constitutes itself in a dual manner as abstract and 'supra-personal'. The material relations take place only if the subjects of law act in conformity with the movement of value. The intercourse reified in the equivalence of circulation and in the form of money demands that the subjects within this social context (a) act as towards a thing, and (b) that they consciously make their own the imperative of this thing.

In the law there emerges, on the side of the subjects, the adequate form of a reified social cohesion and the fixed, 'positive' norms find a material sanctioning instance analogous to the function of money *vis-à-vis* prices: the extra-economic force of coercion.[36]

(This genetic relationship and structural identity between value and law also reveals itself in the parallelism pertaining to the original historical activity of the state. The fixing of weights and measures together with the ensuring of a 'peaceful marketplace' shows the identity of the principles of the form of the rule of law and of money. Weights and measures, as well as later the money standard, are the formal pre-conditions of the exchange nexus. It is precisely because the carrying through of the law of value (principle of equivalence) permits the comparative commensuration of differing value quantities that money as the external standard of value must be fixed, codified and guaranteed.)

The first typifying feature of *politics* we can now identify as being relations of will (actions, 'interactions') between independent, equal subjects of law. These take the *form* of struggles to establish, or disagreements on how to interpret, rights (transferred only later from the 'political' sphere to the separate apparatus of justice); their *content*, however, is 'economic', i.e. dictated by movements of production and value realization.

We must be clear that the abstract categories of commodity production and circulation do not disappear with the emergence of capital as the fundamental social relation; rather they form the general categories of the surface appearance.[37] The inner changes of function emerging with capital alter nothing of this outer form. This is important in understanding the fact that the formality of law and of the state based on the rule of law (*Rechtsstaat*) is a functional requirement of capitalism that does not simply disappear when class structures develop. The basic form of politics too, the struggle for law and for the instance or agency guaranteeing it, the extra-economic force of coercion, is on the basis of class relations no mere illusion but the very form in which the class struggle continuing within the bourgeois state finds political expression.[38]

Private property and the dual structure of the rule of capital

The decisive functional change in the extra-economic coercive force expressed in the shift to the new function of the class state occurs with the (here always conceptual) development of money into capital and of labour into wage labour — both being dependent on the separation of producers from the conditions of production. But here too we must start our analysis from the forms developed above so as not to conceptualize the function of the class state in a crude empirical way as mere brute force.

The principle of equivalence in exchange and of the appropriation of products on the standard of the workers' own 'objectified' labour is broken with the emergence of capital. The exchange relations remain relations of equivalence in form but in content they are unequal.[39] Labour power as a commodity is exchangeable at its value but it produces — by virtue of its use value — a higher value which is appropriated by the capitalist in production. This new value he can then realize in circulation.

On both sides of the circulation this surplus value appears lawful. In the exchange relation between capital and wage labour, all 'labour' appears as paid (because the dual character of labour disappears in the form of the 'price of labour'); in the exchange relation between capitalist and 'buyer', surplus value appears as profit and is seen as a mere addition to the cost (and interpreted in totally differing ways: as a premium to recompense abstinence, as the return on the production factor capital, as the gain resulting from the situation or from business acumen, or simply to be accounted as a residual category).

As the extra-economic force protects commodity production's fundamental right, private property, it protects also:

1. the right of capital and wage labour equally, thus also the ownership of labour power (as a commodity);

2. the right of capital to the product produced in the production process.

To guarantee property when that property relates to the ownership of commodities thus means to guarantee the specific form of the production process: the capital-relation. All this leaves the form of the law unaffected; it bears no mark of a change of function. Formally, property = property (and that too is no 'illusion'! Extra-economic force also protects the right of ownership of labour power). In effect, however, to protect the ownership of capital also means to protect the rule of capital over wage labour in the process of the production of value. This rule, however, has now split itself into two: into a purely material form, the pre-political rule of the conditions of production (as capital) over the producers on the one side, and into abstract, general, public, i.e. fully political rule on the other.

The doubling of social rule finds its expression in the separation between private and public law — between the law (in the narrower sense) relating to the reproduction of bourgeois society (a law which pivots around private property) and the law relating to the structure and jurisdictional competence of public rule. This division of bourgeois law, in the wider sense, into apparently independent areas makes the relationship of economics to politics appear even more external. The protection of private property — and thus private property itself — are seen as being so objective and neutral that it becomes necessary to uncover the points of conflict from which we can interpret the activity of the extra-economic coercive force as functioning in the sense of capital and thus the political rule as functioning in the sense of capital as class-rule. The development of these points of conflict is important because in the slovenly formulations of many Marxist theories of the state 'the functionality of the state for capital by virtue of its essential nature' is so taken for granted that the exact analysis of the struggles, conflicts and crises concerning the changing forms of state (in the narrower sense of government systems) is no longer possible.

First we shall deal with the moments of conflict and then, retracing our steps, analyse the way in which the extra-economic force of coercion affects the varying categories of private property owners.

Legal relations and class conflict

(a) From the character of labour as a commodity there results a fundamental breach of the borderline between purely material relations and relations of legal persons (which, through a long process of mediation, are also political relations). (This breach renders impossible any attempts at delimitation based on any kind of systems theory.) The owners of the commodity labour power carry together with the commodity themselves as concrete beings onto the market: figuratively, the worker as *legal subject* remains for ever in circulation, never entering the factory, never shouted at by a foreman, sitting besuited in his car before the factory gates; the worker as *concrete being* puts on his blue overalls and becomes the 'factor of production', a material function within the system of capital production, he acquires the form of variable capital.[40] As such a factor, he is subservient to the rule of capital: the voluntary act of exchange has become a one-sided subjection to an alien will. The 'voluntariness' of the worker as legal subject is based on his compulsion to sell his labour power as a concrete being so as to reproduce his own life.

(b) The legal guarantee of property in capital guarantees not only the rule of every individual capitalist over his workers but also the reproduction of the relations of capital in that it safeguards the accumulation of capital (legally ensured in the right of free disposal over existing and newly realized ownership of value).

(c) The value of the commodity labour power is not determined in the same way as the value of other commodities. All other commodities represent only a certain quantity of 'objectified' or 'dead' labour. The reproduction of the commodity labour power is, however, the life process of the concrete being with his concrete needs. The value of this commodity, i.e. the quantity of indispensable necessaries required to maintain life must always be a matter for struggle (see *Capital*, vol. 1, Ch. 10, 'The Working Day').

(d) The saleability of the commodity labour power depends on the conditions of the market (as a reflection of the accumulation process). This dependence seems to have the same material 'natural' form as that of any other commodity. If, however, other commodities perish, the labour incorporated in them was in vain; when the commodity labour power perishes, it is man himself who perishes.

All these factors create conflict — the result not of the *objective* movement of capital even if conditioned by it, but of the working class's claim to the right to live. These conflicts, i.e. class conflicts, express themselves in historically varying ways but they are nevertheless the fundamental conflicts from which the relationship of 'politics' to 'economics' is determined.[41]

This relationship has now become an external one and our analysis must therefore pursue the mode in which the forms affect each other as external and trace the general features of their effect on the class relations within production. We must also show the forms of mediation in which extra-economic coercive force can bring itself to bear on the material aspect of the reproduction of capital.

On the dual effect of law in bourgeois society

The abstract and apparently 'neutral' character of the extra-economic force, at the level of the forms of circulation, proves, when we analyse how it affects people (legal persons) according to their class position, to be no longer neutral but related to the capital-relation.

(a) In so far as law lays down only the *procedures* necessary to ensure the operation of the law of value, it regulates the processes of circulation by

guaranteeing that the subjects behave in accordance with the demands of
the material economic process. In circulation the subjects are called upon to
behave as the mere 'character-masks' of the relations implied by this process.
The *formal character* of law applies in effect, not to its subjects but to
things.[42] Accordingly someone who possesses property is protected not as a
person but as the owner of commodities, etc. This protection applies to:

1. the right of free movement of things (above all capital). Freedom in
the sense of 'independence from an alien will' here has the (economic!)
function of making the piece of property free to adapt to the workings of
the law of value (to be sold, or invested in this way or that, etc.).[43]

2. The equality which here emerges as a principle of law is in effect the
equality of treatment (abstract equal validity) of every commodity corresponding to the principle of equivalence in exchange. Here too the principle
applies not to the concrete person but to the legal subject as a necessary
category of commodity production. Through this subject it applies to the
labour materialized in the commodity, to the precise quantity of labour
in each case which in the process of comparison effected on the market gives
the commodity its value and thus its exchangeability. This is the law of
circulation.

(Freedom and equality applied in this sense to labour power leads
necessarily to the proscribing of workers' combinations as happened in
the nineteenth century and in the USA still in the twentieth century; or
alternatively to the political and economic 'recognition' of such combinations at the same time as relying on their ineffectiveness when confronted
with market laws. (Mill 1962, Book 5, ch. 10).)

(b) In terms of production, the law of private property applies to the right
to conform to the objective movement of the law of value in the private
production process (through re-organization, technical change, increase in
productivity) and this not merely formally but through the flexible, free
conduct of affairs. Here labour power counts no longer as the fine, free
legal subject but rather as a factor of production with which the property
owner can do as he wishes, although his 'will' is conditioned by the objective
movement of the economy. In the worker's eyes this movement divests
itself of its pure 'objectivity' and confronts him as the direct rule of capital.
Here we see that for the worker freedom and equality in the production
process are once again suspended.

(c) In so far as 'freedom' and 'equality' as rights were from the beginning
not merely functional in economic terms, but were citizens' rights connect-
ing legal subjects with the extra-economic coercive force (appearing at first
only in the form of subjection, then later in the form of the right to political
participation and to share in the services provided by the state)[44] these rights
concealed within themselves a danger for the bourgeois system. Understood
as the claims of concrete human beings (human rights) they constitute to
some extent the legitimating point at which class struggle can break into

'politics'. This is true in that people derive from the rights to 'freedom' and 'equality' the right to fight for their 'interests'[45] as well as the right to aim beyond the system of the bourgeois mode of production. This feature inherent in the legally constituted state (*Rechtsstaat*) is of vital importance. Emphasis on this, however, should not lead to a naive contraposition of 'state based on the rule of law' (*Rechtsstaat*) to 'class state' (*Klassenstaat*).[46] Instead we must first analyse the dual effect of the bourgeois legal state which protects 'private property owners' generally as well as property in the form of capital.

Extra-economic coercion as class coercion

Now we can attempt to determine the character of the extra-economic coercive force as class coercion in general:

(a) In relation to the commodity nexus and to the commodity owners as legal subjects, the extra-economic force is no more than a neutral, 'third' force (like money) standing over the exchanging parties. Abstract equality is its pre-condition and thus its effect can only be an identical one for everyone. This is expressed in the concept that law is formulated as general principles: that the general norm is the form of law.[47]

(b) In relation to the reproduction of capital, the extra-economic coercive force guarantees not just the possibility of buying and selling but also the compulsion to sell resulting from the division of the producers from the conditions of production. It guarantees the reign of capital in the private production process, i.e. the unrestricted employment of labour power for the purpose of producing surplus value.

The first guarantee protects the relation of capital in general, the second the particular area of operation of individual capitals.[48]

(c) By this analysis of how law and the extra-economic coercive force operate we have in effect developed the concept of the 'particularization of the state'. We have shown *why* the 'state' (as a concrete structure) constitutes in essence a general force of coercion which confronts even the individual bourgeois (individual competing capital) as a separated, neutral instance, but which *at the same time* and only *through* this separation is, by virtue of its existence as a central force guaranteeing the law, a class force.

Precisely in order to be a class force, the state must dissociate or 'particularize itself' (*sich besondern*) from the ruling class.

The basic forms of social relations as mediating forms and limitations on extra-economic interventions in the process of reproduction

Before we investigate the points of departure for an analysis of the structure of the state, we wish briefly to specify the forms through which extra-economic interventions are mediated and their limitations.

We have established that in a commodity-producing society certain basic forms of social relations emerge. Of these we can say:
(a) the material—economic relations present themselves as monetary relations between people;
(b) relations between the subjects of exchange take on the form of legal relations.[49]

The extra-economic coercive force always bases its actions on the specific monetary and/or legal form of social relations or creates such relations for the purpose of its interventions. This means, however, that these attempts to intervene do not directly and immediately shape the relations between the social classes particularly in the sphere of private production, but are mediated through the basic forms.

The analysis of the form of law and of the extra-economic coercive force showed that actions stemming from this force and mediated through law

1. have different effects on the legal subjects according to their position in the reproductive process;

2. can only take effect on the reproductive process from *outside*, mediated through the legal subjects.

Extra-economic force thus 'regulates' the material relations of reproduction externally by establishing standards or norms for behaviour. Only where private property owners are legal subjects (in their relations within circulation) are they subject to the force of the state. In their private sphere, where their property is at their disposal, they are beyond the reach of state authority.

Just as in law, what in money appears as an external 'limitation', can be seen to be nothing other than the autonomization of forms resulting from the laws of capitalist commodity production.

Money as the externalized form of the reproductive process shows the limitations of the 'state' in two respects:

1. 'State monetary policy' (in all its different spheres) affects the subjects as *money-owners*, not in their function in the process of reproduction. From this direction too, the impact on the classes is a varying one (even although the *form* of 'state' activity is the same).

2. Actions *vis-à-vis* the money-owner through the medium of money affect the process of reproduction only externally. Although limitations or demands implemented through 'monetary policy' do have effects on the behaviour in the reproduction process of those affected,

> the qualitative *content* of this effect is something that is not subject to the act of will of the state, something that is an inherent part of the bourgeois subject's freedom of decision and thus subjected to the laws and process of competition. (Wirth 1973, p. 35 f.)

Two objections could be raised, however, to this argument concerning the mediate nature of extra-economic intervention:

1. That the bourgeois state is constituted first and foremost as a coercive force intervening *directly* and 'regulating' class relations. On no account would we deny that the open (and indeed, in certain circumstances, terroristic) use of state force is and has been an actual occurrence and always a possibility. But it is (seen in terms of our general analysis) 'only' force proceeding from the bonds of the legal relations which we have already analysed. Furthermore, this force lies at the basis of legal relations as a guaranteeing force — it is the same justice and the same police, even if through different branches, that tracks down and sentences both traffic offender and 'radical'. This is not contradicted but rather is confirmed by the fact that, as class conflicts become increasingly institutionalized in law[50], even in the direct use of force the state does and must increasingly ensure that its actions respect legal formality.

2. That the state also or principally develops out of the necessity to provide 'general, material conditions of reproduction' and that in this it acts under its own responsibility and is competent for its own organization, i.e. it acts directly, without mediation.[51]

We do not see in this objection any argument against the view that extra-economic interventions in relation to the process of reproduction are in principle mediated and limited. For:

(a) the 'state', in pursuing such concerns, often does not function *as a state* but as *individual capital* (state-run enterprises of very many kinds);

(b) the 'organization' of certain services, such as education, is in fact characterized by its *mediated* relationship to the reproductive process (hence the difficulties in evaluating its function for capital, as the whole Marxist debate over further education has shown).

However, this cannot finally and comprehensively serve to determine the limitations on the extra-economic force of coercion in its relation to the process of capital reproduction. We must attempt to show 'the limitations of the state in the capitalist system' from two sides: that of the economic process as material process of the movement of value (in the form of capital), and that of class relations in so far as they present themselves as relations between 'legal subjects'.

The state and the movement of capital

We must again recall the limits of what can be done at the level of the analysis of form: the investigation of the 'general' and the 'communal', prompted by commodity circulation as the specific form of societization and general surface of society, covering over even the capital-relation, leads to the establishment of a social function which must be formed 'alongside and outside' the special interests contained in the exchange relation. The question of how this function is institutionalized lies beyond the scope of this conceptual level and is, as we have said above, the subject of the historical analysis of the genesis of the bourgeois state. What is important is that the function *is* organized and finds a corresponding structure and thus an agent of action in society. The limit to form analysis consists in the fact that, although the *possibility* of the realization of this 'state-function' is established, the *necessity* for it is not. This limit to analysis is familiar to us from the derivation of crisis, the general possibility of which can be demonstrated even on the level of commodity exchange, but the necessity for which cannot be conceptually determined (cf. TSV, vol. 2, pp. 513 ff) — despite the further development in the presentation of the concept of capital and despite the fact that the conditions for its possibility are developed with increasing specificity.

Here, as we see it, there is a fundamental difficulty in the discussion of the state: it is true that we have described the inner relationship between the mode of production and *one* of its functions, a function presupposing an organization 'alongside and outside' buyers and sellers as parties to exchange. But we have not yet derived *the* state which in our understanding contains a *multiplicity of connections with and functions for the process of reproduction*.

This is, however, overlooked if one starts out from a general concept of the state. If one starts from such a concept the competence for *certain* functions is to some extent accounted for *a priori*. We intend to demonstrate the consequences of such a concept by looking at some approaches to a Marxist analysis of the state which we have already in part cited in connection with the dialectic of state and society. The intention of these approaches is to 'derive' systematically the relationship between the state and the economic process of reproduction and thus to establish how 'the state' *can* at all exist as a particular social form and why it indeed *must* exist as such.

Three attempts at a derivation of the state and their respective determination of the functions of the state

(a) Flatow and Huisken (1973) insist quite rightly that both questions must be answered. They themselves establish the possibility of the formal particularization of the state from the existence of a particular 'sphere of state-hood (*Staatlichkeit*)' (p. 118) which crystallizes out in the structures of problems and consciousness on the 'surface of bourgeois society'. The substance of this sphere comprises the 'general interests' of those drawing incomes, interests which, regardless of the different 'sources' of the incomes, are general and equal as far as the maintenance of the preconditions guaranteeing the incomes is concerned. The content of the concept of 'general interests' is, for Flatow and Huisken, constituted by all that the individuals as owners of a particular source of income have in common, but including also the owners of other sources of income in so far as they share interests other than those conditioned by the material nature of the source of income: security of the source of income against theft, exhaustion, etc.; the guarantee of economic growth as pre-condition of the highest possible income for all; the harmonious, crisis-free functioning of reproduction to ensure continuity of income (pp. 108 ff.).

The category of 'general interest' already conceptually includes the entire empirical gamut of state functions. Thus Flatow and Huisken see 'general' as applying to everything from a characteristic of the form of law (Flatow and Huisken view this on the level of the agent , the property-owner) to a designation for the common interests of any, almost arbitrarily composed group.

Nevertheless, they believe that in explaining the state in terms of the dialectic of general and particular interests, they are deriving the *necessity* of its form independently of the content of specific state-functions. Because the individual property owners are by definition concerned only with their particular interest, and because, on the other hand, the pursuit of these particular interests presupposes the realization of general ones, an instance must emerge which is responsible for these general interests.[52] It is, however, merely a question of definition to say that the pursuit of particular interests excludes the realization of general ones. Marx's presentation of competition shows precisely that the realization of general interest is the unconscious and unsought result of the actions of individual private property owners.[53]

The essential point in this derivation, however, seems to be that the contradiction between general and particular interests is used to establish 'the doubling of society into society and state' and that this state is already a functionally fully determined form: the state is, as it were, merely in search of the general interests which it has to realize. Concerning their derivation of the form of state, Flatow and Huisken point out that 'a methodological constraint to come to a *general* derivation of specific state activities no longer exists in our context' (p. 136). The view, correct in our opinion, that specific functions of the state cannot be derived from the general concept of capital, is argued by Flatow and Huisken by way of a pure dialectic of concepts. For all these state-activities emanate solely from the concept of the general interest — they are as it were, and in our formulation, nothing more than the historically real, outer manifestations of the 'essence' of the bourgeois state.

The functions of the state, i.e. the areas to which state policies relate, and which appear in the division into departments and ministries [a thesis which Flatow and Huisken do not follow up — BJK] do not constitute the essence of the bourgeois state; rather the full spectrum of these areas can only be analysed if one sets out from the concept of the bourgeois state. But, because the concept of the state characterizes its form, it at the same time encapsulates the *general conditions* for the genesis of the functions of the state (the administration of the general interest) (p. 137).

A fatal result of this way of determining the essence of the state is that *contradictions* in its activity in fulfilling its possible functions can no longer be explained from the *general* features of the state. Such contradictions are then correspondingly removed by Flatow and Huisken to the empirical level (they speak of the 'heterogeneity of the empirical actions of the bourgeois state' (p. 124)), whilst what is 'general' in state activity asserts itself only through these heterogeneous empirical elements (in merely linguistic analogy to the oscillation of prices around value).[54]

(b) In contrast to the attempt to explain the essence of the bourgeois state from the structure of the *surface* of bourgeois society, the 'Projekt Klassenanalyse'[55] derives the state directly from the system of social division of labour and the contradiction between the material demands of social production and their bourgeois form as private labour. The 'Projekt Klassenanalyse' sees the necessity of the state as arising from the apparently naturally given fact that labour functions exist 'which *a priori* are communal' (p. 130) and which thus by definition cannot be realized through the unconscious, mediated form of social organization. The state is therefore allocated its place as functional agent of society in the making and securing of the 'general conditions of production'. In this way the formation of the state 'solves', as the authors of the 'Projekt Klassenanalyse' rightly express it, the contradiction between communal and indirectly (i.e. not immediately) social functions.

The construction of an '*a priori* communality' peculiar to certain labour functions is seen to be deficient as soon as the attempt is made to use it as a criterion for differentiation within the division of labour. The criterion given by the authors is tautological: all forms of labour are considered communal which 'directly serve to accomplish communal tasks . . . and which thus cannot be performed under the form of labour that is only indirectly social' (p. 130). We can also see that in the following 'derivation' of the state by Engels (quoted by the authors of the 'Projekt Klassenanalyse') only the problem but not its solution is to be found:

> The matter can be most easily grasped from the point of view of the division of labour. Society creates certain communal functions which it cannot do without. The people appointed to implement them form a new branch of division of labour within society. This means that they represent certain interests *vis-à-vis* their mandatories, they grow independent of them and . . . the state is there. And the same thing happens as with commodity and later with money exchange . . . (Letter from Engels to Conrad Schmidt, 27 October 1890; MESW vol. 3, p. 491.)

But why is it the *state* that emerges and not a new branch of social production within the capital relation? The question remains unanswered as to why the state assumes (*a priori*) certain tasks and why capital should not be in the position to develop forms which do justice to the specific character of labour (of course in its own way, i.e. by conforming without any plan or awareness to necessities of the system which confront it in the form of 'bottlenecks' and 'barriers' of the production and circulation processes). Without wishing to overtax its use as evidence, we must here refer to the so-called 'road-building' example (*Grundrisse*, pp. 524 ff.) where Marx assumed a regression of state production functions in the areas commonly counted amongst the 'general conditions of production' to the extent to which capital developed socially. And we must point out that Marx considered the formation of limited companies, for example, to be a means by which capitalist forms of socialization adapted themselves to tasks that could no longer be solved with the old forms of organization.

What is essential to our argument, however, is the fact that for the 'Projekt Klassenanalyse' too, the doubling of society into society and state establishes the state from the start, without any mediation, in a definite form that is functional for capital. In the 'Projekt Klassenanalyse' there emerges a very simple chain of argument: if the relation of capitalist production by its very nature implies social domination and if the state guarantees it the necessary 'general framework conditions', then the state is proved to be by its very nature repressive; the ruling class can use it as its *instrument*.

(c) A third possible derivation of the state has been developed by Altvater (1973). He too explains the necessity of the form of the state from the relationship between the bourgeois form of the socialization of production and the objective demands of social organization which cannot be realized in its bourgeois form. Alongside competition the state is functionally necessary for total social reproduction. Capital, says Altvater:

> . . . requires at its base a special institution which is not subject to its limitations as capital, one whose transactions are not determined by the necessity of producing surplus-value, one which is *in this sense* a special institution 'alongside and outside bourgeois society', and one which at the same time provides, on the undisputed basis of capital itself, the immanent necessities that capital neglects. Consequently, bourgeois society produces in the state a specific form which expresses the average interest of capital. (Above, p. 41.)

As with 'Projekt Klassenanalyse's' derivation, the state steps in, as it were, alongside competition (which Altvater describes more precisely as being capitalist) in order to perform the necessary tasks which the other form of socialization cannot accomplish. However, to the extent that the state is obliged — here due to *capital*'s limitations, not to pre-determined factors arising from the material nature of these tasks — to take them over, there results not merely a dualism or *juxtaposition* (which would imply no restrictions on the tasks assumed by each side) but an actual *contradiction*.

Although the state is not subject to the limitations of capital as capital, its limitations grow out of its specific relationship to capital. The need to take over certain tasks results here from the 'possibilities and limitations' of capital:

> What the general conditions of production are depends precisely on what cannot, within a given historical situation, be taken over by capital itself.[56]

The 'definition' of the general conditions of production in relation to the level of accumulation and the conditions of valorization erases the difference between them and those social labour functions which, because of the movement of the social rate of profit, can no longer serve as a sphere of capital investment, — that is, the difference between state functions when capital is scarce and when it is abundant. His historical relativization does not mean that Altvater introduces the state as a factor of pure historical contingency. While the system of social labour contains no indication as to which tasks must in their nature be performed 'alongside and outside' the system of particular interests, Altvater's argument leads to the conclusion that it is the state's general function to undertake, should the necessity arise, the tasks involved at any given time.[57]

In a certain sense, the contributions of von Flatow and Huisken, the 'Projekt Klassenanalyse' and of Altvater provide three logical possibilities for deriving the state from an immanent contradiction in capitalist socialization. While the first authors focus on the contradiction between private property and the general conditions of its existence (formulated on the level of interests), and the second on that between unconsciously social and communal production — both starting from the level of commodity production — Altvater specifies the contradiction between capitalist socialization and the material demands of production — and thus takes capital as his starting point.

As regards the determination of the limits of state intervention the external relation to the movement of capital, the form fixation, the movement of rates of profit, etc. and the forms in which these limits appear (stagflation, armaments–budgets, etc.), we agree broadly with Altvater, although we shall try to express the determination of these limits as a problem of method more precisely and systematically. We are here chiefly concerned with showing that it is characteristic of all three variants that whatever the root contradiction, the *result* of the derivation is always the 'state' as a fully determined form — a form which in its turn is seen as the *essence* of the state and thus already embryonically contains all the state's functions, responsibilities and possibilities of action.

The points of relation for the functions of the state

In contrast we deem it of crucial importance not to approach the problem of the individual functions of the state on the basis of a general concept of the bourgeois state, however determined, but to analyse these functions individually in relation to the process of the reproduction of capital.

It is important, therefore, in determining the oft-cited 'possibilities and limitations' of the state in relation to its freedom to mould social structures, not to fall into the vicious circle in which every activity of the state is no more than a manifestation of a determination already contained in its 'essence' — a determination which can thus operate only within boundaries prescribed by this essence. We have uncovered as the result of the 'division' of politics and economy the condition for the existence of an extra-economic instance and this engenders the abstract possibility of an intervention from 'outside' in the spontaneously socialized process of society's material reproduction. The realization of this possibility requires careful historical— empirical analysis reconstructing conceptually the genesis of each of its functions. This would trace the process by which they are detached from particular stages of the reproduction of capital, the conditions which prevent their being carried out as matters of specific private concerns, their centralization and institutional consolidation as a structure which then becomes a 'moment' of the historically specific state. Even though this process cannot be anticipated by form-analysis, it can nevertheless be used to systematize the points of insertion given as available to the state when it relates as an external instance to the process of reproduction of capital, and this allows us to ascertain some basic characteristics of this external relation.

The process of reproduction must present itself in a dual manner to the extra-economic instance: (a) as an economic process mediated in an apparently objective manner; (b) as a system of social relationships. This dual appearance only expresses the condition of existence of that instance (which we have described above as the 'division' of politics and economy).

(a) In his presentation of capital as maintaining and expanding itself through motion, i.e. in the metamorphoses of the circuit of a single capital and in the interweaving of circuits and forms of circuits of the many capitals, Marx uses the category, 'functional forms', in order to draw attention to one particular problem: reproduction occurs through forms which capital must assume in its various stages of production and circulation, forms which *although related functionally* as forms of *capital* to the *total process*, are, *as forms, subject to their own conditions.*[58]

'Functional form' implies both the inner connection and the external lack of connection of the reproduction process — and thus the 'relative autonomy' of the individual forms (of capital), the possibility of their autonomization. Marx develops the functional forms of 'industrial capital', corresponding to the stages of circulation, as money, commodity and means of production/labour (as the factors of production). Suffice it merely to mention that, if examined more closely and if those functions of capital were included that differ from those of industrial capital (*Capital* vol. 2,

p. 83), these forms would increase significantly in number. The important point is that the state relates to reproduction through these forms, and that the forms of the production stage acquire through private property (see above p. 127) a particular state-free status. Money has been characterized by us as a *form of mediation* of state interventions, *vis-à-vis* capital it is a point of insertion; but only from the perspective of capital is it a functional form, which can therefore be understood only from its context, or interconnections.

The way that functions with a specific form operate (in the case of money, its functions as medium of circulation, means of payment and reserve fund; in the case of the commodity: its function of realization) is not obvious with reference to their functions for capital. Thus shortage of money (with the corresponding phenomena in the money form) can 'indicate' completely different, even contrary movements in the reproduction of capital. Marx has described in detail the confusion which this caused in England's banking legislation and monetary policy in the first half of the nineteenth century;[59] the results of G. Lindner's analysis (1973) of the policies of the German Federal Bank can be understood in a similar manner.

As regards the historical development of attempts at regulation by the state, we can at this point surmise that these are *fixated on individual forms* (on the basis of the historically experienced tendencies towards autonomization of these very forms), which thus also come to be seen as a possible cause of crisis or as a factor of control, and that ranges of instruments, criteria of intervention and theories of crisis have been developed corresponding to these form-specific functions. Policy thus fixed in form must necessarily reinforce appearances, i.e. strengthen still more or 'consolidate' politically these tendencies towards autonomization.

A further thesis might be derived from the manner in which such form-fixed state functions are institutionalized: the state structure would have to be understood as a complex system of policies, with only an apparent, external unity, which are by and large initially linked independently of one another to the movement of capital and are only subsequently more or less brought together (for 'less' see the status of the Federal Bank and the various organizational forms of state concerns). These policies, which orient themselves, as we have shown, to the forms in which reproduction is expressed, can contradict or duplicate one another in an unforeseen manner: in the last resort they lead to haphazardly regulated results. *For the inner connection of these policies*, their logic, lies outside their formal unity — the state; *it lies in the movement of capital*.

(b) Just as the state relates, in the matter of material forms, to those of the sphere of circulation, so too in the matter of social relations. It has already been shown how the state relates to individuals, seeing them as subjects of law and as formally free and equal subjects of the market and imposing on them only their own abstract will. Now we cannot separate the 'material' and the 'social' relations of the state to reproduction in such a way that the state intervenes via the first, and via the second only guarantees the laws of appropriation of private property. When it does not employ the material form of money, the state intervenes by dragooning the legal subjects even when the object of the intervention is the material interrelations. At this point the 'system-limit' inherent in state measures (interventions, functions) is revealed — a limit which, as we shall see, is formed in the last resort by that social relation which also constitutes a functional form of capital: the social relation between labour power and means of production, between living and objectified, dead, labour in production.

Private property (and thus the social relations of the sphere of circulation) forms a system-limit only in the wider sense. This limit does indeed characterize the formal independence of the sphere of reproduction, but only the *formal* independence. For there is no doubt that the state intervenes in the sphere of private property — particularly in times of crisis when it forces the working class to sell their labour power at a certain price and thus suspends their right, resulting from ownership of their labour power, to their own conceptions of price.

The system-limit in the narrower sense is production as the functional form of capital and capital's 'material metamorphosis' [60] *in contrast to the purely formal metamorphoses of circulation.* When the state intervenes at the source of production of surplus value, it infringes the limit critical to the survival of the system. The withholding of investment, the removal of production to other countries, the withdrawal of capital are spectacular forms of reaction against such intervention. A critical position is already reached if, for example, anything more than symbolic price controls are attempted (in analogy to wage restrictions). In contrast to wage labour, capital is very well able to steer against this type of intervention with such measures as production cut-backs, demands for compensation, pressures on the working-class and many more. When price controls affect property rights, the equality of such state interventions *vis-à-vis* capital and labour is merely formal.

The system-limit is fixed by the form determinations developing out of the relation of capitalist production and it can therefore be derived on the level of form-analysis.

Discussion of the limits of state autonomy of action must, however, be concretized on the analytical level of historical movement which we reach in the next section.

The State and Class Movement

System-limit and limit of activity [61]

From the external relation of the 'state' to the economic process we determined hypothetically two features which characterize its functional activity:

1. the necessary reference to forms whose functional interrelation within the reproduction of capital is not transparent, and which on the contrary are themselves autonomized and give a false indication of the conditions and requirements of state activity. (A high interest rate can indicate good conditions of valorization or merely a need for means of payment; a steady flow of commodities can mean good opportunities for realization or simply stockpiling by commercial capital.)

2. The theoretical fixation (problem-perception) on,[62] and observation of particular forms leads to opposing policies, since these policies are elaborated within a state structure which is itself a conglomeration of institutionalized functions.

These two features impose on state action 'activity limits' over and above the actual 'system limit'. The system limit can be specified on the level of form determinations, activity limits can only be specified on the level of historical movement.

We cannot here undertake to determine a limit of activity for a particular state with respect to particular functions. Instead we shall analyse more closely the limit of activity which, in our eyes, is the decisive and final one.

The core and thus 'state-free' process of the capitalist mode of production is the 'material metamorphosis' of capital in the production process — that is the process in which not only the substance of the distribution process is generated but also in which primary distribution is already decided upon. The measures taken by the state as 'framework-conditions' of reproduction in the areas of money, trade, foreign trade, economic law, etc., are indeed (for individual capitals more or less) connected with this central process, but they are basically no more than attempts to regulate that which the process of capital 'controls'.[63] The question of the activity limits of the state — whether in the attempt to help capitalist reproduction to continue in the face of its own barriers, or in the attempt to limit the controlling freedom of capital in a manner which 'transcends the system' — must be answered by reference to the conditions of surplus value production. As soon, however, as constellations emerge or state measures are taken which infringe this central process of capital, its relevance manifests itself: capital reacts in a spectacular form, by investment strikes, inflation, etc.

Alternatively, when the workers' (class) struggle (whether confined to the plant or not) restricts capital's 'freedom to control', the state reasserts — if need be, in equally spectacular fashion — the right of capital. If we stress the process of *production* of surplus value as the decisive moment in determining the activity limit and not the rate of profit or conditions of accumulation, etc., which are singled out by most Marxist authors, it is because a functioning process of exploitation in production and the possibility of its extension and intensification (i.e. high rates of profit, high surplus product also for political disposal) alleviate all the state's governmental problems; quite the opposite is the case where the extension and intensification encounters resistance.

The decisive and final limit of state activity is thus set by the working class although it is to some degree first felt and politically transmitted by capital on the basis of falling profits and worsening conditions of accumulation.

We maintain in this context that the limit of state activity will differ depending on whether this activity is directed at wage-labour or capital as the object of intervention. The state can intervene in the rights of the working class with considerably more force (from the point of view of form) because these rights are only covered very generally by private property. Such instances of intervention, however, themselves have limits in the functions of the capitalist reproduction process where an intervention mediated through the regulation of working class rights affects the system of capital reproduction too. Since labour power (LP) functions as a form of capital (v) in the reproduction process of capital, all attempts to intervene in the rights of the person result — because in labour power person and thing cannot be separated — in affecting the movement of the thing. Thus the restriction of working class mobility (as for example in fascism) can lead to the capital represented by v being regulated disfunctionally for the reproduction process of capital. Problems can arise when the elimination of the labour market means that the composition of the capital mass v can no longer be regulated in terms of quantity and quality (training) according to the demands of the process of valorization.

The asymmetry of the limit of activity with regard to capital and labour is a birthmark of the bourgeois state: 'negatively', i.e. directed against capital, the limit of the system is soon reached; 'positively', i.e. directed against wage-labour, intervention is determined only according to the limit which the working class can erect in accordance with the historical phase of the class constellations. And this, in fact, is the decisive historical moment in the investigation of the state's limits of activity. Of course, this phase cannot be separated from the conditions of accumulation and the degree of socialization of labour.[64] Periods of dictatorial rule through the bourgeois state can, however, easily create 'unevennesses', as the German example shows, so that these last-mentioned conditions, which derive from the level of the productive forces and the historical conditions of valorization, are bad indicators of the class constellation. We believe that in characterizing capitalism according to periods, particularly where such problems as the relative autonomy of the state are concerned, one must focus on the features of the long-term, firmly delimited class constellation rather than on features which in the last resort must depend on market structures (competitive and monopoly capitalism, etc.).[65]

Class Constellation as Limit of Activity

(a) At this point the concept of the *surface of the capitalist process of reproduction* becomes relevant, a concept employed particularly by Flatow and Huisken in their derivation of the bourgeois state. We believe we have shown that the *conceptual* derivation of the state cannot begin at this point. However, the 'surface' now becomes relevant since we are concerned with the *historical* constitution of state functions.

Class relations in capitalist society are not merely concealed by the equality and freedom of the private-property owners arising from the forms of simple commodity circulation discussed at the beginning of this study — rather they actually *appear* on the surface of developed competition as the relations between the factors of production and the owners of sources of revenue, i.e. recipients of incomes.[66] These surface figurations must be analysed before the attempt is made to reconstruct the constitution of state functions and thus of the *real* state out of the class constellation. However, because they neglect the *form* of law, Flatow and Huisken overlook that this constitution is in fact the result of an historical process. The owner of labour power as a free wage-labourer with the full and equal rights of a citizen was able to develop only through long class struggles. In no way does he arise from the surface forms of competition, for in these forms the private property-owner always remains an *economic category*. The emergence of a political subject of law corresponding to this economic category, the 'worker citizen', is accomplished in the shape of class struggles, because surface categories always constitute mere *formal* equality while the *material inequality* posited in the production of surplus value continually calls this apparent equality into question. Working-class resistance must develop out of the relations of domination in production and with regard to the state assume certain structures which mark out the framework of state activity.

(b) We should like here, albeit sketchily and on the basis of German history, to characterize the different phases which establish specific 'possibilities and limits' for state activity.

First phase: Here the relation of capital to labour appears as corresponding to the general concept of capital. The worker's full sovereignty over his commodity, labour power, in the exchange process is transformed into the total sovereignty of capital in the production process. In the organization of this process, capital acts with such disrespect for its limits that it endangers its own source of reproduction. The limits which capital was set after the struggle for the eight-hour day are nothing but the safeguard of one of its functional forms against the logic of capital itself. In so far as the state enforces this safeguard, it is an 'ideal total capitalist' (a formula which should be used, if at all, only to derive the content of state action from its *result*; it must not serve as a concept of 'essence' to imply that the state's activity depends on the extent to which it is an ideal total capitalist). With this guarantee the working class has won the right to life as separate indivi-duals based on the sale of their commodity, labour power. The state mani-fests itself as a class state when labour power revolts against its functional character as capital — as a factor of production — and thus at the same time infringes the law (cf. Müller and Neusüss, 1975).

Second phase: Workers' coalitions (trade unions and the like) are recognized by capital and by the state — the working class has won for itself the right to organize. The legalization of trade unions initiates an increasing tendency towards the legal formalization of the relations between capital and wage labour (now as a collective subject of law) and towards the institutionalization of class struggle.[67] Although we cannot here go into the process by which working-class forms of organization are legalized, we shall nevertheless make some remarks about the necessity of this development with regard to capital reproduction so as to avoid the impression that this movement is based merely on *political* power constellations. The legalization of the trade unions and the legal formalization of the social conflicts between capital and labour were the preconditions for a social truce which had become indispensable for the reproduction and development of capital. The reason for this is not only that the working class acknowledges the 'system-limit' through the institutionalization of class conflict and that its struggles lose the character of a negation of the capitalist mode of production. Indeed, in the first phase, *open repression* already served as the alternative to a *political inte-gration* of the working class. The essential point is that, with the develop-ment of the capitalist mode of production, or in other words with the in-crease in the organic composition of capital — an expression denoting the relation between 'living' and 'objective' labour in production and thus the conditions of its capitalist valorization — the comprehensive planning of developments in material and in value terms, the continuing flux of the forms of capital, the calculability of the rate of surplus value become ever more necessary.[68] In the face of these conditions, the *cost of integration* weighs more lightly, that of *repression* weighs more heavily than in the phase marked by smaller units of capital.

The institutionalization of class conflict thus means in economic terms a (certain) calculability of the rate of surplus value and the capability to plan production in the face of the actions of the wage-labourers: the pre-planned, pre-announced conducting of wage struggles in accordance with the set timetables and deadlines, the obligation to keep the industrial peace, etc.; politically it means a (certain) capacity to plan and foresee even mass arti-culation. Here the problems of mass loyalty enters into the picture. It is evident that mass articulation, political mass movements that is, can be foreseen and pre-planned only to the extent that they do not pursue an autonomous course. Hence the need to integrate not so much the working class as such but rather its organized expression, the workers' parties and the trade unions.

Concepts such as 'institutionalization', 'legal formalization', etc., refer to a change in the relationship between state and social relations. The haphazard regulation of class relations through the economic process is partially replaced by regulations guaranteed by the *state*. In contrast to the character of law as a form of mediation (analysed above) through which the state relates to 'private property owners', now law involves the state in the social relations of production — albeit within the limits peculiar to law.[69]

For our investigation of the relationship between the bourgeois state's system-limit and its limit of activity, this type of 'involvement of the state in the process of reproduction' (a familiar 'Stamocap' formulation with a different theoretical intention) means that its limit of activity *vis-à-vis* the working class is more narrowly drawn: the rights, institutions and organizations won by the working class hinder, for example, the pressure on wages. And further: the acts of intervention in the rights of the working class, for instance in the regulating of the different funds which ensure the reproduction of the commodity labour power, will meet with considerably stronger resistance simply because the organized working class is present in the state sphere. This presence refers as much to the existence of workers' parties in the political system as to the existence of specific functions in the state apparatus which cause the latter to be divided even with regard to the act of intervention (social bureaucracy, etc.).

Third phase: The state proclaims a 'quasi-right' to employment. We intend to comment only briefly on this, although the extraordinary circumstances of West German post-war development have created a kind of customary right in this respect which makes it appear at least politically risky to 'allow' 'purgative crises' as a means of bringing pressure to obtain a desired rate of surplus value.[70] That such a right for workers leads to a change of function in the unions which now themselves become a means of bringing pressure against the autonomous demands of the wage-labourers — that the unions move closer to the state structure both institutionally and in their own self-awareness, this has been plentifully discussed since the 'Concerted Action'.[71] Unresolved, however, is the question of how far new limits of state activity have arisen out of this shift of structures between political classes and economic relations.

To sum up regarding our 'phases and integration model': if one attempts to attribute the legal formalization of the basic social conflict to the development of a new 'function' of the state, this function could be described as the establishing of a social truce in order to bring about a more constant and plannable process of reproduction (the conditions which determine the possibility of this lie outside its 'power' but this consideration must be strictly distinguished from the attempt and its underlying theoretical consciousness. If one seeks to characterize the basic problem or basic contradiction of this state function, then it consists in the fact that with this social truce the state has to uphold the contradictions between capital and labour which endanger it; it may not do away with them.

It would be (theoretically and practically) a fatal mistake to consider the level of integration to be a law determining the development of the relation of politics and economics. Any reader with the slightest knowledge of German history will notice that we have left out a particular phase: the different countenance of the bourgeois state in fascism. The repression employed in this phase shows that a level of rights once attained can only be reserved with difficulty, and in fact the relations between capital and labour were not restored in their (conceptually) pure form; rather, fascism in its conception of the corporate state referred *formally* to the degree of integration already attained.[72]

We have stated that, in our opinion, the institutionalization of the social conflict between wage labour and capital is a necessary process, that the development of production as labour process and process of valorization makes autonomous, unplannable movements of wage labourers ever more disruptive so that the costs of integration finally become necessary social costs for capital. This perception is of course only arrived at through the struggles of the working class which, precisely, are to be limited and made calculable. A question to follow up is whether in the course of time the institutionalization of class conflicts within the bourgeois sytem causes a level of organized politics to arise which would make the cost of an open repression of labour power and of a descent from this level appear too high and whether, as a result, fascism in certain countries is becoming historically ever more unlikely.

We would like merely to gather together a few arguments that would counter this conclusion and which at the same time — corresponding to the experience of real fascism — speak against the notion that fascism is a creation of the bourgeois state in its function as 'ideal total capitalist' (in the sense of the determination of its essence: the state as guardian of the long-term, competition-transcending interests of the bourgeois class).

It has been shown that when, in a crisis, attempts are made to prop up the system of capital reproduction on a short-term basis, this may lead to acts of state intervention in the rights of the working class, which in themselves, i.e. ex post, may appear as 'irrational' in the context of the whole system. The calculability of such risks may have become greater — parallel to the integration of the working class (cf. the trade unions as an early warning system). In the crucial borderline case, however — where the necessary rate of surplus value is threatened — capital will even today still have to throw every consideration for the working class overboard.

Reasons for this 'short-sightedness' may lie in the fact that, in the interests of the reproduction of individual capitals and of the whole capitalist system, acts of intervention in working-class rights are possible which *only later*, in the course of the accumulation process, prove to be dysfunctional for capital in the sense indicated above. For:

1. functional equivalents to a free labour market can emerge (in fascism, e.g., black market, private recruitment, etc., as well as the partial reactivation of the DAF (German Labour Front) to 'represent' the interests of the workers);

2. the costs of such acts of intervention can be shifted (for example through pursuing a policy of military conquest) (cf. Mason, 1966; Sohn-Rethel, 1973);

3. the act of intervention and its dysfunctional consequence are widely separated. The struggle for the normal working day, for instance, showed that individual capitals can reproduce themselves and accumulate very satisfactorily (the 'control' here takes place within a much shorter space of time), whilst, in the long-term perspective, the working class is destroyed. The limit which is critical for this function becomes visible only later (from the point of view of the whole);

4. the limits to such acts of intervention depend on the condition of labour power also in quantitative terms: as long as a large reserve army and a growing, poorly qualified population exist, there is hardly a necessary 'limit' — in such cases, the workers might as well starve (e.g. Third World).

Concluding Remarks

To conclude our thoughts on the historical constitution of the functions of the bourgeois state, we should like to return to the methodological question of how the levels of historical development and general conceptual determination of the state interrelate. In almost every analysis of the 'role of the state' two obligatory contentions are to be found:

First that, *after* the general conceptual determinations, one must investigate the specific historical, national, etc., particularities in order to explain the real historical phenomena and *second* one must of course, *alongside* the economic considerations, always take note of the functions of the state relating to class struggle. Even where the *inner* interrelationship is referred to, as by Altvater ('The character of the state as a bourgeois class state permeates all its functions; they all finally serve to preserve and strengthen the capital relation as a relation of domination and exploitation of the working class' (1973a, p. 82)) — even here the significance of this interrelationship is not worked out.

We for our part have tried to clarify this meaning and the consequences of a particular historical constellation of class relations for the role of the state, i.e. its 'relative autonomy', 'possibilities and limits', etc. This enquiry has only an exemplary character; with regard also to other problems and developments of concrete, historical capitalist societies, the determination of the specific class constellation is an essential analytical step; but to reach the level of the historically concrete, it is not enough. Thus the concept of the 'limit of activity' of the state, which we derive from the specific class constellation, lies on the historically concrete level; this limit is not quite, however, that which appears empirically in an individual case. For this, problems such as the internal decision-making structure of the state, the scientific and informational foundations of political decisions, the legislative machinery, the specific interests of parties and associations, etc., could be decisive. If we do not go any further into this level, encountered in traditional enquiries of political science, it is not because we consider it irrelevant with regard to the 'role of the state in capitalism'. We were here particularly concerned to develop systematically the division of politics and economics and thus the limits inherent in an enquiry focusing on the internal structure of organization and of conflict in the state.

  For just as the forms of appearance of the political process cannot be relegated as 'mere superstructural forms' to the realm of historical particularity (in the sense of given data which cannot be explained in terms of political economy) and presented as irrelevant for the general laws of motion of capitalist society[73] — so those forms of appearance cannot be understood without analysis of the historical, material substance of the political process and without the specific form determinations of social reproduction.

7

Class Conflict, Competition and State Functions

Heide Gerstenberger

It seems time to point out that the development of the historical—materialist theory of the state has still not got very far. Furthermore, the theoretical approaches that have been tried do not offer any firm basis for future work. So far, the discussion of the problematic of the constitution of the bourgeois state has been generally characterized by an over-hasty analysis, in the various 'derivations', of the relation between economics and politics. In fact the reason for the inadequate conceptualizations of this relation on which the theories rest is that until now in the state—theory discussion, reality has been looked at only in order to provide a mere *illustration* of any given theory. The theoretical bases for a concrete *analysis* of the bourgeois state have not yet been established, and it seems doubtful whether they can in fact be built by continuing along the lines developed so far. These doubts will be developed below. They form the basis for some suggestions for a strategy for further research; but these suggestions do not claim to add to the systematic approaches already mentioned yet another view of the theoretical foundations of the bourgeois state.

Despite many differences in detail, the existing theoretical analyses of the state can be divided into three main groups. They will not be set out in detail here yet again (that has been done many times recently), but will only be discussed in order to consider how far they can provide us with a theoretical preparation for concrete analysis.

The starting-point represented best by Sibylle von Flatow and Freerk Huisken (1973), as well as by the Munich AK (1974),[1] sees the foundation of the bourgeois state in the particular relationship which people have with each other in bourgeois society. The state for them is not to be derived from the general concept of capital, since in the latter individuals cannot be contained as citizens. It can only be derived from the economic forms of intercourse and the relationships between people which these forms create on the surface of bourgeois society. But at the level of appearance of bourgeois society the economic forms of intercourse present themselves as those of simple commodity circulation, and people appear as possessors of various revenue-sources. For Flatow and Huisken the bourgeois state is derived from the common interest in a high income; for the AK it is based on the recognition of contradictory special interests. Both views start from the premise that the theory of the state can be adequately developed at the level of a systematic explanation. For this form of historical materialism history does not exist. But if, as the AK correctly state, there cannot be an adequate theoretical explanation of the state on the basis of its empirically ascertainable functions, then equally its systematic explanation should not stand in contradiction to historical reality. Only those who deny the importance of class struggles, and thus of history, for theory, can run the risk as theoreticians of being duped by current issues, as has happened to these theoreticians. If today a largely integrated working class sees the state actually as the protector of its interests, this is in no way proved to be the case for the whole duration of bourgeois society. Workers on strike who, in the nineteenth century and even in the twentieth, were attacked by armed and mounted police presumably had little experience of the recognition by the bourgeoisie of their particular interests. It is just as difficult to reconcile this conception of the state with the long periods of fascist and authoritarian bourgeois rule. The theoretical transposition of conditions of simple commodity circulation into political forms of intercourse is based on reasoning which, because it is unhistorical, is short-circuited.

It is the *particular form of the bourgeois state* which results from the economic forms of intercourse, that form which distinguishes it from all other states: to that extent we can agree with the writers we have mentioned. In fact, the very basis of this form is that the economic movements on the surface of bourgeois society appear as those of simple commodity circulation. For, as distinct from other forms of exploitation, the capitalist form consists precisely in converting labour-power into a commodity which circulates freely. The coercive character of this society consists in ensuring that the possessors of the commodity labour-power are in a position to take only its exchange-value to market. Hence the class character of the bourgeois state is also established as soon as the state does not distinguish between the possessors of different 'revenue-sources'.[2]

What can be ascertained from the analysis of the surface of bourgeois society (aside from the preconditions for commodity circulation itself, hence for the reproduction of capital) is the conclusion that the state must guarantee the phenomenal form of economic movements as being that of simple circulation. But the conditions for this guarantee are given too much theoretical weight, while the *social* reproduction of relations of production is correspondingly underestimated. It is not ideology that is the most important stabilizing factor, but rather the naked force that lurks behind the form of appearance. Thus, it is not definitely settled that the capitalist mode of production *requires* formal equality, universal suffrage and democratic structures.[3] True, Marx's early writings, which these writers frequently refer to, do tend towards such 'determined' conclusions. But these works arose from the development of a concrete strategy for emancipation, and from the point of view of what forms of bourgeois rule would offer the best pre-conditions for the preparation of the socialist revolution (*Introduction to the Critique of Hegel's Philosophy of Law; On the Jewish Question*). Any reliance on Marx's early works for theoretical purposes must take into account both this strategic moment and the period in which they were written (see Reichelt, above). Once historical and systematic analysis are harmonized, the neces-sary correspondence of economic and political forms of intercourse in bourgeois society is much reduced; what must be maintained is the illusion that the bourgeois state is functional[4] and, connected with this, the illusion of the universality of the norm. The precondition for the stability of bour-geois society is not that the state *actually* appears as the guarantor of all interests, but that it should seem possible to make it become such a guarantor; and this, no less, is also the content of revisionism, which provides a theoretical justification for the actual integration of the working class into bourgeois society. The stabilization of bourgeois society does not require the existence of, but only the struggle for universal suffrage. And since the actual implementation of formal freedom and formal equality in the end undermines the hopes which could, prior to that, be placed in the improve-ment of the bourgeois system, it is not at all to be seen as the guarantor of stability for this society, but rather the precondition for momentous convulsions.

The explanation of the functions of the state in relation to valorization has become more influential for the current debate than the derivation of the bourgeois state from the surface of bourgeois society. Although seldom thought through in the theories (it is clearest in Altvater 1973), this approach has nevertheless shaped the whole of the debate on the left in recent years.

Admittedly, the manifold restrictions on the activity of the state have been repeatedly analysed in the meantime,[5] but in the discussions of state functions the aims of state activity are still treated as the *adequate* expression of a situation of valorization (for the most part still viewed as limited to economics). Since class rule has found its organizational embodiment in the state, it is deduced not only that the interests of capital prevail in class conflicts (usually quoted to illustrate the functional relation between valorization and state activity), but it is also fundamentally implied (with-out discussion) that the interests of capital are represented by the state. This must then mean that the real structure of national capital finds in the activity of the state the representation adequate to it at any moment. The analysis of the bourgeois state is thus conceived of as the *continuation* of the analysis of capital. First of all, the average or mean form of the state is developed from the general analysis of capital; this analysis is then supposed to ascend to the concrete by explaining concrete state functions from the concrete movements of accumulation. But since at present the analysis of the concrete processes of accumulation is still not very advanced, the concrete development of the bourgeois state is generally in a supplementary way still derived from those general conditions of the capitalist mode of production (above all from the law of the tendency of the rate of profit to fall), which however as such give precisely no information about their concrete historical content.[6]

However, the historical development of the functions of the state can even less validly be derived directly from general theory than this can be done for the concrete development of the processes of accumulation. It is wrong to believe that a breakthrough in the general theory of the state will at last enable us to derive the politics of the family, of education or of welfare with satisfying finality from the conditions for valorization. It is the obvious starting-point for materialist analyses of the state that a relationship exists between the movement of capital and the activity of the state. The assertion of such a general relationship does no more than remind us of the basic research strategy formulated by Marx in 1859 in the Preface to the *Critique of Political Economy*. That is to say that concrete analysis consists precisely in working out in every particular *how* such relationships are produced. And the reference to class struggles is no solution to the difficulty unless it has a decisive effect on the actual analytical approach.

Class struggles and concrete competition strategies grow out of conditions of valorization[7] and take place in the framework of a definite political structure. The assumption that out of such conflicts there is established an exact correspondence between the situation of capital valorization and the activity of the state, or even that the state can in general be characterized as the administrator of a concrete collective interest of capital — these are suppositions with which we have not only made the realistic analysis of the state superstructure much too easy for ourselves, but also with which we deny the historical importance of concrete class struggles.

The assumption that state activity (at least at the outset) can in general be characterized as functional for capital as a whole could be theoretically justified in three ways. First, it could be argued that the representation of different interests not only leads to an ascendancy of capitalist interests, but that differences in the interests of capital also result in a compromise of interests among the capital fractions, which would coincide with or approximate to the interest of capital as a whole.[8] But this implies processes of compromise which even in periods of pre-monopoly capitalism could correspond only to a *model* of bourgeois society and to faith in the working of an 'invisible hand'. The interest of capital as a whole could perhaps be said to have resulted from concrete struggles most nearly in those instances analysed by Marx in an exemplary way in his chapter on the eight-hour day: in the struggle of the working class over the conditions of reproduction of

their labour-power (*Capital* vol. 1, ch. 10). But here too it is questionable
whether, with the increasing inequality of their development, the individual
capitals are not confronted in very different ways with the conditions of
reproduction conceded through struggle (e.g. in-service training), or whether
particular demands of this kind could not even transcend the conditions of
reproduction of capitalistically-exploited labour power. The second possible
argument that the interest of capital as a whole is expressed through the
activity of the state comes from the competition between nation-states.
Competition on the world market is one of the basic characteristics of the
concrete historical development of capitalism, and state organization is a
vital instrument of world market competition strategies. This nation-state
argument does have something to be said for it. For we can safely assume
that both governments and officials of the state administrative apparatus
are conscious of the responsibility of ensuring the competitiveness of
national capital on the world market — a responsibility which today must
generally lead to the needs of so-called growth industries being given special
treatment in state measures.[9] Even if we do not start from the hypothesis
of some of the Stamocap theoreticians of an alliance between monopolies
and the state, a result of the classical historical function of the bourgeois
state of guaranteeing external representation is that government departments must obtain information and advice from those representatives of
capital who are important for the current position of the nation on the
world market. Yet such a general line of thought does not tell us much
about concrete state activity. It cannot take into account a case where
leading capitals are compelled to make contradictory demands of the state
(cf. the energy crisis); nor does it help us to indicate what concrete decisions
might be taken when it comes to establishing the competitive position on
the world market of a particular branch through state support. And lastly,
it completely ignores the necessity for state authorities to balance the
needs of competitiveness on the world market against internal political
stability. To characterize the concrete results of such a balancing process
generally as the adequate expression of the current interests of capital as a
whole would again involve a series of fairly objectionable assumptions.

The third conceivable possibility of establishing an adequate correspondence between the interest of capital as a whole and the activity of the
state has been foreshadowed, and comes back to the role of officials of the
state apparatus. At one stage in the debate on the political economy of
education it was thought that substantial relationships could be proved
by showing personal links (e.g. of members of the Scientific Council) with
certain capital interests. To expose individuals as the puppets of definite
interests is quite inadequate for the analysis of real relationships, and
moreover it is virtually irrelevant. The connection between the state apparatus
and capital interests is indeed established partly through the typical selection
and socialization processes — described in particular by Miliband (1969) —

and also to some extent through conscious obligations. But in systematic terms what is relevant above all is the connection that necessarily establishes itself behind the backs of the persons concerned. And this necessity is mediated in the developed bourgeois state through the voting mechanism. A government will only be elected or re-elected if a majority of the electorate hopes that it will pursue their interests (in a way that is sometimes rather loosely understood).[10] Unless they are willing to do entirely without the acclamation of the ballot, governments must try to maintain the appearance of neutrality in various ways;[11] they are also, as capitalism develops, increasingly obliged to alleviate its crisis-ridden character. That members of the government and officials in the administrative apparatus are both fully conscious of the task of crisis management is a fact that can certainly be taken into account in the analysis of the state. However, in the present stage of capitalism this does not only mean, in very general terms, the favouring of the interests of capital over those of wage earners, the aim is rather to improve the profitability of particular capitals and fractions of capital, due to the importance of competition on the world market. As regards the analysis of the occurrence of state activity, we thus find ourselves once more at the point reached earlier. It is only possible to trace a mere outline of the occurrence of this activity, unless we can ascribe to the state apparatus a quasi-mystical knowledge of the concrete interests at any given time of capital as a whole.

In opposition to the dominant contemporary approaches, the AK have correctly pointed out that the analytical decomposition of the state into economic categories theoretically denies the particularization of the state from bourgeois society (1974). For them it follows from this that the analysis of the state must start from the phenomenal forms in which the movements of capital present themselves on the surface of bourgeois society. But this adhesion in theory to the inverted appearance of bourgeois society unnecessarily restricts the analysis of the state. That the movements of capital could present themselves as those of simple circulation on the surface of bourgeois society was not only an historical achievement (in the phase of primitive accumulation) but also necessitates constant state action. This is because the successful reproduction of capital is the precondition for the reproduction of the particular appearance of bourgeois society, and in every phase of bourgeois society this has required state measures (contrary to simplified stages models).[12] For this reason, the analysis of state functions is an essential part of an historical—materialist theory of the state. This analysis does not provide a complete explanation of the bourgeois state, and it also remains unsatisfactory unless it actually brings into theoretical analysis both class struggles and the levels of mediation through which the movement of capital and state action are related. More on this below.

A further approach to the analysis of the state has recently been put forward by Hunno Hochberger[13] (it is also to be found in a similar form in the work of Ulrich K. Preuss (1973)) on the development of the German constitution. In Hochberger's view the class character of the bourgeois state is not satisfactorily established in existing works. The derivation of the state from the logic of the economic system, he writes, means that a class nature must be attributed to the state without any mediation whatever. This shows, he says, the limits of a purely logical analysis, and makes it clear 'where history comes in'. He then develops this approach in particular by elaborating on the difference between the administrative apparatus and forms of intercourse in bourgeois society. He argues that the bureaucratic apparatus originates as a class instrument to carry out proletarianization during primitive accumulation. Consequently, the autonomization of state power must be the result of the situation of class struggle in capital's primitive accumulation phase. Apart from the historical objection that a separate administrative institution can be shown to have originated in much earlier historical periods, it is only an historical proof of the class character of the bourgeois state to show correctly that the state apparatus was an instrument of class struggle during primitive accumulation. But historical analysis only tells us about structures, and not about the necessity for them to exist. What distinguishes the phase of primitive accumulation from that of the development of bourgeois society is that it has an overt class character. But just because it was overt at the start does not suffice to explain its existence in a later camouflaged form. And materialist analysis is inadequate so long as it cannot decipher the class character which lies in the very universality of the law, in the universality of the norm. In spite of this criticism, two points in this decidedly historical approach are worth noting: first, its objection to the claim implied by systematic derivation, to seek to comprehend all phenomena of the bourgeois state from the conditions of bourgeois society alone. In fact, the creation of the institutional apparatus precedes the establishment of bourgeois society. And in view of the fact that the state is not a direct component of the capitalist mode of production, we cannot take it for granted that there do not cling to it features which can be accounted for by the conditions of its formation. Hence the approach we have cited leads us to the following thought: if the political sphere in bourgeois society must in fact be analysed as one separated in a certain way from the economic, and accordingly if the categories for this analysis are not available fully formed from the developed general theory of capital, then it would seem necessary (to a limited extent, since the particularization of the state does not break through the general social framework) to repeat that process of research which precedes the analysis of capital: the processing of historical material and the critique of bourgeois theory. What this implies is a certain scepticism towards the striving for a systematic theoretical structure in the current state of this debate.

The state as the precondition for the reproduction of the community[14] develops in relation to the social division of labour and simultaneously with the regional demarcation of production; also, the character of class domination is extracted and conferred on the state by all sorts of exploitative oppression. Marx and Engels worked with both these formulations (Marx, *Grundrisse*, pp. 472 ff; Engels, *Origins of the Family*). This does not mean that the analysis of the state is completely absorbed into a form-analysis of bourgeois society. Rather, what the latter is concerned with is the particular form which is assumed by the state in bourgeois society: 'It is always the direct relationship of the owners of the conditions of production to the direct producers — a relation always naturally corresponding to a definite stage in the development of the methods of labour and thereby its social productivity — which reveals the innermost secret, the hidden basis of the entire social structure, and with it the political form of the relation of sovereignty and dependence, in short, the corresponding specific form of the state' (*Capital* vol. 3, 791).

During the period of its formation, the bourgeois state distinguished itself from earlier forms of state at first only as regards its functions and not in its basic structure. It formed the organization for carrying out the common interests of the ruling class(es) and for the institutionalization of a new system of economic exploitation. At the stage of primitive accumulation the state can, therefore, be described as the committee for managing the common affairs of the ruling classes, a description which the *Communist Manifesto* polemically gives it in relation to the whole bourgeois epoch. The oppressive character of the state in that period was as overt as in all previous forms of political organization. Why does the state change its form in the bourgeois epoch? Why does it become, in form, the state of society as a whole? This is the question which must be answered by analysing the basic structures of bourgeois society.

The formation of the specifically bourgeois form of the state is historically the result of primitive accumulation. Only after the state — in the form of an institution acting undisguisedly in the interests of the ruling classes — had furthered the proletarianization of a large part of the population and the rapacious accumulation of capital did it change its phenomenal form. (For an amplification of this see Gerstenberger 1973). Capitalist relations of production are already established at that period, if not always very extensively. Thereafter it is no longer so much a matter of establishing but rather of reproducing these relations. Whereas in all previous epochs of production the overt fixing of power relations formed part of the process of reproduction, the reproduction of capitalist relations of production must take place as far as possible without the application of overt force. For the result of the establishment of the structure of exploitation in the form of an overt relation of force is the extensive immobilization of labour power. But this is very hard to reconcile with capitalist accumulation determined by competitive processes.[15] Hence the reproduction of capitalist relations of production does not merely presuppose the availability of labour power (which could already have been achieved by the forcible withdrawal of the means of self-subsistence); it also presupposes that workers should view their situation as not in any way brought about by force, but rather experience it as the result of an act of exchange into which they have brought their labour power. In previous historical epochs personal misery could perhaps be understood as a punishment from God, but never before could the system of exploitation be rooted in the consciousness of the exploited in such a way that they had to understand their predicament as the consequence of their own incapacity, as determined by the particular qualities of their labour power. The precondition for the reproduction of production relations to appear to the consciousness in this manner was historically (and is systematically) that the state should no longer overtly appear as the organization of the rulers. Once the state ceases to compel vagabonds and inmates of debtors' prisons forcibly into work, but comes forward as the guarantor of the (legal) regulation of exchange relationships, it formally withdraws from society and at the same time becomes the state of society as a whole. (Historically this process is expressed, for example, by the abolition of the estates and the establishment of the unmediated character of state power). What the state guarantees in this way is the appearance of freedom of contract, which comes to be expressed in bourgeois law. This appearance can however only be maintained because in wages it has a basis which can be materially experienced (cf. Negt 1973). Only because wages create the appearance that all work is paid for can the capital relation establish itself on the surface as an exchange relationship. The concealment is brought about not by the legal form but by the capitalist mode of production. But since capitalism has succeeded in concealing the system of exploitation in the organization of production itself, it has become possible for the political—legal regulation of relationships between people in bourgeois society to develop in formal abstraction from the social organization of production. Hence the state does not indeed guarantee justice, but nothing more than the application of formal principles.

Once we explain the abstraction of the political—legal forms of intercourse from the structures of production as arising from the concealment of the relationship of exploitation by wages, we have already established the particularization of the state from society and the most general form of the bourgeois state. But this tells us very little still about the concrete historical development of the bourgeois state. For from the form of the bourgeois state we cannot directly derive its functions.[16] Rather, *the relationship between form and function of the bourgeois state involves a contradiction*; this grows out of the requirement of the capitalist mode of production not only for particular modes of intercourse, but at the same time for the provision of material preconditions of production. Their general character can be ascertained from the competition between capitals (and between national-state groups of capital); their particular form is a result of the historical-concrete conditions of valorization of capital. These relationships have been discussed by Elmar Altvater. The provision of material (as opposed to legal— formal) conditions of production requires economically determined state action. This creates a vital threat to the safeguarding of capitalist relations of production by means of the particularization of the state from society.

There are three ways in which this contradiction between the form and function of the bourgeois state is reconciled:

1. The formally equal participation of all citizens in the process of determining the collective will serves to conceal the class content of state measures concluded in legal form. (We have already argued above that the struggle for equal participation can have the same effect.)

2. The establishment of definite, formal, judicially reviewable procedures as operational standards for the bureaucracy serves to subject state action to the principle of the universal norm. (This does not in real terms establish any limitation on the scope for state action, as has been shown most clearly above all by Luhmann 1973).

3. As a result of class struggles state actions come to include not only formal but also real interests of the working class (welfare-state illusion).

Although we cannot go into it here, we must point out that in the course of historical development it becomes necessary for an increasing amount of state business not to be channelled through legislative procedures, in order to ensure the provision of the material preconditions of production (cf. Preuss 1973). But at the same time the bourgeois state, as a result of class conflicts, increasingly represents itself as the real defender of all interests. Thus bourgeois society is able to secure the relations of production in a way which surpasses (or increasingly replaces) that which is constituted by the particularization of the bourgeois state from society.[17]

The first task of concrete analysis must be to show how the contradiction between the form and function of the bourgeois state unfolds concretely, and in what ways it is partially reconciled. Only after an extensive process of historical research — which has hardly begun yet — will a systematic construction of theories be possible. The basis for this will not be provided by the kinds of historical description and attempts at systematization so far put forward by the proponents of the theory of state monopoly capitalism, nor do the critical discussions of these works provide a really adequate starting-point. (The rejection of the stages models of Stamocap theory does not free us from the necessity of working out what are the changes that result from the process of development of bourgeois society.)

We have generally limited ourselves, in the concrete analysis of the bourgeois state, to recognizing the general connection with the conditions of valorization of capital. Class struggles are brought in to explain the establishment of this connection at any given moment. We have emphasized above the problems involved with this procedure. It consists of the theoretical (and hence also political) reduction of class struggles to nothing

more than the implementation of general laws. At the same time the necessary result of this procedure is the interpretation of state activity as functional for the concrete situation of capital valorization.

An attempt to break through the limitations of previous state analysis
would introduce on the analytical horizon factors whose analysis Marxists
have hitherto left exclusively to political science. It would involve, for instance,
the more detailed investigation of those members of bourgeois society of
whom Marx once said that they regard the state as their private property
(*Introduction to the Critique of Hegel's Philosophy of Law*, MECW, vol. 3,
p. 187). (The conceptions of bureaucrats have always been a factor left
out of systematic analysis, although presumably they are the very ones who
mediate the translation of the needs of the reproduction of capital into
state action.) But above all, class struggles must no longer be looked at, in
the framework of state analysis, with regard only to their objective basis
and context, but also in terms of their concrete course and results. This
gives analytical significance to those particular conditions which are at the
same time the result of previous class struggles in a society, and also influence
the actual pursuit of political strategies. They are partly consolidated into
the concrete constitutional structures of the state (in the present form of
the state), but they are also embodied in certain traditions and typical
modes of conduct. It is not that such structures determine the content of
class struggles; but they are important for state analysis as channels through
which economic and political strategies are as a rule pursued in a society.
Just because a concrete strategy may be possible in one country (say, the
setting up of the 'concerted action' in the Federal Republic of Germany)
does not make it in any way one that can be implemented in a corresponding
form in another country — even if the general conditions of capital valorization are in every way similar (e.g. Great Britain, in the case of the above
example of political class compromise).

The approach put forward here, that the concrete activity of the state
should be grasped as the result of social confrontations which are mediated
through a wide variety of channels into the state apparatus,[18] only makes
theoretical sense if we think it conceivable that on the basis of such mediations actual state activity is not always the adequate expression of the
interests of capital as a whole. Not that the interests of capital are not in
general implemented; but in a concrete analysis we should not assume in
advance as a certainty that in a concrete case the ensuing state activity will
further the possibilities for accumulation of national capital to the fullest
extent possible under capitalist conditions. This methodological emphasis
on the concrete course of social strategies could be opposed in particular by
pointing to the increasing activity of the state in planning, which results from
the acceptance of the responsibility for initiating the development of stabilization strategies. But the transference of planning responsibilities to government departments does not itself create a kind of capitalist super-intelligence.

It is therefore not only a matter of analysing the economic limits of state activity; we must go further and show the limitations to which state activity is subject in its functional possibilities for capital accumulation, limitations which arise from the connection between state activity and the crisis-ridden development of capitalism. The difficulties of gathering information, which are customarily stressed in this context, can only be mentioned here. But assuming the very best collection of information, where would the responsible advisers suddenly acquire analytical ability? We will illustrate these points with only one, but a rather important, example. Today, the most able growth theorists are absolutely clear that predictions about the concrete connection between definite infrastructural investments and economic growth are only possible as speculation. But even factors whose importance is not denied (e.g. the limited nature of oil reserves, or the long-term effects of environmental pollution) do not thereby become guiding principles of state action. Where suitable plans do exist in desk drawers (let us say, an energy policy less exclusively based on oil), they can only be implemented even as plans either if they are in the interests of a fraction of capital, if the working class presses them forward as massively supported demands, or if an acute crisis makes clear the necessity for them. That is to say, new problems must first become problems for the state; this is brought about through the channels for the articulation of interests and/or through crises. The state reacts to both largely *ad hoc*; and as a rule its measures create the preconditions for new crises. The logical analysis of the conditions of capitalist development certain provides no basis for understanding how state activity, which on closer inspection is amazingly unsystematic, always establishes, as if by a trick of reason, exactly that which can be regarded as functional at the time for the concrete conditions of capital accumulation. For this reason it is questionable whether the commonly assumed *degree* of dependence of the capitalist accumulation process on *certain definite* state measures would stand up to fundamental analysis. We can equally suppose that for some state activities no direct connection can be shown with the conditions for the valorization of capital. If such considerations are taken seriously and not just put down to historical accident, this poses problems for the materialist analysis of the state which we have not yet begun even to think about.

8

On the Analysis of the Bourgeois Nation State within the World Market Context. An Attempt to Develop a Methodological and Theoretical Approach

Claudia von Braunmühl

The imperialist system, particularly in its metropolitan regions, is characterized to an increasing extent by the contradiction between internationalization and nationalization of the process of accumulation,[1] a contradiction which manifests itself today in the appearance of internationally operating capitals, such as multinational corporations, and in the constant intervention of the state apparatus in the reproduction of the national capitals. In attempting to come to an analytic understanding of this contradiction, every analysis of imperialism, whether empirical or theoretical, is confronted by the double dilemma of the covert conservativism of the dominant concept of imperialism and the inadequacy of those attempts which up to the present have been made to investigate it.

The current definitions represent imperialism as a 'spill-over' problem of one form or another: a national capital which was once essentially internal in scope reproduces itself externally to a growing extent and thus produces imperialism. Such a conception[2] contains latent bourgeois elements. Imperialism has the specific partition of the world market into national states as a precondition, and such a use of the concept consolidates this in such a way that it takes on an almost normative character. The accumulation of national capitals suddenly acquires its own legitimacy in the face of the intervention of external capitals. Rather than assessing the quality of the intervention from the nationality of the capital or of the capitalists it should be a question of determining the effect of the intervention on the chances for revolutionary change, and establishing the part played in this by boundaries, by the process of accumulation of national capitals, by the national development of productivity and by the national state apparatuses. It is, in other words, a question of giving the concept of imperialism added precision along the dimensions of the international division of labour and class struggle as these are determined by the historically changed function of national statehood, and in this the specific mould of the international division of labour as it is structured by metropolitan capital is of particular importance.

The problematic of the current concept of imperialism is reflected in the attempts which have so far been made to investigate it, and which try to provide a conceptual account of the relation between the world market movement of capital, imperialism and the state. In particular, Marxist-oriented accounts have tried to free themselves from the traditional point of view that sees the state as determined in the first instance by internal processes to which external determinants are, as it were, appended *a posteriori*. In analysing the process of capital accumulation as an international one, they conceive of the contemporary state as the political representative of 'national' capitals in relation to intensified contradictoriness (alterations of form, loss of function, expansion of function), as well as the tendencies towards new forms of statehood and the conditions for their realization. Although this shows an analytic regard for more recent developments, a methodological procedure which focuses on the national capital and its state is retained.

Numerous accounts have developed from this position in which the 'development of underdevelopment' is elevated to the central object of research.[3] Here the formation of the capitalist mode of production and its world-wide expansion is seen as a process taking place within international contexts and on an international scale, and its 'other face' is analysed as the decisive factor determining the course and form of developments in the peripheral regions. Thus although the integration of national independently organized economies in the world market is seen as a phenomenon historically inseparable from capital, this insight is, however, confined to the extreme disparities exhibited in relationships between the metropolitan areas and the peripheral regions where this context is, of course, particularly obvious.[4]

This insight, however, must be raised to the level of theory. It must be formulated there as a question regarding the international determinants of state interventionism. The insight into the way in which the world market mediates national accumulation and development of the productive forces, which first received theoretical attention as the international context of crisis, makes it in fact theoretically impossible to consider national economic development and the activities of national state apparatuses as being to a large extent internally determined. And this raises the question of the relation between the national economy and the world market, or in other words, between the bourgeois national state and the imperialist system.

This question is, however, quite insoluble within models of increasing, externally induced, loss of autonomy by a politico-economic unit, i.e. the nation state, which, as such, is structurally unaffected — as for example is the case in the debate over Multinational Corporations versus the Nation

State. The old model of the bourgeois nation state as a bounded entity
with external relationships, which must act in conformity with international
standards to the extent that it has external economic and political commit-
ments, and which receives an additional impulse for state activity from
these, has become untenable in its treatment of the real process of inter-
nationalized accumulation. The evident untenability of the model makes
it clear that the model in no way captured the essence of anything, but
merely, unaware of its own restrictions, circumscribed a particular period
of history.

An international system is not the sum of many states, but on the contrary the international system consists of many nation states. The world
market is not constituted by many national economies concentrated together, rather the world market is organized in the form of many national
economies as its integral components. 'The methodological primacy of the
totality over individual instances (Lukács 1971, p. 9), must also be maintained at this level of the argument.

Any national economy can only adequately be understood as a particular
instance turning more or less upon its inner configuration, but which, nevertheless, is an integral element of the world market; so, therefore, the nation
state, and the bourgeois state as a general phenomenon, can only be properly
determined in these dimensions. Similarly the influence of the internationalization of capital accumulation cannot be understood if it is thought of as
an external factor acting upon national statehood and the actions of the
nation state, but must be conceived of as a process taking effect within the
national economy as part of the world market.[5] It may be asked whether
the theory of imperialism should not take the world market as the *a priori*
level of analysis from which conclusions then might be drawn, rather than
taking national capital and the state associated with it as its starting point.
In the 'Urtext' of the *Grundrisse* Marx writes: 'the appearance of exchange
value as a simple point of departure upon the surface presupposes the whole
system of bourgeois production' (*Grundrisse*, German edn., p. 907);[6] in the
Introduction he makes the celebrated remarks about the only seeming correctness of beginning with 'the real and concrete'[7] and asserts that the emergence
of the concept of labour in its 'simplest abstraction' requires the fullest
practical development of 'the most modern society' (*Grundrisse*, p. 105).

It does not seem unreasonable to take these remarks of epistemological
validity, directed towards the analysis of the commodity form, also to
apply to the *level* on which analysis should take place and to take them to
be similarly valid for the world market.

> As a rule, the most general abstractions arise only in the midst of the
> richest possible concrete development, where one thing appears as com-
> mon to many, to all. Then it ceases to be thinkable in a particular form
> alone . . . .. The simplest abstraction, then, which modern economics
> places at the head of its discussions, and which expresses an immeasur-

ably ancient relation valid in all forms of society, nevertheless achieves practical truth as an abstraction only as a category of the most modern society (*Grundrisse*, pp. 104–5).

This is valid not only for the construction of politico–economic categories and their articulation in deductive schemata, but also for the determination of the level at which the categories as an expression of the social totality are situated. To determine the essence of things from their most fully developed form of appearance thus means that the nation state as a particular form should no longer be taken as the level on which the movement of capital is to be analysed; this should be the world market as a totality.

This does not demand the wholesale reconstruction of the categories which Marx devised, but rather what might be called the epistemological transference of the dialectical method and the dialectical form of presentation to the designation of the *level* at which individual capitals act upon one another. The level of capital movement, or, in other words, the dimensions of the extent of the unity of the many, must itself be systematically deduced from the necessary determinants of the process of accumulation seen as class struggle. Rather than springing in conceptually unarmed at some level which is taken to be factually given – whether this is the nation or the world market – and trying to trace the movement of capital in the development of its laws within it, the aim should be to determine the relation between the two of them both in the conditions of the possibility of their relative separation and in the concrete terms of the history of accumulation.

> The tendency to create the world market is directly given in the concept of capital itself (*Grundrisse*, p. 408).

This tendency becomes more and more clearly manifest. The world market is the place 'in which production is posited as a totality together with all its moments, but within which at the same time, all contradictions come into play (*Grundrisse*, p. 227), it becomes the sphere of a global context of production and exchange in which capital is in the process of constituting itself as historical real world capital.

> In accord with this tendency, capital drives beyond national barriers and prejudices as much as beyond nature worship, as well as all traditional confined, complacent, encrusted satisfactions of present needs, and reproductions of old ways of life. It is destructive towards all of this, and constantly revolutionizes it, tearing down all the barriers which hem in the development of the forces of production, the expansion of needs, the all-sided development of production, and the exploitation and exchange of natural and mental forces (*Grundrisse*, p. 410).

This tendency, understood in terms of accumulation theory, must be analysed at world market level. In other words, the accumulation of capital must be reconstructed conceptually in the world market context. *Vis-à-vis* this totality, historical partitions, divisions, the political coming together of capitals in the bourgeois nation state, national state apparatuses and their activities are to be analytically determined as the particular. The world market should thus be related as the one proper sphere of the circulation of capital to the national spheres of circulation as particularizations, and defined in this relation.[8]

The appropriate analytical level is thus that of the world market,[9] and the task before us is to explain its differentiation as national capitals and its organization as nation states. Thus, rather than investigating the extent of the diffusion of national capitals into capitals acting and merging on a world scale, which is conditioned by the process of accumulation, and the consequences which arise from this by either a methodological or analytic procedure — and thus remaining focused upon the bourgeois nation state — attention should be turned to specifying the conditions under which capital — the movement of which is international in its very essence — is particularized into national capitals and their delimited political organization in the national state.[10] A further topic for examination is how the world market context of capital in the period of the internationalization of production influences class relations so as to unify or further differentiate them, given that these class relations are themselves to be understood as an international ensemble with nationally located centres of gravity (cf. Leucate 1975, pp. 96 ff).

In working out such an approach serious methodological and conceptual problems must be confronted. The categories developed by Marx in *Capital* vol. 3 which are concerned with the unity of the plurality and which contain competition as an effective factor entering into the constitution of the categories — such as the average rate of profit, the organic composition of capital, the tendency of the rate of profit to fall, etc. — are categories derived from the concept of capital in general[11] which, if they are used in concrete historical analysis, must be related to a context of production and exchange. Within this context the conditions of their existence, the mobility of capital and of labour, must be established. At the time that Marx wrote *Capital*, the only unit which embodied these conditions necessary for the constitution of the categories was the bourgeois nation state or the internal market established within boundaries partly given in advance and partly achieved as the result of struggle. Since the boundaries of the complexes of production and circulation of the interrelated capitals were thus largely identical with those of the bourgeois nation state, the categories, such as the average rate of profit, could only find empirical reference as categories reflecting an historical reality in a national framework. The concrete contradictory unity of the many had, corresponding to the historical unfolding of the development of the productive forces and the division of labour, its historically most highly developed form of appearance in the national capital.

This does not mean, it must be stressed, that Marx developed these categories belonging to the concept of capital in general in a national context and that it is necessary to 'dehistorify' them through a complicated process of decontextualization and abstraction, but simply that he relates them in moments of empirical concretization to the national framework. This is partly for reasons to do with the historical nature of accumulation, but partly, however, also because the conceptual development of competition was insufficiently differentiated to allow for a view of the state as the political form of organization of competing capitals gathered together in historically formed systems of reproduction.[12]

Thus Marx defines the average rate of profit on the basis of the methodological presupposition of the same degree of exploitation of relative and absolute surplus value in 'a given country' (*Capital* vol. 3, p. 142), stressing that 'What we want to show in this part is precisely the way in which a general rate of profit takes shape in any given country' (*Capital* vol. 3, p. 143). He speaks of the process of the equalization of the rate of profit 'in a given national social formation' (*Capital* vol. 3, p. 196) and thus applies the concept of 'total social capital' in a concrete manner only within a national framework. In fact, he cannot conceive of the world market as anything other than an aggregation of national units,[13] and his explanation of 'National Differences in Wages' (*Capital* vol. 1, pp. 524 ff.) is based on this.

The concept of a national capital combines an economic concept, subject to its own laws, with a political concept which in its essence is contingent to the economic. As a result it seems all too easy for the political concept, a short every-day expression, to become a substitute for systematic consideration of the conditions (understood from the point of view of accumulation theory) required for the constitution of this specific historical form of appearance of the unity of capital. In the course of the process of accumulation, of the extension, differentiation and intensification of the social division of labour, of the increasing establishment of international capital mobility and supranational interpenetration, the unity of the divided complexes of reproduction (i.e. national capitals), previously established selectively and essentially in the sphere of circulation, coheres increasingly to become a real, unified, global complex of reproduction. To the extent that this development arises from the process of the valorization of capital itself, it marks a new historical and concrete form of appearance of the unity of capital, which, *vis-à-vis* the previous unity, shows itself to be a process of particularization which must be determined historically. The analysis of the movements of capital must start from the level of that new unity within which capital movement actually takes place.[14]

If the movement of capital and with it of the law of value are to receive conceptual analysis at the world market level, then the derivation and determination of the form of the *bourgeois state* must be introduced on this dimension, or perhaps can only be accomplished at this level. In the light of the fact that the sphere of motion of capital and of the law of value is the world market and that the law of value, in accordance with the

inner laws of capital, progressively realizes its tendency towards world-
wide effectiveness, the form of the *bourgeois nation state* — the political
organization of separate complexes of reproduction, the political con-
densation of national capitals — cannot be derived from the merely internal
dimensions of a commodity producing class society alone. It is not just a
question of the derivation of the state in general, but of the derivation of the
specific political organization of the world market in many states, or, in
other words, of explaining the particularization of capital in national
capitals each with their own political organs and their own features. This is
an indispensable prerequisite for any analysis which has the forms of appearance of contemporary imperialism and the problems of state interventionism as its object.

Marx himself never touched upon this problem at length, much less
offered possible solutions to it. His only remarks on the topic are essentialist,
underived and unfounded quasi-analytic statements which are ultimately of
a rather descriptive nature.

> It [i.e. bourgeois, or civil, society, C. v. B] embraces the whole com-
> mercial and industrial life of a given stage and, in so far, transcends the
> state and the nation, though, on the other hand again, it must assert
> itself in its external relations as nationality and internally must
> organize itself as state (*The German Ideology*, MECW vol. 5, p. 89).
> But it [i.e. the state, C. v. B] is nothing more than the form of organiza-
> tion which the bourgeois are compelled to adopt, both for internal and
> external purposes, for the mutual guarantee of their property and
> interests (*The German Ideology*, MECW vol. 5, p. 90).

Or in the description which bundles a whole range of historically diverse
forms together:

> The 'present society' is capitalist society, which exists in all civilized
> countries, freed in varying degrees from the admixture of medievalism,
> modified in varying degrees by the particular historical development
> of each country, and developed to a varying degree. In contrast to this,
> the 'present state' changes with each country's border. It differs between
> the Prusso—German empire and Switzerland, between England and the
> United States. '*The* present state' is thus a fiction.
> Nevertheless, the various states of the various civilized countries,
> despite their motley diversity of form, do have this in common: they
> all stand on the ground of modern bourgeois society although the degree
> of capitalist development varies. They thus also share certain essential
> characteristics. In this sense one can speak of 'present states' (*Critique
> of the Gotha Programme*, MESW vol. 2, p. 32).

In each of these the multi-state nature of the world market is presupposed,
never examined.

Thus materialist theory in its present stage of construction and reconstruction hardly provides points of contact for the presentation, in the context

of a rigorous derivation, of the specific statal organization of the world
market. Neither, on the other hand, can a reasoned argument be produced
to show that such a derivation is impossible. Nor is the answer to be found
by taking some concept of the state and making a plausible deduction of
its plurality and applying it in historical concrete modification. Any such
deduction would remain unsatisfactory; the modifications would still
have to be explained.

The most suitable way to achieve the conceptual clarification outlined
would seem to be through historical analysis informed and accompanied
by systematic reflection.[15]

The world market must be seen as an international, state-organized and
specifically structured, all-encompassing effective international context
of competition, within which statehood arises and consolidates itself and
states form their characteristic economic, social and political structure.

The concreteness of the particular nation state and its economic form
determination is to be explained in terms of the particular historic circumstances and preconditions under which the various total national capitals
develop. Of these factors a *dominant role* must be assigned to position
within the world market context. But this concreteness, in spite of being
in essence contingent to capital, nevertheless had a decisive effect historically
upon the actual formation of the accumulation process within specific
bounds. Thus it in turn played a decisive part in the determination of the
particular pattern of development of the productive forces, of class relations
and, last but not least, the specific configuration of the state apparatus, its
functions and its perception of its function as much as its position in the
context of a class society. The particular pre-existing territorial features
of the pre-capitalist system of reproduction and the structure of its administrative apparatus of rule are similarly of central importance.

Conceptual reflection must be introduced in the analysis of the formation of bourgeois society in the context of the world market — which is
'the basis and the vital element of capitalist production' (*Capital* vol. 3,
p. 110) — of the connection between the growth of national systems of
reproduction and the development of the world market and of the influences,
mediated through the world market, upon the specific features and modes
of action of the national state apparatus. The historical account of the
origin of the capitalist mode of production in the particular form of national
capitals and of the world market assuming the form of organization of
political nation states requires the discovery and reconstruction of the systematic conditions for the constitution of the categories. For if, as is here
being maintained, the world market *is* the appropriate analytic *level*, in relation to which effectively delimited spaces of the movement of capital are
to be determined, then this designates a dimension which, within capitalism,
is historical only in relation to the effectiveness of the delimitation, not as
regards the appropriateness of the level of analysis. In other words, it is a

question of reconstructing as substratum of the categories, as it were, the effectiveness of the world market context as manifested from the onset of the capitalist mode of production right up to its development in monopoly and imperialism.

The existence of regionally delimited political entities exercising sovereignty was from the start the precondition and the specific bearer of the constitution and consolidation of a complex of exchange based on the division of labour, on the basis of the capitalist mode of production, and thus also of the unfolding of the laws of capital. But, at the same time, the establishment of the capitalist mode of production presupposed the world market, on the one hand in the sense of the capturing of wealth and the absorption of commodities; on the other hand, the world market was the vital element of capital in such a manner that the disunited processes of accumulation did not form themselves into a single unit, but rather, using and changing the function of pre-existing boundaries and apparatuses of domination, they assumed political forms of organization — those of the bourgeois state — which relate competitively to one another.

> The colonies created world trade, and world trade is the condition of large-scale industrial enterprise (*The Poverty of Philosophy*, MECW vol. 6, p. 167).

Owing to their dual function as providers of raw materials, precious metals, luxury goods and slaves, and as a market outlet for predominantly manufactured products (cf. Gerstenberger 1973, p. 207), the steady expansion of the world market, initially in a time of still predominantly feudal structures,[16] acted as a powerful driving force in the accumulation of treasure, the circulation of money and commodity production for an expanding market (cf. Kaemmel 1966; *The Poverty of Philosophy*, MECW vol. 6, pp. 184—5). The world market is an integral component of those processes which have as their result primitive accumulation and the industrial revolution, in other words the assertion of the capitalist mode of production and its laws. That is to say that right from the origins of the capitalist mode of production, the world market is integrated into the national economies, in which this process takes place.

In the course of securing and maintaining the material basis of its supremacy, the political apparatus of feudal rule was transformed into the absolute state, which, partly in objective and partly in direct coalition with merchant and manufacturing capital, undermined its own economic and social foundations to act as midwife to the capitalist mode of production.[17] The 'centralization and organization of state power' (*Moralizing Critique and Critical Morality*, MECW vol. 6, p. 312) achieved by the absolute state, precondition for a wide-reaching series of measures aimed at increasing wealth and centred on the rising bourgeoisie,[18] required the definite establishment of state boundaries, which gradually lost their dynastic character and acquired a growing economic significance, becoming the framework within which the bourgeois nation state was gradually formed.

With the implementation of a state-supervised monetary system (cf. *Grundrisse*, pp. 873–4) and the expansion of channels of commerce and trade etc., the absolutist state promoted the unification of the conditions of circulation. 'The bureaucracy maintained the notion of unity against the various states within the state' (*Contribution to the Critique of Hegel's Philosophy of Law*, MECW vol. 3, p. 79).[19] Admittedly, in its social dimension, this unity was confined to the property-owning bourgeoisie who sustained the bourgeois nation state; confined, in effect, to capital; but it necessarily also contained within itself the class antagonism which negated that unity. In its territorial dimension it comprised the space within which capital moved as complex of circulation and production based on the division of labour, a space which was provided and formed by the actions of the absolutist state.

In its external affairs the absolute mercantilist state was still fully committed to the theory that wealth was to be achieved through trading. It functioned as the executor of a system of 'state regulated exploitation through trade, which played an exceptionally important role at the time of the onset of capitalist industry. It was in essence the economic policy of an age of primitive accumulation, (Dobb 1963, p. 209). The modest productivity of labour did not permit a concept of surplus value to develop; profit was understood to be the result of an advantage gained as the result of differences in prices, and on the national level this meant importing as little and as cheaply as possible, and exporting as much and as expensively as one could. As a result the central aim of mercantilist policies was a monopoly control of export markets and a structure of production in the colonies geared to the needs of domestic manufacture and industry. Thus a comprehensive. system of state regulation, expression of the still extreme need of the capitalist mode of production for protection and support, provided for the furnishing of the requisite labour power and the promotion of industrial life (cf. *Capital* vol. 1, pp. 686 f; Kuczynski 1961, vol. 22, pp. 101 ff; Bondi 1958, p. 3 ff). The protective external borders became a defensive tariff wall for production and the internal market for as long as, and to the extent that, ascendant capitalism required protection within these borders in order to 'manufacture capitalists' (*Capital* vol. 1, p. 717; cf. also *Speech on the Question of Free Trade*, MECW vol. 6, pp. 450 ff).

Through its policy of optimal strength on the world market, the mercantile state achieved the systematic integration of the world market into the national economy and the structuring of the national economy for the world market. In its external policy — and not just in the waging of war, but also in the provision of legal guarantees in international exchange operations — the state appears clearly as representative and guarantor of the dominant mode of production. Thus the political and military strength of a state within the international system served from the first the immediate interests of the rising bourgeoisie.[20] In the course of the development of a system of international law, states came to recognize one another as the political representatives of separate, bounded complexes of production and circulation the unity of which, developing upon an antagonistic basis, constitutes the bourgeois nation state.[21]

Just as the world market was the necessary basis of primitive accumulation, and just as its precondition was the territorial delimitation and sovereignty of the emergent bourgeois national state, so the industrial revolution was also accomplished along the dimension of this contradictory unity of the two elements. Neither did the old mode of production suffice for the international 'extending markets and still more rapidly extending competition of the capitalists' (*Capital* vol. 1, p. 443) — extended by merchant capital and manufacture — nor did the developing national capital ever at any time remain within its frontiers. 'On the one hand, the immediate effect of machinery is to increase the supply of raw material in the same way, for example, as the cotton gin augmented the production of cotton. On the other hand, the cheapness of the articles produced by machinery, and the improved means of transport and communication furnish the weapons for conquering foreign markets. By ruining handicraft production in other countries, machinery forcibly converts them into fields for the supply of its raw material. In this way East India was compelled to produce cotton, wool, hemp, jute, and indigo for Great Britain. By constantly making a part of the hands "supernumerary", modern industry, in all countries where it has taken root, gives a spur to emigration and to the colonization of foreign lands, which are thereby converted into settlements for growing the raw material of the mother country; just as Australia, for example, was converted into a colony for growing wool. *A new and international division of labour, a division suited to the requirements of the chief centres of modern industry springs up, and converts one part of the globe into a chiefly agricultural field of production, for supplying the other part which remains a chiefly industrial field*' (*Capital* vol. 1, pp. 424–5; my emphasis — C. v. B.).

Thus with the industrial revolution, the country undergoing industrialization became actively caught up in a structure of international division of labour, and, operating in accordance with the dynamic of the valorization of capital, wrought permanent changes upon it.[22] In the violent process by which the structure of the international division of labour was established, the trade and production structures of the colonies were formed so as to suit the requirements of manufacturing and industrial capital (cf. *Capital* vol. 1, p. 705), and thus achieve the accumulation necessary to secure the capital expenditure needed for the success and prosperity of the capitalist mode of production in the metropolitan regions.[23] The structure of international relationships became 'the expression of a particular division of labour' (Marx, *Letter to Annenkov*, MESW vol. 1, p. 520) and altered in accordance with it; separate and particular histories became subsumed and condensed, into a single world history. (*The German Ideology*, MECW vol. 5, pp. 50—51).

This process, which was initiated in England with the support of a state apparatus with active international involvement,[24] was to the advantage of British capital and detrimental to the autonomous reproduction of those countries where the unevenness of political and economic development made for feudal relations which were much more stable and far more resistant to external influences. Once the world market had come into being, and once the capitalist mode of production was established, the remaining European states were compelled to open up to them on pain of economic stagnation or the loss of the material basis of their authority; where the social preconditions were lacking, this opening up was achieved through the active involvement of the state apparatus which owes to a large extent its specific shape and its specific location in class society to just those interventions in the service of the establishment of capitalist relations of production. 'Since 1825 the invention and employment of machines is simply the result of the war between entrepreneurs and workers. And even that is true only of England. The European nations are compelled to adopt machinery by the competition to which they are subjected by the English as much in their domestic markets as on the world market' (*Letter to Annenkov*, MESW vol. 1, p. 521).

Whereas England was in world market competition with states which were still at the stage of an almost pure merchant capitalism, the European states were confronted in both domestic and external markets by a technologically superior competitor with extensive world market connections which was permanently in a position to effect value transfers through profitable unequal exchange. They were thus forced, on the one hand, to create a complex of production and circulation subject to their own control and protected as far as possible from external influences by means of protective tariffs,[25] and on the other, to revolutionize economic and social relations in order to introduce capitalist relations and promote the development of competitive conditions of production, or in a word, to develop a national capital which would be competitive on the world market. The less the pre-capitalist relations of production were already in a state of decay, the more the state-mediated acceleration of accumulation contributed to the petrification of pre-capitalist class relations, and the more the active state apparatus became autonomous. Thus in every metropolitan country which underwent primitive accumulation and an industrial revolution in the wake of England, class relations and the relation of the state apparatus to society bear in a specific manner the imprint of that country's position on the world market.[26]

Whereas in England the bourgeoisie in coalition with an extensively capitalized aristocracy was able to secure its influence over the state apparatus with relatively little force or bloodshed,[27] in France, in contrast, it required an economic crisis, mediated by the world market and resulting in revolutionary convulsions, for the bourgeoisie to gain an influence upon the structure and activity of the state apparatus. Moreover, the bourgeois republic as historical political expression of the consolidated capitalist mode of production was able to establish itself in France only some forty years later than in England. In Prussian Germany, on the other hand, with its oft-cited 'late start', the confrontation between relatively stable feudal relations and the necessity for self-assertion on the world market developed in forms of forced accumulation (in which a relatively developed banking system played an important role,[28] the protracted and for a long time incomplete penetration of the capital-relation and the persistence of feudal conditions.[29] The political action of the state apparatus eliminated those obstacles to primitive accumulation and industrialization which, although they had not yet become barriers to internally determined economic and social processes, had proved to be limiting internationally. In total contrast to the German state which never fully overcame the lack of development of its class relations and the relative autonomy of its state apparatus, the American state can be seen as almost the direct result of the measures towards the outside world which have to be taken by a relatively developed bourgeois society in an historical situation where class antagonisms are deeply distorted and hidden and where there are unusually favourable conditions for autonomous reproduction (cf. *Grundrisse*, p. 884). Lacking any objectives over and above society, the state apparatus in the USA developed in administrative reflection of the necessities of the economic and political processes and with the closest of ties with the clientele affected.[30]

The study of the historical material[31] dealing with the establishment of the capitalist mode of production makes it clear that the capitalist mode of production in general can only arise within the context of a world market established by merchant capital. The world market is the precondition, 'the basis and the vital element' of capital (*Capital* vol. 3, p. 110), and therefore logically inseparable from the concept of capital, although in its real concrete form as a space permeated and structured by capital, it depends upon the concrete historical unfolding of capitalist relations of production. In the transformation of pre-existing territorial boundaries into the bourgeois nation state, as political form of organization a necessary basis for the operation of capital, the world market retains its characteristic principle of organization, the general realization of which reflects the penetration of capitalist relations of production. Of compelling importance as a constitutive element, the world market at all times remains a real influence and conditioning factor in the process of the development of nationally organized capitalist complexes of reproduction, and asserts its dimension within the nationally organized process of accumulation both in periods of prosperity and in crisis.[32]

If the world market is the basis and the integral scope of the capitalist mode of production, the bourgeois nation state is also the basis: the bourgeois nation state is both historically and conceptually part of the capitalist mode of production.[33] The economic relation of force in the capitalist relations of production has always required, for its continued profitable domination as well as for its establishment, the exercise of political force, localized in the apparatus of the bourgeois state, to intervene and to protect it. That this state force is not a *single* central one, congruent in its domain with the development and extension of the capitalist mode of production; that it appears as a plurality, and imposes on the world market the principle of organization into national states — this is essentially due to the *domination which characterizes* relations within all previous societies and to the specific form this domination takes under capitalism. The existence of a state apparatus is in itself the admission by a society that its reproduction is organized along the dimension of domination, that it is a class society (cf. Engels, *Origin of the Family*, MESW vol. 3, p. 327). Ultimately it is the conditions of the material interchange between man and nature and the development of the productive forces which give to the statement that 'the history of all hitherto existing societies is the history of class struggle' (*Communist Manifesto*, MESW vol. 1, p. 108) its specific historical concrete form, referred to by Marx and Engels as social formation (*Preface to the Contribution to the Critique of Political Economy*, MESW vol. 1, p. 504), to which there corresponds in each case a specific form of the exercise and preservation of authority.

The pre-capitalist state formations with their historically contingent frontiers strongly dependent in their extent on the development of the productive forces are characterized equally by the nature of their internal domination and by the rivalry of their external power struggle. The border marked the end of one and the beginning of the other. The capitalist mode of production then comes into being within these pre-existent bounded territories, where authority and competition prevail. In the capitalist mode of production, domination is reproduced in the mechanism of economic functioning itself and yet needs *politically* regulative and repressive safeguarding precisely because as anarchically exercised authority it is incapable of being adequately assured by the operation of the laws of production. Many centres of capital arise, reproduction and accumulation take place within limited areas, capital avails itself of the existing political apparatus of force to impose and safeguard itself, reforming and expanding it according to its own needs. In the nation state the bourgeoisie constitutes itself as a unit operating politically on the world market in a competitive relation with other national bourgeoisies, just as within the framework of national borders fractions of the bourgeoisie 'only constitute politically active units through their relationship to the state' (Hirsch 1976).

The political complexes of production and exchange have a specific density which stabilizes borders and gives them their economic relevance only to the extent that they partition capitals historically to constitute a national total capital. Through the national state apparatuses the fractioned bourgeoisie organizes *state interventions* of the most diverse forms in the world market movements of capital. Whether such interventions are domestically focused or whether they involve action directed outwards depends upon the particular imperatives of valorization and the particular class constellations.

Thus there are preexistent structures of authority whose economic bases are transformed with the establishment of the capitalist mode of production. Once it has embarked upon the process of its development, capital imposes its laws upon the rulers within a defined territorial area, on pain of losing their power through the gradual erosion of its basis, mediated through either internal or external assault. The existing apparatuses of power, in acting to maintain the material basis of their authority, function as the objective vehicle of the capitalist mode of production and as the administrative executors of 'the historical dissolution process and as the makers of the conditions for the existence of capital' (*Grundrisse*, p. 507). To this extent they are based on the previously predominantly politically determined sphere of authority, whose boundaries increasingly lose their purely political character and come to comprise the complex of production governed by the division of labour, the unity of competing capitals which finds its conceptual expression in the national average rate of profit.

The universal character of the capitalist mode of production also asserts itself in the fact that it brings forth and strengthens the bourgeois nation state as a reproduction complex of a specific density separated off from other bourgeois nation states, as a partial centre of accumulation.

Once the capitalist mode of production had established itself in England, less developed forms of national production in other countries began necessarily to be rendered obsolete by English large-scale industry (cf. *Grundrisse*, German edn., pp. 917 ff). The specific establishment of the capitalist mode of production in France and Germany shows in an exemplary manner the necessity of forming nationally determined centres of capital accumulation, mediated through the state apparatus. The necessity was derived from the *political* premise of autonomous economic and political authority, which was maintained at the cost, naturally, of the transfer of that authority from the hands of the feudal classes into those of the bourgeoisie.

The relevance of the formation of politically bounded centres emerges even more clearly from a consideration of the coming into existence of the USA. The conflict between the colonies and the mother country broke out at the precise point in time at which a decisive divergence of views occurred over the authority to dispose of the capital generated by primitive accumulation, and at which the economic disposition favourable to England centrally threatened the autonomy of the economic and political authority of the colonies. The political independence of the ruling classes in the USA required the constitution of a bourgeois state of their own as the precondition for providing an economic basis for that rule via the capitalist mode of production. At bottom, all the pathetic rhetoric of freedom which the War of Independence produced was no more than the legitimating screen of competing claims to rule, which here still required that formal constitution which in Europe was already provided by territorial sovereignty.

The form of the bourgeois nation state, of the world market organized as nation states, acquires, as a bounded, legally sovereign centre of a capitalist complex of exchange and production, the function of securing, both internally and externally, the politico—economic power of the bourgeoisies competing in the 'international system'. The form, however great its economic significance — 'The relations of industry and trade within every nation are dominated by their intercourse with other nations, and are conditioned by relations with the world market'[34] — is ultimately not comprehensible without recourse to the *political moment of domination* which is implicit in the economic relation of force between wage labour and capital, and without reference to the *competing claims to rule* advanced by rival bearers of authority. This political moment here acquires a fundamental significance in as much as without its introduction in the schematic derivation of the political from the economic — competition between national bourgeoisies as a mere reflection of competition between national capitals — the constitution of this capital as national, the insistence on its own foundation and exercise of authority, as opposed to the theoretically conceivable profitable participation in non-national authority, cannot be established.

In the national organization of the world market, with all its implications for the development of power and for its exercise, there is nevertheless an admission, the admission again that domination lies at the core of the capitalist mode of production and with it the antagonistic and competitive striving to maintain it by whatever means. The bourgeois nation state is indeed the primary location for the social reproduction of class relations: it is here that repressive political measures for their preservation are carried out, and this becomes ever clearer with the growing coincidence in the scope of economic and social reproduction. On the other hand, political self-assertion in a specific national state and the arsenal of means of power which go along with it is indeed the precondition for long-term economic self-assertion. However neither the considerations of economic nor of social reproduction are adequate to explain the refusal of one national bourgeoisie to accept the politico—territorial subjection to another. Even in cases of extensive economic dependence, in the ever-fragile union of the national bourgeoisie with its own nation state, class society is revealed as a nexus of domination.

The complexes of reproduction centred within the boundaries of nation

states define themselves as nationally autonomous complex of authority
principally through the ownership of the means of production and the overall direction of the process of production on the part of the national bourgeoisie, who in the state apparatus have created an organ of authority which
will represent their own interests. In so far as the basis of this authority is
grounded in the continuous appropriation of surplus value, national bourgeoisies will compete with one another for the surplus value produced on
the world market, and the extent, the forms and the strategy and methods
used in this competition are centrally dependent upon the process of accumulation and crisis as an increasingly international process. The nation
state is thus not merely the historical form of organization within which
capital first develops and grows into a nationally centred complex of production and exchange, it is also — mediated through the national development
of the course of accumulation, mediated above all through the state
apparatus — an indispensable instrument necessary to secure the profitable
outcome of the valorization of national capital in its competition with the
many other capitals combined together in nation states. It is the guarantor
and regulator of the conditions necessary for the reproduction of capital
within the framework of the nation state and at the same time also the
apparatus for the repression of national labour power. As is stated in the
Communist Manifesto, the class struggle is 'though not in substance, yet
in form . . . a national struggle'.[35] Even if the internationalization of accumulation involves the increasingly international determination of exploitation, and the direction of the particular national production processes are
structured by the conditions of international competition and differences
in productivity, the authority which safeguards this exploitation still continues to be mediated nationally. It is precisely the actualization of the
international complex of accumulation and crisis, functioning as a pressure
towards the equalization of the different national levels of productivity,
which activates the national bourgeoisie's interest in safeguarding the basis
of its rule, which, as an imperialistic one, itself transcends national frontiers;
it mobilizes the state apparatus in its defence and thus, in spite of the
growing non-coincidence between accumulation processes and state
frontiers, consolidates the organization of the world market into nation
states.[36]

The relation between the world market and the nation state is therefore
to be understood as an historical continuum internal to capitalism and to be
determined with reference to the laws unfolding in the process of accumulation of capital — in a specific concrete historical form. In this context, it is
necessary to reach a more precise understanding of the extremely blurred
concept of the world market. Marx uses the concept to describe the location
of those international trading relationships which in a centuries-long process
helped to accelerate the destruction of feudal relations (cf. *Capital* vol. 3,
pp. 238–9). When, however, he writes of 'the entanglement of all peoples

in the net of the world market, and with this, the international character of the capitalist regime' (*Capital* vol. 1, pp. 714—5), the world market is envisaged as the fully developed domain of capital movement. Clearly a theoretical distinction must be drawn here between two separate states of affairs, which are linked by capital's development according to its own inner laws, and distinguished by the historically different level of accumulation and the different structuring of the international division of labour. Part of the task of any theory of imperialism is to undertake to account for these historically differentiated determinations on the basis of a theory of accumulation.

Notes to Introduction

1. It should be clear from our definitions that 'economic determinism' cannot be identified with the work of 'economists', nor 'politicism' necessarily with the work of 'political theorists'. We develop this point later in the Introduction.

2. It is seen also by Poulantzas as a more general work embracing the overall articulation of the capitalist mode of production and the development of basic concepts such as mode of production, relations of production, etc. Our point of criticism, however, is that the categories developed specifically in *Capital* (value, surplus value, accumulation, etc.) are seen as being concepts specific to the analysis of the *economic* level.

3. Cf. e.g. Poulantzas 1975, p. 15. In our view developed below, production relations or relations of exploitation, are neither economic nor political; in capitalism they appear as distinct economic and political forms of social relations, but the task of Marxist theory is precisely to criticize and transcend these forms.

4. It is significant that in his treatment of fascism, as in his other works, Poulantzas deals with the various classes in separate chapters on the 'dominant classes', the 'dominated classes', etc. This allows him to pass over the systematic analysis of the all-important conflict *between* the classes which is the source of all historical movement. The political implications of this emphasis on the contradictions within rather than between the classes is particularly evident in his treatment of Greece and the fall of the military junta in his most recent book (1976b). For a discussion of this, see the paper presented by Loukas Politikos to the Conference of Socialist Economists' working group on European integration, 'Internationalization of Capital, European Integration and Developing Countries' (December 1975).

5. It is true that Poulantzas has repudiated to some extent his earlier views on method, criticizing his first book for conveying 'a certain view of instances as being to some extent partitioned from and impermeable to each other' (1976a, p. 81), and now emphasizing more the unity of the two separate 'instances'. It may well be that Poulantzas, partly under the influence of the German debate, is groping his way towards a dialectical and materialist theory of the relation between economics and politics, but his recent books (1975, 1976b) do not show very much progress in that direction. As we have seen in his treatment of European integration, there is still no analysis of the historical development of the relation between political and economic forms. Poulantzas is unable to develop a theory of the unity-in-separation of politics and economics precisely because he rejects the task of historical materialist theory to grasp as a totality the capitalist development which provides the basis for that unity.

6. Cf. Negri's treatment of both Poulantzas and Miliband as 'neo-Gramscians': Negri 1976.

7. For a recent full account of the controversy, see Fine and Harris 1976b.

8. For a fuller discussion of Gough's article, see Holloway and Picciotto 1976; Fine and Harris 1976a.

9. In view of their stress on surface categories, it is perhaps not surprising that their work, like Poulantzas's, is characterized by a general hostility to what they regard as 'historicist' or 'Hegelian' interpretations of Marx: see in particular Hodgson 1976.

10. The problem of form analysis is further complicated by the need to grasp the essential nature of social relations which present themselves in certain *phenomenal forms*. On this see Blanke, Jürgens and Kastendiek, below ch. 6 footnote 21.

11. The problem of form, the understanding of Marxist analysis as the materialist critique of bourgeois categories as forms of social relations, has been greatly neglected by Marxists in this country. In West Germany, however, the analysis of form was given central importance by a number of influential studies which appeared in the late 1960s and early 1970s. Thus Rosdolsky, in his excellent commentary on the *Grundrisse* stresses that: 'It is thus the specific social forms of production and distribution which constitute in Marx's eyes the proper object of economic analysis.' (1968, p. 105.)
Thus Backhaus talks of 'the central theme of Marx's analysis of the value form: why does this content take this form' (1969, p. 132). Thus Reichelt introduces his work by stressing that: 'the critique of political economy differs from all — even present-day — economic theory in the question it asks: what . . . is concealed in the categories themselves; what is the particular content of the economic form determinations, i.e. of the value *form*, of the money *form*, of the capital *form*, of the *form* of profit, of interest, etc. While bourgeois political economy is generally characterized by the fact that it takes up the categories externally, Marx insists on a strict derivation of the genesis of these forms.' (1970, p. 16, emphasis in the original.)

12. It is a great pity that Pashukanis has been so neglected by Marxists in Britain: this is perhaps partly due to the relative inaccessibility of the existing translation (see bibliography) and partly due to the appalling quality of the translation (which speaks of 'goods' for commodities, 'worker strength' for labour power, etc). In citing Pashukanis here we have therefore retranslated where appropriate.

13. It would be wrong to personify the debate, but the proponents of this first approach are generally associated with Berlin and the journal *Probleme des Klassenkampfs*.

14. For references to recent developments by Marxist theorists of law, see Blanke, Jürgens and Kastendiek's essay.

15. One interesting aspect of the German debate is the fruitful stimulation it has received in the critique of theories of state monopoly capitalism: for a specific treatment of these theories, see particularly Wirth 1972; 1973.

16. For a very full discussion of the general conditions of production see Läpple 1973.

17. Blanke, Jürgens and Kastendiek also make this criticism: see below, p. 132.

18. It was originally intended to include the article by Flatow and Huisken, but the authors subsequently withdrew permission.
19. If the first approach can be loosely identified with Berlin, then this approach can be associated with Frankfurt and the journal *Gesellschaft*.
20. The term 'capital logic' has been rather loosely applied in Britain to any analysis which bases itself upon the contradictions of capital; it should be clear from this Introduction, however, and certainly from a reading of the book, that it would be extremely misleading to apply the tag 'capital logic' to the whole of the debate presented here; that, although all the authors do start from the analysis of capital, there are very great differences in their approach to the 'derivation' of the state and their understanding of the 'logic' of capital.
21. The pursuit of the second course (the analysis of the 'missing link') is to some extent foreshadowed in the last pages of Hirsch's essay, and articulated in his more recent work: Hirsch 1976.
22. See in particular Gerstenberger's (1977) discussion of Hirsch 1976.

Notes to Chapter 2

Editors' note: The full article from which this extract is taken originally appeared in 1970 *Sozialistische Politik* 6–7, pp. 4–67, and was reprinted in *Probleme des Klassenkampfs*, Sonderheft 1, 1971. A complete translation in English was published in *Telos* 1975, 25, together with pieces by Offe and Habermas which constitute a reply to the criticism of them developed in this article. Although we have here retranslated these extracts from the original, we have obviously not been uninfluenced by the existing translation, by R. V. Heydebrand, whose work we willingly acknowledge. However, we differ from him in the translation of some terms, in particular the central term 'Sozialstaatsillusion' of the title, which he renders as 'Illusion of the Socialist State'.

1. Marx, *Grundrisse* p. 108. Cf. also *The German Ideology*, MECW vol. 5, p. 90: 'Since the state is the form in which the individuals of a ruling class assert their common interests, and in which the whole civil society of an epoch is epitomized, it follows that all common institutions are set up with the help of the state and are given a political form. Hence the illusion that law is based on the will, and indeed on the will divorced from its real basis — on *free* will.'
2. *Critique of the Gotha Programme*, MESW vol. 3, p. 25. Cf. also *Contribution to a Critique of Hegel's Philosophy of Law*, MECW vol. 3, pp. 99, 101: '. . . what is the *content* of the political establishment, of the political purpose — what is the purpose of this purpose? . . . What power does the political state exercise over private property? . . . This, that it *isolates* private property from family and society, that it turns it into *something abstractly independent*. What then is the power of the political state over private property? The *power of private property itself*, its essence brought into existence. What remains for the political state in contrast with this essence? The *illusion* that the state determines, when it is being determined.' 'The "*inalienability*" of private property is one with the "*alien-*

ability" of the general freedom of the will and morality. Here property
no longer exists "in so far as I put my will into it", but my will exists
"in so far as it lies in property". My will here does not possess, it is
possessed.' Thus Marx in his early writings shows that the bourgeois state
itself creates the appearance of its independence in a particular manner,
and that the capitalist mode of production is the basis of the illusion of
the state. He shows at the same time that this illusion that the state has
an unlimited scope for action is already inaugurated with the fiction of
the freedom of will of the owner of private property, the capitalist.

3. Marx very early on showed that the contradictions of society are condensed into contradictions of the state itself, in relation to the example
of the state bureaucracy, in *Critical Marginal Notes on the Article by a
Prussian*, MECW vol. 3, p. 189: 'The *contradiction* between the purpose
and good will of the administration, on the one hand, and its means and
possibilities, on the other hand, cannot be abolished by the state without
the latter abolishing itself, for it is *based* on this contradiction. The state
is based on the contradiction between *public* and *private life*, on the
contradiction between *general interests* and *private interests*. Hence the
administration has to confine itself to a *formal* and *negative* activity, for
where civil life and its labour begin, there the power of the administration
ends. Indeed, confronted by the consequences which arise from the un-
social nature of this civil life, this private ownership, this trade, this
industry, this mutual plundering of the various circles of citizens, confronted by all these consequences, *impotence* is the *law of nature* of the
administration. For this fragmentation . . . of civil society is the natural
foundation on which the *modern* state rests . . .. If the modern state
wanted to abolish the *impotence* of its administration, it would have to
abolish the *private life* of today. But if it wanted to abolish private life, it
would have to abolish itself, for it exists *only* in the contradiction to private
life.' In contrast the theory of state monopoly capitalism today states, for
example: 'It has been pointed out that the monopolies must make use of
an instrument, the state, which in some circumstances can be used against
them.' (In Herbert Meissner, ed. 1967, p. 422). The theory of state
monopoly capitalism forgets, even though it pays lip-service to the contradictions of capitalist society, that these contradictions are present in a
condensed form even in the state apparatus and its political possibilities of
action. Therefore this apparatus cannot be a monolithic instrument which
in itself is neutral and hence can be used by any class in its own interest.

4. Lenin, *State and Revolution. The Marxist Teaching on the State and the
Tasks of the Proletariat in the Revolution.* (Written in Aug./Sept. 1917);
in *Selected Works* vol. 2, pp. 301–400. (But cf. the reservations expressed
below.) In his *Critique of Hegel's Philosophy of Law*, hence in his critique
of Hegel's mystical view in which the state appears as the embodiment of
reason, Marx himself first made it clear that only the proletariat as the
contradiction of bourgeois society can be the subject which overcomes
the contradictions of that society. See Karl Polack 1968. In the *Critique
of Hegel's Philosophy of Law* Marx perceived 'that contradiction, class

struggle, is the ruling principle of reality, and that political power, that is to say the state, is the expression of this contradiction and this struggle' (Polack p. 51). Further, 'The dictatorship of the Jacobins was the attempt to overcome through political power the contradictions of bourgeois society; it did not, and could not, succeed' (*ibid.* p. 42).

5. Cf. on this point the essays by F. Deppe and J. Agnoli in *Neue Kritik* VIII (1967) (44), pp. 48–66; IX (1968) (47), pp. 24–33. Also Pannekoek, Lukacs, Friedländer and Rudas, *Parlamentarismusdebatte* (West Berlin, 1968). Bernd Rabehl and the study group on the DKP at the Freie Universität Berlin discuss the debate in their publication, 1969. They present and criticize the tradition and contemporary forms of revisionist state theory and its consequences for political strategy. They draw analogies between the revisionism of German social democracy and of Austria in the 1920s (Otto Bauer, Karl Renner, Rudolf Hilferding, Edward Bernstein, Karl Kautsky *et al.*, and the thesis of an 'organized capitalism' as a new and potentially crisis-free perfected form of the capitalist mode of production), and they draw similar analogies between the DKP's modern theory of state monopoly capitalism and the political sociology of Habermas and Offe, who are continuing the tradition both of the social-democratic state-theory of the Weimar republic and of bourgeois sociology since Max Weber. The revisionist theories of the state which we have been able to summarize only briefly here are given in greater detail as to their different forms and contents in pages 65–119 of that book. Cf. also the Introduction to the new edition of *Gegen den Strom* by P. Lapinski *et al.* Their repeated insistence on a 'historical-genetic' analysis of the capitalist state, echoed also in the DKP book, is however not complied with in that publication itself (which was perhaps not to be expected). Due to the attempt to give a complete survey of revisionist political ideas, criticism is directed constantly to the specifics of each viewpoint, in which it is generally accurate since it is based on the tradition of the critique of revisionism in the workers' movement; but in this process the systematic relationship of revisionist theories is lost from sight, as well as the relationship of the critique to them. Hence this account does not provide a theoretical starting-point for a truly materialist analysis of capitalism and class.

6. This essay is an attempt to begin this analysis; cf. also Elmar Altvater's conjunctural analysis in *Sozialistische Politik* 5, 1970. [A developed version of this 'conjunctural analysis' of West Germany, by Altvater, Hoffmann, Schöller and Semmler, was presented to the Conference of Socialist Economists in Britain in 1973, and published in its *Bulletin*, spring 1974. Editors' note.]

7. Does not revisionist theory express above all the consciousness of those officials of bureaucratized workers' organizations, who no longer personally experience the conflict with capital, but are essentially characterized by their partially successful activity as mediators for important organizations and the state administration? In contrast, does not the mass of the workers still have that 'dichotomized consciousness' ('them and us') which countless investigations have shown is still prevalent? Does not our

previous account rather carelessly equate the consciousness of the organized and that of the organizing apparatus? Is it even possible to explain the development of a revisionist consciousness without giving an account of the organizational forms through whose mediations class struggle actually takes place? Can one speak of 'actual experience' without referring to the organizational level and the precise social situation where such experiences take place? These questions indicate aspects which we leave open.

8. For the trade union apparatus the decisively important experience was that of its own indispensability, of the 'successful' cooperation with the state apparatus during and after the First World War (which went so far as the denouncing of insubordinate workers). The illusions of an 'organized capitalism' were importantly fostered by the memory of the so-called 'war socialism', the war economy organized by the state (i.e. essentially by the representatives of the large armament firms); this applies e.g. to Wissel and Hilferding. Cf. on this point the essay by Lapinski cited above, which deals in detail with the institutionalized collaboration between classes during the First World War, and shows how it developed under the Weimar Republic. The establishment of the Zentralen Arbeitsgemeinschaft (Central Council of Labour) by the trade unions and businessmen in November 1918 with the aim (for different motives) of forestalling the revolution is only a highlight of the whole process. Cf. also Deppe *et al.* 1969, and the FU project on the DKP cited above, at p. 182.

9. We have chosen this heading although it is at first hard to understand, because the debate has shown that the apparently easier formulation 'the particularized existence of the state' can imply the notion of the *independence* of the state. Our meaning will become clear in our argument. [It is for the same reasons that the word '*Besonderung*' has been translated as 'particularization' and not as 'separation' or 'autonomization'. Even though though 'particularization' and 'particular existence' are perhaps even clumsier in English than the German equivalents, it is essential, as these authors go on to argue here, to describe the relationship of state and society without confusing the actual nature of that relationship with the apparent (and illusory) independence and autonomy of the state that it creates. Editors' Note.]

10. The formulation in this early work does not completely exclude the mistaken interpretation that the bourgeois as bourgeois might be something other than the mere character masks of capital (i.e. that they consciously adopted this form of state organization).

11. This is still today the fiction of all constitutional provisions, e.g. the German Fundamental Law, in which however the fiction is particularly transparent, since all the fundamental decisions affecting society had previously been taken, namely the restoration of capitalist relations. [Readers in Britain in 1977 perhaps need no reminding of the role of another 'social contract', again a transparent fiction, in attempting to establish a legitimizing base for the restructuring of capitalist relations. Editors' note.]

12. Cf. Engels, *Anti-Dühring:* 'But the transformation, either into joint-stock companies, or into state ownership, does not do away with the capitalistic nature of the productive forces. In the joint-stock companies this is

obvious. And the modern state, again, is only the organization that bourgeois society takes on in order to support the general external conditions of the capitalist mode of production against the encroachments as well of the workers as of individual capitalists. The modern state, no matter what its form, is essentially a capitalist machine, the state of the capitalists, the ideal personification of the total national capital. The more it proceeds to the taking over of the productive forces, the more does it actually become the national capitalist, the more citizens does it exploit. The workers remain wage-workers — proletarians. The capitalist relation is not done away with. It is rather brought to a head. But, brought to a head, it topples over. State ownership of the productive forces is not the solution of the conflict, but concealed within it are the technical conditions that form the elements of that solution.' (p. 382.)

13. No emphasis in the original. That this characterization is still strikingly accurate and most topical is shown by the laborious attempts to enact laws for the 'conservation of air and water', and the feeble agitation against the continual increase of noise pollution by cars, planes, etc. Recently there was a report of an estimate that the nuclear power plants already projected would alone, once in full operation, increase the temperature of the Rhine to 50 degrees Centigrade (122° F), and cause the destruction of the climate, the river environment, exterminate the fish, pollute the air, etc. Are such projects conceivable in the GDR?

14. See generally, A. Gurland's thesis, 1928.

15. For a full account see *Grundrisse*, pp. 471 ff. Here Marx contrasts the original *unity* of labour and its material pre-conditions, mediated through the community, with the *separation* in the relationship of wage-labour and capital.

16. Cf. Marx and Engels, *Communist Manifesto:* 'When in the course of development, class distinctions have disappeared, and all production has been concentrated in the hands of a vast association of the whole nation, the public power will lose its political character. Political power, properly so called, is merely the organized power of one class for oppressing another' (MESW vol. 1, p. 127).

Notes to Chapter 3

Editors' note: The full article from which this short extract is taken appeared in *Probleme des Klassenkampfs* (1972) 3. A slightly edited version appeared in English in *Kapitalistate* (1973) 1. The main participants in discussions on the article were Karlheinz Maldaner, Wolfgang Müller and Christel Neusüss. It also resulted from debates in seminars at the Otto-Suhr Institute.

1. We cannot here go into the meaning of this category, and refer to what is still the best treatment, in Roman Rosdolsky (1968) pp. 24–124, esp. 61 ff.

2. This is expressed clearly by Marx in the twelfth chapter of the first volume of *Capital:* 'It is not our intention to consider, here, the way in which the laws, immanent in capitalist production, manifest themselves in the movements of individual masses of capital, where they assert themselves as coercive laws of competition, and are brought home to the mind and

consciousness of the individual capitalist as the directing motives of his operations.' (p. 300.) Marx is concerned to establish the immanent necessity of the production of surplus value, but not to elaborate the details of the mechanism through which the individual capitals carry out the immanent necessity of the production of surplus value. However, this is not so in his more complex treatment of the formation of the average rate of profit in the second part of the third volume of *Capital*. We cannot here go into this. In the treatment of competition a distinction must be made between two aspects of the concept of competition: 'capital as itself and its own level of surface appearance, as a dynamic unity of being and appearance, which yet finds its expression in conceptual terms; and then capital in historical reality. This second aspect is completely disentangled' (Helmut Reichelt 1970, p. 85).

3. Marx writes in the *Grundrisse*: '(2) however, capital in general, as distinct from the particular real capitals, is itself a real existence. This is recognized by ordinary economics, even if it is not understood, and forms a very important moment of its doctrine of equilibrations, etc. . . . While the general is therefore on the one hand only a mental mark of distinction, it is at the same time a particular real form alongside the form of the particular and the individual . . .' (p. 449).

4. Karl Marx and Friedrich Engels, *The German Ideology*, MECW vol. 5, p. 90. Marx and Engels establish the separate existence of the bourgeois state from the 'emancipation of private property from the commonwealth', i.e. from the historical development of bourgeois society and its state, from the emancipation from pre-capitalist forms of social organization.

5. The state 'is nothing more than the form of organization which the bourgeois necessarily adopt both for internal and external purposes, for the mutual guarantee of their property and interests . . . in which the individuals of a ruling class assert their common interests, and in which the whole civil society of an epoch is epitomized . . . ' (MECW vol. 5, p. 90).

6. This is itself a criticism of positions such as those involved in different variations of theories of state monopoly capitalism, according to which the state is the tool of the most powerful monopolies, or those advanced by most bourgeois theories, which claim the state to be an autonomous subject which regulates. It should be pointed out that theories of state monopoly capitalism are very divided precisely on this question. At times they maintain that there is a unified mechanism which includes the power of the monopolies and of the state, or the intermingling of monopoly power and the state; at others the state is conceived simply as the 'tool of the monopolistic bourgeoisie'. Cf. for instance 'Der Imperialismus der BRD' (1971). It cannot be denied that state and capital are combined in a unified mechanism, but the important point is to investigate exactly how this 'mechanism' works. This is the question that the theoreticians of state monopoly capitalism have still not resolved. Cf. as an example of the most developed version of the theory: Paul Boccara (1972); Werner Petrowsky (1971).

7. Friedrich Engels, *Anti-Dühring*: 'And the modern state, again, is only the organization that bourgeois society takes on in order to support the

general external conditions of the capitalist mode of production against the encroachments as well of the workers as of individual capitalists. The modern state, no matter what its form, is essentially a capitalist machine, the state of the capitalists, the ideal personification of the total national capital' (p. 382). However, we cannot agree with Engels's next statement: 'The more it proceeds to the taking over of the productive forces, the more does it actually become the national capitalist . . ..' Although the state does indeed become a real capitalist by taking over capitalist production processes, it does not become the *total* capitalist. As a capitalist producer the state is subject to the contradictions of individual capitals among themselves, as are other *large* individual capitals. As will be shown, it is precisely the establishment of the state as a real capitalist that is problematic for capital.

8. This is one of the points not taken into account by Projekt Klassenanalyse. So they state (p. 197): '*Any* social production, however, involves a general framework of conditions for the process of reproduction. These conditions are general, *regardless* of in what way, to the extent that they are general conditions for a greater or smaller part of social production.' (Emphasis by E.A.) The question however is why general conditions cannot be provided by capitals, and this is the basis for the particular way in which general conditions of production are provided in capitalist society, and of their successive historical phases of development.

Notes to Chapter 5

Editors' note: This article consists of Part 1 and Part 5 (Conclusions) of Hirsch's book, *Staatsapparat und Reproduktion des Kapitals* (1974), the remainder of which deals with state policy for science and technology. Part 1 is a revised version of the article *Elemente einer materialistischen Staatstheorie*, which appeared in Braunmühl *et al.* 1973.

1. For a detailed examination of these theories, see Hirsch 1974, parts 2 and 3.

2. From the perspective of this approach, some of the 'derivations' of the bourgeois state which claim to be Marxist should be criticized as being 'idealist' in the strict sense. They neglect this moment of the objective emergence of the political form from the conditions of the material process of social reproduction, and instead — starting from the surface of bourgeois society — they openly or implicitly construct a 'general will' of the subjects of society which constitutes the particular form of the state — whether these subjects be the universal private property owners, the private commodity producers or the competing individual capitals (cf. Flatow and Huisken, 1973; Altvater, 1972 (see above, p. 40); Projekt Klassenanalyse, 1973). In all these approaches, the form of the state has to be derived from specific generalized functions — that results necessarily from the assumption of a 'general will' emerging from the inverted shape of the surface of bourgeois society. This means, however, that the fulfilment of the functions abstractly attributed to the state (provision of the

general external conditions of production, safeguarding of the sources of revenue, etc.) is always already tautologically presupposed, which means that the central problem of state analysis, namely the question whether the state apparatus is at all able — and if so, under what conditions — to carry out certain functions and what consequences this has, is conjured out of existence. A critique of the individual approaches mentioned is not, however, included in this essay.

3. See also Neumann 1957, ch. 2, 'The Change in the Function of Law in Modern Society'.

4. On this, see Gerstenberger 1973a — although she neglects the aspects of the constitution of the bourgeois state which proceed from the character of the reproduction process itself; see also Braunmühl, below, p. 160.

5. These elements of form were already worked out clearly by Max Weber (cf. Weber 1964, pp. 1034 ff). See also (with bibliographical references) Blank 1969.

6. Riehle (1974) has attempted this. It is clear that the absence of this derivation in this essay leads to certain short-cuts, which would have to be made good in a developed theory of the bourgeois state.

7. A stringent derivation of this relation has been undertaken by Riehle (1974).

8. Close attention must be paid to Engels's formulation. There is a difference between the state's actions against the workers as a class and its sanctioning of intervention against *individual* capitalists. The bourgeois state cannot intervene against the bourgeoisie as a class.

9. Therefore it also makes no sense to go directly from a general characterization of the form of the bourgeois state to drawing up a list of its tasks. These can then only be the empirical generalization of existing state functions on the most general level, which must necessarily stand in a purely abstract relation to the 'derivation' of the state.

10. Cf. for this also Robinson 1956.

11. 'If one looks at the economic development of the last hundred years, the enormous development of the productive forces and the huge accumulation of capital as well as its ever-rising organic composition, then, in view of the law of the tendencies of the development of capital accumulation, the problem lies not in the question whether capitalism will one day collapse, but, on the contrary, one must wonder why it has not already collapsed.' Grossmann 1970, p. 289. Grossmann's work appeared in 1929, shortly before the outbreak of the world economic crisis in which this collapse of the capitalist system almost became reality for the first time. [For a contemporary critique recently republished in English, see Pannekoek 1977; editors' note.]

12. Cf. *Capital*, vol. 3, pp. 232 ff; *Grundrisse*, pp. 745 ff; Grossmann 1970, pp. 287 ff; Mattick 1969, p. 57; Mattick 1959; Gillman 1969; Wygodski 1972, pp. 232 ff.

13. Authors like Gillman or Baran and Sweezy, who try to derive the crisis of capitalism from the difficulty of realizing a growing surplus, adopt an approach which is limited to the forms of appearance and thus inverted, an approach which can explain neither the basic dynamic of capitalist

accumulation nor the mechanism and function of crisis. Above all, they are unable to show the basis of the development of the productive forces and the course of technical progress. This must be brought in — just as in bourgeois economic theory — as a positive datum. Cf. Gillman 1969; Baran and Sweezy, 1966.

14. Cf. also Grossmann 1970, pp. 294, 307; *Grundrisse*, p. 319.
15. Grossmann 1970, p. 290; Mattick 1969, p. 70.
16. We do not here go into the question of how far the quantitative and qualitative changes in state activity in 'late capitalism' have set in motion a process which makes for the long-term reorganization of the conditions of production at least partially through administrative mediation, thus modifying the 'classical' course of the cyclical crisis.
17. Cf. Mattick 1969, p. 100.
18. That is the general objection to all attempts to prove the effectiveness or ineffectiveness of the law by direct empirical evidence, by real price quantities. Cf. e.g. Gillman 1969; Wygodski 1972, pp. 239 f, 269.
19. Cf. Dobb 1937, p. 97; 1959.
20. To this extent, Mattick is wrong when he says: 'To speak about a "tendential decline of the profit rate" and of "counter-tendencies" to this decline, means to speak simultaneously in terms of value analysis and concrete reality. This is permissible when one keeps in mind that only the "counter-tendencies" are real phenomena and reveal by their existence the unobservable tendential fall of the profit rate.' (Mattick 1959, p. 35.) Capitalists do actually experience from time to time the 'reality' of the fall in the rate of profit.
21. Cf. *Capital*, vol. 1, p. 340; Gillman 1969, pp. 83 ff; RKW, 1970, pp. 72 ff, 120 ff.
22. 'The tendency to create the world market is directly given in the concept of capital itself. Every limit appears as a barrier to be overcome. Initially, to subjugate every moment of production itself to exchange and to suspend the production of direct use values not entering into exchange, i.e. precisely to posit production based on capital in place of earlier modes of production, which appear primitive from its standpoint' (*Grundrisse*, p. 408; cf. also pp. 539 ff; and *Capital*, vol. 3, p. 245).
23. On this cf. especially Lenin, *Imperialism, the Highest Stage of Capitalism*; Hilferding 1968, pp. 321, 421 ff; Grossmann 1970, pp. 297 ff.
24. Cf. Lenin, *Imperialism, the Highest Stage of Capitalism*; Grossmann 1970, p. 269.
25. *Capital*, vol. 3, p. 238; cf. also Grossmann 1970, pp. 505 f; Mandel 1962, p. 477; Bukharin 1972b, pp. 82 ff; *Grundrisse*, p. 872.
26. 'According to the materialist conceptions of history, the ultimately determining element in history is the production and reproduction of real life. More than this neither Marx nor I have ever asserted. Hence if someone twists this into saying that the economic element is the *only* determining one, he transforms that proposition into a meaningless, abstract, senseless phrase. The economic situation is the basis, but the various elements of the superstructure: political forms of the class struggle and its results, to wit: constitutions established by the victorious class after a successful

battle, etc., juridical forms, and then even the reflexes of all these actual struggles in the brains of the participants, political, juristic, philosophical theories, religious views and their further development into systems of dogmas, also exercise their influence upon the course of the historical struggles and in many cases preponderate in determining their form. There is an interaction of all these elements in which, amid all the endless host of accidents . . . the economic movement finally asserts itself as necessary. Otherwise the application of the theory to any period of history one chose would be easier than the solution of a simple equation in the first degree.' (Engels, Letter to Joseph Bloch, 21 Sept. 1890. MESW, vol. 3, p. 487.)

27. The weakness of Flatow and Huisken's approach lies above all in the fact that they do not succeed in establishing the mediation between the 'appearances on the surface' and the contradictions of the capitalist process of reproduction. So long as one determines the 'particularization' of the state and its modes of appearance simply from the hypostatization and ontologization of false consciousness and not from the historical-materialist conditions of production and reproduction, one can hardly come to a 'materialist' derivation of the state. Cf. Flatow and Huisken 1973.

28. Marx defined the development of the commodity as a similar form of 'reconciliation' of contradictions: 'We saw in a former chapter that the exchange of commodities implies contradictory and mutually exclusive conditions. The further development of the commodity does not abolish these contradictions, but rather provides the form within which they have room to move. This is, in general, the way in which real contradictions are resolved. For instance, it is a contradiction to depict one body as constantly falling towards another and at the same time constantly flying away from it. The ellipse is a form of motion within which this form of contradiction is both realized and resolved.' (*Capital*, vol. 1, ch. 3, sec. 2a) [the translation is here, exceptionally, taken from the 1976 Pelican edition, p. 198, which provides a more appropriate translation here].

29. Cf. Maitan 1970.

30. On this, cf. Katzenstein 1973; Wygodski 1972.

31. In this sense: Neusüss 1972.

32. For more on this, see Braunmühl, below, p. 160.

33. Cf. Wygodski 1972, pp. 79 ff; Zieschang 1956; Zieschang 1969; Magri 1970; Boccara 1973.

34. This means redistribution of revenue (by the state or through the mediation of the state) with the aim of raising the accumulation rate of big capitals, as opposed to the merely subsidizing equalization of the rates of profit.

35. Of course in practice even the informational basis of the state's forecasting and planning activity is considerably limited — quite apart from the effectiveness the 'instruments of economic policy'. Cf. Ronge and Schmieg 1973, pp. 53 ff.

36. Cf. Kidron 1968, p. 104; Mandel 1969; Shonfield 1965; Galbraith 1967;

Huffschmid 1969.

37. See especially the Annual Reports of 1972—73 and 1973—74 and the Special Report of Autumn 1974, where the (Federal German) Council of Experts (a committee of 'neutral' economic advisers), in agreement with the Federal Government and the employers and readily calling in aid the so-called oil crisis, recommends to the workers and trade unions a wages policy to maintain 'stability', which in practice means a reduction of real net incomes. For the first time even the DGB [German equivalent of the TUC] felt that it had to attack the political role of the 'Experts'.

38. On this see Cogoy 1973; Ronge and Schmieg 1973; and on the question of arms expenditure, Kidron 1968.

39. On the tax system and its class character, see Ronge and Schmieg 1973.

40. Not least because management of the economic cycle must necessarily begin with the existing structure of fixed capital and therefore tends to strengthen disproportions in production. Cf. Katzenstein 1967, pp. 187 f.

41. In Altvater's 'derivation' of the state which starts from the external preconditions of production of the competing individual capitals and implicitly assumes a subsidiary relation between individual capitals and state, this question has no place — even if one does not want to understand Altvater as simply assuming the always 'harmonious' fulfilment by the state of the 'objectively' necessary infrastructural demands — which nevertheless lies in the logic of this approach. See Altvater, above p. 40. and 1973b.

42. The much-discussed road-building section in the *Grundrisse* (pp. 524 ff) is to be interpreted in this context. On this see Läpple 1973, pp. 180 ff.

43. Cf. Altvater 1973b, pp. 117 f; Läpple 1973, pp. 148 f. The table of criteria drawn up by Stohler can also be interpreted in the sense of the factors mentioned — although the author himself does not do this; cf. Stohler 1965, p. 238. It should be noted that in some cases it can be the technically conditioned monopoly position of the 'infrastructural' establishments and the consequent possibility of obtaining excessive monopoly profits which makes a takeover by the state be in the interest of the other capitals. This factor played a role, for example, in the nationalization of the railways in Prussia in the 1880s and is one of the reasons for the frequently encountered state or state-controlled management of enterprises which provide energy.

44. For the moment we make no distinction here between 'general material' conditions of production in the narrower sense, e.g. roads, canals, and 'general' conditions of production which for capital are incorporated in labour power and which refer to this incorporation: maintenance of living labour power (e.g. health service), education, also research in the broadest sense. We embrace both within the concept of material-substantial conditions of production, in so far as living labour power of a specific quality related to the technological process of production is also a 'substantial' condition of production, i.e., a condition having a special use-value character. Läpple in particular has established that this distinction should not be blurred; but we will only later go into these specific features.

45. Cf. the Annual Report of the Council of Experts for 1967—68, where,

as a measure to raise the entrepreneurs' inclination to invest, apart from the obligatory 'incomes policy', above all the rapid expansion of the 'infrastructure' is proposed.

46. Cf. OECD 1970a, 1970b, 1971.
47. Cf. Rödel 1972; Cogoy 1973.
48. Cf. Leontief 1961; Nelson, Peck and Kalachek, 1968.
49. Cf. OECD 1970a, 1971.
50. Cf. Klein 1967; Nikolajew 1972; Cartellieri 1967—69.
51. Cf. Marx's examination of the struggles for factory legislation and the normal working day in England, which shows very clearly the mediated and contradictory manner in which the objective necessities of capitalist reproduction assert themselves in the political process. *Capital*, vol. 1, ch. 10.
52. Cf. esp. Luhmann 1968, 1969; Naschold 1968, 1969. For a discussion of these attempts to reformulate political theory, cf. Hirsch and Leibfried 1971.
53. Cf. especially Poulantzas 1974, 1975.
54. To this extent, the theories of state monopoly capitalism do contain a correct and doubtless wrongly neglected element. What is missing in them is a correct theoretical concept of state and class, with the help of which the phenomena of fusion which can actually be observed might be interpreted and politically evaluated. The reasons for these deficiencies have been extensively discussed and do not need to be repeated here.
55. The so-called 'oil crisis' of winter 1973—74 would be worth a case study on this relation and the way in which the directors of the bourgeois state were ridiculously swindled by the monopolies.
56. Cf. especially Läpple 1973. What we have not dealt with in this context is the question of the effect on the class position of what is called the scientific-technical intelligentsia of the ever stricter and partly state-mediated functionalization of science production for the ends of capital valorization and 'protecting the system'. Certainly the living and work conditions of this group are considerably affected by the growing industrialization and functionalization of the research for ends which are set externally and not subject to control (integration into complexes of production characterized by an extreme division of labour, increased job insecurity, etc.). However, the effects of these general changes in structure must be examined in greater detail and in a specific manner for the different groups affected before satisfactory statements can be made about possible political effects.
57. To this extent, 'political crisis theories' focusing on 'deficits of legitimation' do have a correct aspect. When they theoretically deny the possibility of class struggles, however, the whole matter can only appear to them under the aspect of the problematic creation of legitimation by the state apparatus. Cf. especially Habermas 1975, and Offe 1972.
58. The fall of Brandt and the end of the era of reform openly proclaimed by the Schmidt—Genscher government is to be interpreted in this sense.
59. Lacking an even sketchily developed theory of the process of development of society as a whole, neither Habermas nor Offe can derive with any

consistency their theses of the legitimation-diminishing effect of forms of socialization or invariant 'world view structures' established through the state apparatus and to this extent 'dysfunctional' *vis-à-vis* the capitalist exchange relation. When Habermas postulates that 'state activity could find a coercive limit only in the legitimation at its disposal, unless we want to have recourse to economic crisis theories', he is unable — if we leave aside the hidden tautological structure of such sentences — to establish a foundation for his 'unless'. Both he and Offe can be accused of not criticizing theories of economic crisis developed on the basis of Marx's theory on the theoretical level reached by these, but — e.g. as concerns the validity of the theory of value — claim to operate with an acceptance of them. This blinkered behaviour has, however, its unambiguous consequences as far as the political implications of the theory of social science is concerned: the attempt to negate class struggles theoretically in a time of their evident intensification lays itself open at least to the charge of political opportunism.

60. Habermas does indeed correctly point out that the systematic limitation of communication and suppression of interests capable of generalization is the decisive repressive achievement of bourgeois ideology. But it is pure illusion to want to oppose this with the institutionalization of a kind of lawyerly discourse between theorizing intellectuals (1976, pp. 111 ff). The creation of the preconditions for a practically effective arrangement concerning suppressed needs and interests must be taken in hand, one way or another, by the masses themselves, through their political organization. On this problem, see Negt and Kluge 1972.

61. Cf. especially Poulantzas's analysis of the exceptional state: Poulantzas 1974.

Notes to Chapter 6

Editors' note: this paper was published in *Probleme des Klassenkampfs* 14—15 (1974).

1. Marx, *Capital*, vol. 3, p. 792. Marx here uses the concept of 'principal conditions' for the 'economic base'. We think that such principal conditions (basic functional requirements) exist also with regard to other forms of socialization in capitalism.

2. Remarks on the Paper of BJK, Bielefeld Seminar paper No. 3. In the following we refer to several written contributions in which objections to our analysis were raised. These objections have, however, also been raised in many discussions which can hardly be 'cited'.

3. Minutes of a seminar discussion in Bremen (Döppel, Schroer); seminar paper in Berlin.

4. On the juridical discussion on the organizational forms of state activity, see Preuss (1969).

5. On the different currents and concepts of function in functionalism, see Schmid (1973).

6. As an example see the analysis of the 'social function of the state' in the state theory of Hermann Heller, an analysis impressive for its combina-

tion of historical, sociological and legal research: Heller, 1963 (1934), pp. 199 ff.

7. On the concept of 'capital in general', see Rosdolsky (1968) esp. vol. 1, pp. 61 ff; and Reichelt (1970).

8. On the relation between logical and historical analysis, see especially Zeleny (1968), esp. pp. 103 ff.

9. The 'problem of the state' has — crudely speaking — been a topical issue during three phases: during the discussion on the programme of German social democracy in the nineteenth century; during the Russian revolution (Lenin, 'State and Revolution'); during German social democracy in the 1920s and in the face of fascism. The topicality of the recent state discussion resulted principally from the experiences of the extra-parliamentary protest movement, particularly its experience of the repressive character of the bourgeois state, which it tried to analyse theoretically in a wide variety of ways.

10. The debate sprang up again in the mid-sixties. Cf. the controversy in *Das Argument* 41 and 47 and more recently: Kadritzke 1973; Sohn-Rethel 1973. The discussion on the 'autonomy of the state' was based on Marx's writings on developments in Bonapartist France. Cf. also 'Projekt Klassenanalyse' 1972.

11. Above all Müller and Neusüss (1970) (see above, p. 32). This problem seems also to be the real starting point of the analysis of Flatow and Huisken (1973), but it is so well hidden in a 'state derivation' that it is difficult to find this thread. Naturally, there was discussion of the 'welfare state' before this: we are referring here to the Marxist discussion.

12. Hirsch (1973) (and 1974: see above p. 57), and Funken (1973) base themselves directly on such a general concept of the state; indirectly, yet against their own methodological premises, Flatow and Huisken (1973).

13. Flatow and Huisken 1973, p. 121. Apart from the early writings, the following are often cited in the Marxist discussion of the state:

1. Engels — *Socialism, Utopian and Scientific*; *Anti-Dühring*; *The Origin of the Family, Private Property and the State*. On reading Engels it must be stressed that Engels understands the state in his writings *as a class state* and that precisely this *immediate* determination is avoided in the recent discussion because it leads to the questions outlined in the introduction to our article. On the other hand, Engels's writings also contain a determination of the state as a force for order (*Origin . . .*), which leads to the question of the 'general' character of the state — in regard to which, in the recent discussion, the formulations from the early writings are preferred.

2. The *Communist Manifesto* and the *Critique of the Gotha Programme*. Here the state is characterized as *political state* — certainly as class power, but also as public power. In the *Critique of the Gotha Programme*, Marx specifies only that the different states in the existing capitalist societies have 'certain essential features' in common. Dieter Läpple (1973) starts from these definitions and comes to a derivation similar to our own. However, he associates this definition of the 'public power' with that 'general concept' which we have criticized here.

14. This concept haunts the essay by Funken (1973), who interprets Marx's plan of construction in this sense.
15. On this see Reichelt 1970; and more recently Bischoff 1973, pp. 114 ff.
16. C. B. Macpherson 1962. In our opinion, Macpherson overinterprets Hobbes, Locke, etc., in so far as he does not distinguish clearly enough the political determinations of private property from the economic.
17. 'Every juridical theory of the state [must] necessarily posit the state as an autonomous force separated from society . . .. Precisely in that consists the juridical aspect of the theory' (Pashukanis, p. 189).
18. Such new categories are: the owners of revenue (Flatow and Huisken 1973), the competing individual capitals (Altvater 1972, see above p. 40), the private producers working under the division of labour (Projekt Klassenanalyse 1971).
19. Already seen in Marx's critique of Hegel. Cf. also Godelier 1967. Legal equality as the basis for the theory of the state as general interest was taken particularly by Lorenz von Stein as the starting point for the 'positive' transcendence of social inequality and class division in the state (von Stein 1972, esp. pp. 268 ff).
20. Flatow and Huisken 1973; Funken 1973, p. 110, gives the state the general competence to regulate 'the disturbances in the functional mechanism of the particular system of reproduction in the interests of the exploiters as a whole'. Then why consider the possibilities and limits of state interventionism? On the problem of state functions, see below, pp. 131–139.
21. Our recourse to the category of form has caused most confusion among Marxists — obviously because we have not operated with the concept of 'capital in general'. We would point out, however, that for us the whole debate about this 'general concept of capital' is concentrated in the discussion of the specific Marxist concept of form (e.g. value *form*, capital *form*, etc.). In this respect, we think it necessary to build on the work of Reichelt, Rosdolsky, Backhaus, Wolfgang Müller, Bischoff and others, and develop it in relation to the analysis of the state. — A problem remains in the frequent equivocation of form and *form of appearance*. The distinction between 'essence' and 'form of appearance' designates a relation between steps within the general concept of capital: the step-ladder of mystification of social interconnections in capitalist reproduction. Thus, for example, profit is the form of appearance of surplus value; the reification of social labour is expressed in profit just as in the determinations of income, the origin of which in labour is no longer visible. The distinction between 'essence' and 'form of appearance' thus does not apply to the difference and relation between 'theory' and 'history' (as though empirical reality were merely the appearance of an essence working underground in history).
22. This general concept of capital used in Marx's theory is still 'abstract-general' in so far as it is still unmediated in relation to the given historical-concrete totality of capitalist societies and the forms of appearance on their surface. The mediation of 'individual' and 'general' requires an analysis of the concrete historical constellation and a corresponding

concretization of the general concept. To take an example, one cannot analyse adequately the course of the accumulation process in West Germany after 1945 by confronting statistical trends directly with general categories like relative surplus value or profit. Beyond the general 'problem of translation', one has to reconstruct the specific constellation which capitalism had reached in West Germany: the world market context, the relative power of the classes, level of technological development, etc.

For real analysis, on the basis of Marx's concepts, two questions are relevant, which we can only formulate, but not answer:

1. Has the 'general concept of capital' been 'finalized' once and for all; or — by analogy for example with Marx's analysis of absolute and relative surplus value — could a further development of this general concept be envisaged, albeit following logically on from the concepts already developed?

2. Which moments of a concrete-historical totality must be theoretically developed so that empirical events can be analysed methodically with some degree of exactness? (Below we adduce as an essential moment the state of class relations on the basis of a certain stage of accumulation; what other moments must be added?) That the totality can ever be theoretically analysed to such a point that all forms of appearance can be 'derived' as appearances of this particular totality is a pious wish; but there is a temptation in Marxist discussion to pretend that this has been achieved by presenting Marx's theory as if it provided this totality.

23. The distinction between 'system limit' and 'activity limit' is for us provisional — as also are the statements on the relation between form analysis and historical analysis — and require particularly critical discussion.

24. As regards starting from the 'surface', see Flatow and Huisken 1973, pp. 93 ff; Marxistische Gruppe Erlangen 1972. On 'freedom and equality' at the level of simple commodity circulation, cf. *Capital*, vol. 1, p. 172.

25. The consequences of such a derivation are particularly clear in the theories of state monopoly capitalism, which are implicitly and explicitly based on the view that the growing 'state intervention' in modern capitalism is a result of the increasingly crisis-ridden nature of capitalism. By reasoning *a contrario*, this leads to the view that capitalism in its 'normal form' (competitive capitalism) does not really need the state. Cf. Wirth 1973.

26. The category 'extra-economic coercive force' appears to be pleonastic (coercion, force), but actually has a twofold meaning: it is a question of 'coercion as . . . a command of one person to another, supported by force' (Pashukanis, p. 187). The coercion of subjects of law, which must be organized outside the 'coercions' of circulation (extra-economic), makes necessary a force (here still as function) which imposes the coercion. That is what Marx and Engels called 'public force'. We have not yet used this concept because a determinate principle of form ('public') is already used in it — a principle which itself must be derived (see again Pashukanis, p. 181 ff). In what follows we also use the abbreviation

'extra-economic force'. In contrast to a 'functionalist' approach (see above p. 113), we consider that we have reconstructed this function neither out of empirical findings nor formally, but out of determinate forms of an historically specific form of society. 'Extra-economic coercive force' therefore does not imply general applicability — in the way that common definitions of sovereignty already contain a 'primacy of politics'. We are referring to a function of the material process of reproduction, by means of which the material movement *can* be transformed into 'binding decisions', a function which, however, is therefore neither 'autonomous' nor 'sovereign' in the sense that it 'can do anything it likes'. — A remark on the 'juridical concept of the state' must also be made here: if the law as form and the 'extra-economic force' as function are derived, the way is then free for a further development of the principles of form of the bourgeois constitutional state, principles contained also in this concept of the state. In the dialectic of 'general' and 'particular' interests, both were originally comprised: the general, central force *and* the institutional—constitutional organization of the process by which it acts and exerts influence.

28. The distinction between 'economic' and 'political' relations may sound 'un-Marxist'. Apart from the fact that in his analysis in the *Grundrisse* of the notions of freedom and equality as they result from 'simple commodity circulation', Marx speaks of 'legal, political and social relations', in which those notions are 'only this (economic) basis in another power' (*Grundrisse*, p. 245), we would emphasize two moments:

1. This 'division of politics and economics' is both consequence of and pre-condition for the system of bourgeois society. It is bound to conditions which lie essentially in the structure of the consciousness of the producers. So long as the wage labourers see their 'economic' existence as ordained by nature, as material necessity, and do not relate it to their political existence, this dividing line will remain stable. On the reproduction of this division in various structures of the 'public sphere', see Negt and Kluge 1972, esp. ch. 2.

2. This division of the political and the economic system is also usual in systems-theoretical approaches. They are, however, incapable of showing the specific mediations because they always merely try to draw exact boundary lines. Cf. Narr 1969, pp. 170 ff; Schmid 1973.

29. Pashukanis has already been quoted as an example. A similar criticism however, also applies to Stucka (1969, pp. 85—101) and, as it appears to us, to many contributions to the recently resumed Marxist discussion of law. The pre-determined concept of the state contains two factors: that of class rule and the problem of the state in the transition to socialism.

30. Proof of this parallelism can also be found in the retention of Roman law and of the division of public and private spheres in the transition to 'modern times' Cf. G. Radbruch 1969 ch. 12 on private law, pp. 88 ff; Pashukanis pp. 182—3.

31. We feel that Heide Gerstenberger does not bring this out sufficiently.

There the sovereignty of the principalities (to be used by the bourgeois for its own ends) appears as an empirical quantity serving as a precondition for the emergence of bourgeois rule. It is rather the reverse: the development of this sovereignty (absolutism) should itself be developed from the transition to commodity and money relations.

32. Pashukanis p. 167. This and the following statements do not claim to present a foundation for a Marxist theory of law. We develop the concept of law only in relation to our enquiry into the *functions of the* state; moreover we refer here implicitly to the *German* legal tradition.

33 This parallelism should undoubtedly be pursued further so as to clarify one question in particular: when, following upon the debate of German jurists in the 1920s on the concept of 'a law', for instance by Habermas, this concept was loosely linked to that of competition, this quite obscured the inner connection between commodity *form* and the *form* of law (see particularly Franz Neumann: 'The Changing Function of Law in Bourgeois Society' (1937) in Neumann 1957.)

34. Concerning the two factors involved in the legal guarantee: certainty as to the content of law and certainty of enforcement, cf. Hermann Heller 1963, p. 222. In speaking of 'legislative and executive functions', we are not arguing on the level of specific historical structures, i.e. division of powers. In the classical bourgeois tradition these functions were actually first conceived of as *functions* (particularly by Locke); only in the course of the bourgeoisie's struggle for a constitutional voice, out of the struggle for adequate functions of law and out of the need of the existing social classes to seek some accommodation, did the concrete, given structure yield a division of powers as a compromise. The functionalist discovery of the 'division of function and structure' (see G. Almond 1966, p. 876) held in such high esteem today should thus in fact be credited to classical bourgeois theory. The extent to which the 'separating off' of the juridical from the executive function is itself a product of this class struggle and constitutional struggle would be well worth investigating. An important point for the *historical* analysis (see Gerstenberger 1973) is that certain functions could shift to the feudal overlords; they thus (a) become instrumental in establishing commodity production and (b) simultaneously achieved a change of function: the feudal lord became the territorial prince.

35. On general principles of law and the 'change in the function of the law' (F. Neumann) cf. Ulrich K. Preuss 1973.

36. The analogy between money and power, prices and norms is widely to be found in modern functionalist literature. There, however, it is a mere analogy; of a genetic connection of the kind attempted here there is no sign. It is — with reference to Marxist discussion — a mistake to conclude from the guarantee of a money standard any guarantee of money value (cf. Margaret Wirth 1973, p. 37), even if, in actual politics, the state would appear to guarantee the value of money because it guarantees its standard.

37. Cf. footnote 21. Surface in the sense of the necessary form of appearance.

38. Pashukanis's error is prototypical in that he under-estimates the role of

extra-economic force in the relations posited by the commodity, can
grasp the state only as class state, i.e. as a concrete organization and
instrument; p. 172. Cf. in contrast Seifert 1971, pp. 195 ff.

39. On the divergence between relations of property and those of exchange
and thus between formal and real equality. Cf. Flatow and Huisken
1973 pp. 98 ff.

40. Marx analyses this transposition (or reversal of roles in modern terminology) particularly clearly in *Capital* vol. 2, ch. 20, section 10, 'Capital
and Revenue'. Against systems-theoreticians and lovers of complexity
it must be said that if the specific forms of capitalist society grow increasingly independent of each other, this does not mean that they are
not the modes of life and action of the self-same individuals which cannot simply be studied separately according to a scheme of roles (analogous
to 'subsystems') where the abstract individual always relates contem-
platively to himself beyond the reach of any role. This is an intensely
(in the literal sense) bourgeois conception whose 'pure form' only those
of independent means can represent and only the theoretician can
entertain. And only from such a perspective can the production process
be regarded as something purely material, as 'unpolitical economy' and
an outcry raised when the economy is 'politicized' by workers or social
scientists. The wage-labouring class must oppose this and demand the
removal and overcoming of the particular form of complexity in capitalism in order to realize their potential as human beings. One should note
in this respect the well known fact that the number of cases of
schizophrenia is particularly high among working-class people.

41. These relations, dealt with here on the most general level, should be seen
in connection with Part V of our study, 'State and Class Movement'.

42. This is revealed in the fact that every capital is in effect a 'legal person'.

43. This is very neatly expressed in the neo-liberal apology for the price
mechanisms *and* private property.

44. For the development and rationale of these rights cf. George Jellinek
1905, esp. pp. 81 ff.

45. Flatow and Huisken base their whole investigation on the question,
formulated in the legal terminology we have criticized, of how the state
originates out of the contradiction between general and particular
interests (cf. Flatow and Huisken 1973, p. 95). Because of this, they
have at once to associate with the concepts of freedom and equality
their *emphatic* meaning (pp. 99 f) and as a result they miss the fact that
it is only the meaning of these concepts in terms of legal relations which
provides the logical starting point for the derivation of the state. We
in no way wish to detract from the importance of the concept of 'interests'
which plays the essential role in the work of Flatow and Huisken but we
believe we have proved that for the 'state' a different derivation must take
necessary precedence.

46. Serving as a prototype for this conception is a particular tradition, that
of the 'welfare state based on the rule of law' ('sozialer Rechtsstaat'), in
German constitutional debate.

47. We understand 'general norm' as Peter Römer has formulated it in his

critique of Müller and Neusüss (1972): 'The general and abstract elements in the law are always founded upon the conscious non-consideration of the particularity of the individual case. Since Max Weber the formal rationality and the functions of certainty and calculability in the general principles of law have been continually stressed; this calculability applied first and foremost *vis-à-vis* the authority of the state.' He says that under the rule of general principles of law there has emerged a multiplicity of private and state-issued legal decisions. We said above that the law of value constitutes the rule of law; now we can say that, in analogy with *money* as external form of value by which the fluctuations in value production are put into effect and thus the different species of social labour mediated in the law of value — in analogy to money, it is precisely the *general* law under whose auspices the most varied relations between subjects of law are interconnected and, faced with the individual case, become reducible to norms.

48. Put in different terms: state sovereignty and the sovereignty of capital become identical. (cf. B. Blanke 1973).

49. Here we do not go into social relations which are *not* mediated through exchange (or the structure of law). We should not, however, be misunderstood as subsuming *all* social relations under either the monetary or the legal spheres. The following are not mediated through these forms (although they stand in a relationship to them which can be analysed in each case):
    1. The production process as the labour process in the plant. This can interest us from the point of view of the state only in its external aspect;
    2. The process of socialization in its narrower and wider senses. This is permeated in a particularly complicated way by relations of money and law (family law, etc., school law, etc.).
    Originally we had referred to money and law in this section as 'media' (as does Margaret Wirth 1973, pp. 32 ff). However, this concept, intended to describe how actions originating from the state are mediated, awakens associations with other 'media' (language, ideology, the public sphere). We should at least mention here that these (especially the last) are also forms of mediation between economy and politics.

50. This expression *Verrechtlichung* comes from Otto Kirchheimer. Cf. Seifert 1971, p. 187. We shall deal with this aspect later on in this article.

51. The contrast between 'general law' and 'particular measure' unconsciously leads Preuss (1973) to argue in a similar way. However, Preuss forgets that what he calls 'the concrete use of force to a particular end' occurs precisely in the sphere of 'state-interventionism' in the *forms* of law and of money. Even a 'particular measure' has the form of law and for its 'translation' into behaviour to be successful, capital (for instance) must keep to certain state-issued directives. However, this is only guaranteed so long as these directives do not contradict the functional demands made by the reproduction of capital; the 'state' must have already absorbed these demands into its 'measures' as fundamental conditions.

52. The literal text is as follows (Flatow and Huisken, p. 119): ' . . . a general

interest cannot be realized in the form of the pursuit of its particular
aspect: the particularizations [which ones? those of the general interest? —
that would be pure Hegelianism! — BJK] do not mount up but cancel
each other out in the dynamic of competition.'

53. 'Each pursues his private interest and only his private interest, and thereby serves the private interests of all, the general interest, without willing
or knowing it. The real point is not that each individual's pursuit of his
private interest promotes the totality of private interests, the general
interest . . .. The point is rather that private interest is itself already a
socially determined interest . . .. It is the interest of private persons; but
its content, as well as the form and means of its realization, is given by
social conditions independent of all' (*Grundrisse*, p. 156). These social
conditions independent of all are in no way 'the state' but unconscious
forms of socialization such as the law of value, etc. Flatow and Huisken,
however, posit the state at this point: 'In so far as the general interests
are in content the means or preconditions for the pursuit of the particular,
there exists the necessity of realizing the contents of these general
interests in a manner other than that given by the possibilities of action
of private individuals' (1973, p. 119).

54. Flatow and Huisken's attempt to escape the tautology that 'general
interests' are precisely those which the state has 'taken up, administered
and realized' (p. 129) through its own actual activity — their argument,
that is, that these interests stem from the 'depths' (in contrast to the
'surface') of the capitalist structure — is hardly convincing. A *general*
interest, they maintain, must be directed to the development of pre-
conditions for production and circulation which assert themselves as
as barrier to the development of *capital as a whole*. The problem
of reception remains quite unsolved, because the general interest in this
sense can, according to Flatow and Huisken, sometimes also be articulated
by a small minority of private property owners who become aware of
the general barrier to capital development. But how can 'the state' then
differentiate between real and false general interests as articulated by
all the differing groups?
    At this point it indeed becomes clear that the point of departure for
the derivation of the state *cannot* be the surface (no matter how important the surface forms might be for phenomena such as interest factions
and political parties, etc.). For, as Flatow and Huisken quite correctly
see it, the differences between the owners of revenue are on the surface
purely quantitative (expressed in monetary form) or material (related to
the labour process) so that the decision as to whether an interest is
general or not can in fact only be quantitative. The measure of this
quantity is then in the last resort, power — which is a (bourgeois) consequence of the very kind that Flatow and Huisken wish to avoid
drawing.

55. 'Projekt Klassenanalyse' (1972) particularly pp. 125 ff; the general
statements on the state and on the relationship between politics and
economy are almost identical with the article by 'Projekt Klassenanalyse'
(1971); we had no time to deal with the Projekt's book which appeared

in October 1973, *Materialien zur Klassenstruktur der BRD*, First Part. Berlin 1973.

56. Altvater above, p. 40. Altvater does not, however, use the concept of the general conditions of production consistently in this sense. Cf. Läpple 1973, p. 97.

57. The careful attempt by Läpple, starting from a critique of Altvater, to define what is 'general' in the general conditions of production comes to the conclusion that these conditions of production gain in importance with the increasing socialization of the production process, but that their assurance is by no means a general function of the state and that therefore it does not constitute the state form.

58. On the concept of 'functional form', see *Capital* vol. 2, esp. Part 1: The Metamorphoses of Capital and their Circuits. Taking money capital as an example, Marx shows the errors which arise from this form: 'In the first place the functions performed by capital-value in its capacity of money-capital, which it can perform precisely owing to its *money-form*, are erroneously derived from its character as capital, whereas they are due only to the money-form of capital-value, to its *form of appearance as money*. In the second place, on the contrary, the specific content of the money-function, which renders it simultaneously a *capital-function*, is traced to the nature of money (money being here confused with capital), while the money-function premises social conditions . . . which do not at all exist in the mere circulation of commodities and the corresponding circulation of money' (p. 32; our emphasis — BJK).

59. Cf. *Capital* vol. 3, Part 5: Marx shows here how a specific circuit of capital, the circuit of loan capital, also leads to specific notions about the process as a whole (e.g. the bankers' logic which confuses demand for money with demand for money capital. This logic leads to the confusion of the rise in the demand for money in times of overproduction and stagnating commodity sales, which indicates a flow of capital back into the money form, with the demand for capital and thus to a false interpretation of this development as a sign of good conditions of valorization. Cf. the answers of the banker Overstone in the hearing of the House of Lords Committee to investigate the causes of the crisis of 1847: *Capital* vol. 3, pp. 419 ff).

60. *Capital* vol. 2, p. 53. This system-limit on state interventions in the process of capital accumulation has been demonstrated in earlier works by Müller and Neusüss (1975) in the relation between income distribution and the circuit of capital, and by Semmler and Hoffman (1972) in the relation between capital accumulation, state interventions and the movements of wages.

61. The distinction between system-limit and activity-limit seems to us an important step in the so-called 'restriction analysis' — a term coined by Kirchheimer which is often used in the recent discussion on the state and which is directed to the question of the 'possibilities and limits' of the state.

62. On the question of problem perception, see Ronge and Schmieg 1973;

Wirth 1973.

63. By 'control' we understand here the determining influence of one 'system' on another; by 'regulate' the *attempt* to oppose influences, weaken them or strengthen them (cf. Schmid 1973, p. 242).

64. James O'Connor, 1973b, attempts to establish the connection between class constellation, the structures of capital reproduction (monopolies, etc.) and the limits on the activity of the state, which he brings together in the concept of the fiscal crisis. However, he works with very crude aggregates: monopolized *v.* non-monopolized industry, etc.

65. The relevance for our question of the discussion on monopoly and rates of profit is undisputed. We do not deny at all the later capitalism problematic of changed market structures and power structures and of 'new' forms of appearance of capital reproduction. The question of the changed character of modern capitalism and of the essential features which make up such a change comes down, however, in current Marxist discussion to the question of which 'basic contradiction' each author declares to be the decisive dynamic force of capitalist development: the contradiction between wage labour and capital resulting from surplus value production, i.e. the *form* of production which makes the dominant mode of production capitalist; or the contradiction between 'productive forces and relations of production', between the 'socialization of production and the private form of appropriation'. In our opinion, the discussion of the 'state problematic' can only start from the capital relation. On stamocap theory, see also Wirth 1972, esp. pp. 162 ff. On the two 'basic contradictions' see Godelier (1967).

66. Cf. *Capital*, vol. 3, Part 7: 'Revenues and their Sources'. On the development of this surface we agree to a large extent with Flatow and Huisken. Our model of phases corresponds roughly to their characterization of the three general interests of the owners of sources of revenue: maintenance of the source, high revenue, continuous flow. But it is important to emphasize again that these interests must assume a legal form in order to become relevant for state function and intervention. Flatow and Huisken do mention that (pp. 123 ff), but have to introduce 'the law' without having derived it beforehand.

67. The following considerations on institutionalization are based in part on Agnoli 1975.

68. Flatow and Huisken completely overlook this moment when they deal with the interest of the 'revenue owners' in securing the continuous flow of revenue (1973, p. 115) only on the level of the movement of income. The securing of the continuous flow of surplus value can require precisely for many of the owners of the commodity labour power (as a source of revenue) either that a phase of non-realization of the revenue source come in the shape of unemployment or that the equally 'general' interest in high revenue suffer injury in the shape of cuts in real wages. In such a situation, the state is bound to the conditions of surplus value production, so that the interest administered by it stands *opposed* to wage labour.

69. Peter Römer (1972, p. 88) points to the change in the function of the

law in this context: 'The generality of the law could only be implemented by reason of the fact that the substantial differentiation was carried out through the state's quasi-delegation to private subjects of law of the competence to establish norms.'

70. This is the root of the problem of 'mass loyalty' indicated above all by Offe in relation to the functional conditions of the political system.

71. The 'concerted action' of German trade unions and employers and the state, since 1967, involves a 'tripartite' action on 'prices and incomes' similar to the Social Contract in Britain [editors' note].

72. This was clearly shown by Fraenkel 1966; Kahn-Freund 1966; and Herrmann Heller, 'Europa und der Faschismus', in Heller 1971.

73. The historical movement of the capitalist mode of production does not only posit particular moments as result and expression of its essential laws. In the course of historical development, as soon as forms have particularized themselves, structures have taken shape, institutions and social bearers of action have arisen, there are also new conditions for the implementation of the general laws. Certainly, the new moments can be 'derived' from the old, which means nothing more than that their formation can be grasped in thought. But that cannot mean that in the analysis of historical concrete phenomena they are applied in an unreflected way. We do not think it a legitimate analytical procedure to treat a real problem first 'in the light' of the general concept, in order afterwards to add a few saving clauses and remarks on historical particularities (the so-called 'modifications', the frequent introduction of which indicates that authors are in fact working with a *ceteris paribus* clause) and to attribute it to these if the problem does not present itself as it ought to according to their concept of it.

Notes to Chapter 7

Editors' note: This article appeared in *Gesellschaft* 3 (1975).

1. Argued also by Margaret Wirth 1973, pp. 31 ff.

2. This is to counter Offe, whose view is that the class character of the bourgeois state at any time can only be determined retrospectively, on the basis of definite state measures: see Offe 1972 esp. pp. 69 ff.

3. Argued mistakenly both by Margaret Wirth in the article cited (1973, p. 31) and also by myself (1973, p. 208).

4. This clarification originated in a discussion with Reinhold Zech and Helmut Reichelt.

5. This enabled the discussion on the left to leave behind the phase which had become effectively dominated (though not consciously in the theories) both by Keynesianism and by corresponding approaches in the theory of state monopoly capitalism.

6. This is most suggestively so in Paul Boccara 1971; but equally Elmar Altvater 1972.

7. Since these represent the basis, it is my view that the suggestion of Blanke, Jürgens and Kastendiek, that periodization should be based on the condition of class struggle and not the competitive situation, will

not lead very far (1973 manuscript pp. 40–51). Cf. in this connection the difficulty of analysing fascism.

8. Naturally I do not misunderstand the interest of capital as a whole to be the average interest; I am here arguing as to the theoretical possibility that the interests of the whole could be represented by the state.

9. Cf. the outcry of the middle-class economic associations at the 'concerted action'.

10. The objection can be made to the theoreticians of the legitimation crisis that diminishing credibility can mean the end of a government but not at all the end of bourgeois society.

11. James O'Connor has given actual examples of this (O'Connor 1973a).

12. For this reason also, once the distinction between historical and logical analysis has been made, it is hard to justify a simple derivation of the bourgeois state from the bourgeois forms of intercourse: cf. AK Munich 1974, p. 157.

13. Hunno Hochberger 1974, pp. 155 ff. Hochberger seems to rely there partly on my essay (Gerstenberger 1973). This was however methodologically no more than an attempt at a systematic description. The only theoretical ideas that entered into it corresponded at most to the functional approach criticized above.

14. The approach taken by Projekt Klassenanalyse (1972) is for that reason valid, provided that it is not limited to the form-analysis of bourgeois society.

15. This does not preclude the continued historical reliance of capitalist production also on forced labour.

16. Blanke, Jürgens and Kastendiek wrongly draw this conclusion. Having established the state as the extra-societal guarantor of law, they derive from this that the actions of the state must remain external to the process of reproduction (but their own later arguments contradict this statement). See Blanke, Jürgens and Kastendiek (p. 129 above).

17. The article by AK Munich does not reveal the historical nature of this process.

18. It should have become clear from my earlier arguments that I am not propagating an approach via a theory of influence which would presuppose the real neutrality of the state as theoretically possible.

Notes to Chapter 8

Editors' note: This article was specially revised for this collection from a manuscript which appeared in an earlier version in *Gesellschaft* 1 (1974).

1. This position was formulated as early as the First World War by Bukharin, who interpreted the war itself in this light. See N. Bukharin 1972b; see also the controversy between Mandel and Nicolaus in *New Left Review* 54, 1969 and 59, 1970.

2. A consideration of the various accounts of the derivation of the alteration in the form of capital movements which constitutes the basis of imperialist phenomena is beyond the scope of this essay.

3. See, e.g.: Frank 1967; Cordova 1973; Cardoso 1971; Furtado 1970.
4. This is less true of the relevant aspect of the discussion of imperialism in France. See Palloix 1973; Emmanuel 1972; cf. Klaus Busch 1973. But here the emphasis is rather more on the problems of the lowering of productivity, of unequal exchange and the formation of values internationally. The present problem of the relationship between the world market movement of capital and the state is touched on only implicitly, if at all. It is therefore unnecessary to consider them further here (although they merit more detailed study than they have so far received, at any rate in the FRG).
5. Cf. Poulantzas 1975. For a partial criticism of Poulantzas's position, see Christian Leucate 1973.
6. Translator's note: The English translation of the *Grundrisse* omits much supplementary material included in the German edition.
7. *Grundrisse*, p. 100. These remarks have become the centre of an extensive debate on the relationship between logical and historical methods of analysis. See Helmut Reichelt 1970; Roman Rosdolsky, 1968; Joachim Bischoff, 1973.
8. Karl Marx/Friedrich Engels, *The German Ideology*, MECW vol. 5, p. 89: 'Bourgeois society embraces the whole material intercourse of individuals within a definite stage of the development of productive forces. It embraces the whole commercial and industrial life of a given stage and, in so far, transcends the state and the nation, though, on the other hand again, it must assert itself in its external relations as nationality and internally must organize itself as state.'
9. There is, of course, the danger of failing to keep the appropriate question in mind and allowing the problem posed to be argued away in an unrigorous manner, so that a more or less undifferentiated and unorganized world market, in which capital movement takes place practically free of state influence, is taken as a starting point. Herrmann Bruhn, Dirk Wölfing and Bernd Koch 1974, make this mistake.
10. Only when the problem is posed in this way is it possible to reach a determination of 'barriers' in the sense of the quotation above, and to discover the circumstances under which they may be overcome.
11. On this point the *Neues Rotes Forum* criticism of Neusüss is justified. If, however, it is the case, as the *NRF* admits, that the category of the average rate of profit is in general already given with the development of the level of the world market, it is difficult to see why *NRF* does not regard the question of autonomization into national capitals as posing a problem. See *Neues Rotes Forum* 1973.
12. On the problem of the development of competition in Marx see Winfried Schwarz 1974.
13 Bruhn *et al.* 1974, etc., are all based upon the adoption of this methodological and theoretical pressupposition.
14. For the concept of unity used in this context, see *Grundrisse*, pp. 159, 161.
15. An attempt has been made in this direction by Heide Gerstenberger. See Heide Gerstenberger 1973a. In this she embarks, more or less explicitly,

upon a conceptual analysis of the form of historical development. Rejecting the kind of theoretical derivation of these forms now under discussion, she tries to establish the relevant components of the determination of the function of the bourgeois state from the reconstruction of the historical course of its coming into being alone. This abstract generalization of historical processes, carried out without the added dimension of conceptual reflection, contributes little to the understanding of particular concrete phenomena, and does not allow of their determination as expression of the laws governing the whole structure of the social formation, or as specific autonomizations, themselves in need of explanation.

16. Abraham Leon 1970, pp. 38 ff. Leon has, in particular, shed light on the social significance of 'stagnant' defeudalization.

17. In this the interests of the monarchy and the bourgeoisie coincided in particular in the system of national debt. See *Capital* vol. 1, pp. 706 ff; Kaemmel 1966, pp. 212 ff; Jürgen Kuczynski 1961, vol. 22, p. 40.

18. The German Ideology, MECW vol. 5, pp. 69 f; Josef Kulischer 1929, pp. 138 ff; Leo Hubermann n.d., pp. 158 ff.

19. Karl Marx, *Contribution to the Critique of Hegel's Philosophy of Law*, MECW vol. 3, p. 79.

20. See Kulischer 1929, pp. 102 ff; Gerstenberger 1973, pp. 213 ff. Hilferding's claim that the bourgeoisie only develop an interest in the strength of their state during the monopolistic phase of capitalism seems ill-founded. See Rudolf Hilferding 1968.

21. Whereas for hundreds of years non-European states recognized no principle of sovereignty or national integrity and intervened extensively in one another's affairs in a quite open manner. See Rudolf Arzinger 1966, pp. 20 ff.

22. 'Thanks to the machine the spinner can live in England while the weaver resides in the West Indies. Before the invention of machinery, the industry of a country was carried on chiefly with raw materials that were the products of its own soil; in England — wool, in Germany — flax, in France — silks and flax, in the East Indies and the Levant — cotton, etc. Thanks to the application of machinery and of steam, the division of labour was able to assume such dimensions that large scale industry, detached from the national soil, depends entirely on world trade, on international exchange, on an international division of labour' (Karl Marx, *The Poverty of Philosophy*, MECW vol. 6, p. 187).

23. Kuczynski 1961, vol. 22, pp. 181 ff; Hobsbawm 1968, p. 37.

24. Using the example of the system of double government over the territory ruled by the East India Co., Marx shows the necessity and the administrative origins of a state presence to ensure reproduction. The essay also illustrates the necessary change in function of dependent economies from pure areas of extraction to centres of exchange, and the role which the state apparatus assumes in this process in providing the necessary political mediations. Cf. Marx, *The East India Company, its History and Results* (Marx, *Political Writings* vol. 2, 1973, p. 307).

25. On the problem of protective tariffs, see Marx, *Speech on the Question of Free Trade*, MECW vol. 6, pp. 450 ff; *Letter to Annenkov*; Marx/

Engels, *The German Ideology*, MECW vol. 5, pp. 73 f.

26. This should not be construed as a variety of monocausalism. Rather, it is a question of giving due weight to a determining factor which has been disregarded for too long.

27. Michael Freud 1951; Kaemmel 1966, pp. 250 ff; Kuczynski 1961, vol. 22, pp. 215 ff; Hobsbawm 1968, pp. 63—5; *Capital* vol. 1, pp. 702 f.

28. See Alexander Gerschenkron 1962, pp. 14 ff; Paul Bairoch, 1973, pp. 541 ff, 548 f.

29. 'The independence of the state is only found nowadays in those countries where the estates have not yet completely developed into classes, where the estates, done away with in more advanced countries, still play a part and there exists a mixture, where consequently no section of the population can achieve dominance over the others' (Marx/Engels, *The German Ideology*, MECW vol. 5, p. 90).

30. For the historical process of the constituting of the American federal government, see Heide Gerstenberger 1973b.

31. On the historical process of the interrelationship of the world market, the nationally centred introduction of the capitalist mode of production, the bourgeois national state and the specific expression taken by the state apparatus and its relationship to bourgeois society, see Claudia von Braunmühl 1976.

32. This is a factor that Marx and Engels always took the most thorough account of in their historical writings. The reviews written for the *Neue Rheinische Zeitung* between 1848 and 1850 are exemplary in this respect. See the *Neue Rheinische Zeitung* articles in the collection *Revolutions of 1848*, 1975.

33. Enough has been said on this point in the course of the discussion on the theoretical derivation of the bourgois state. It has become generally accepted, and it is not necessary to go into it further here.

34. Karl Marx, *Die revolutionäre Bewegung*, MEW vol. 6, p. 149. The close interconnectedness of the industrializing nations is also to be seen in the over 70% increase in world trade within Europe between 1840 and 1850. This was an unprecedentedly rapid increase, unsurpassed in the whole of the nineteenth century.

35. Marx/Engels, *Manifesto of the Communist Party*, MESW vol. 1, p. 124. This distinction, first made by Marx and Engels, has been taken up in the French discussion of imperialism and applied in connection with the differentiation between economic and social reproduction. It has as yet made little impression on the West German discussion.

36. Poulantzas attempts to deal with this by means of his distinction between the concept of internal bourgeoisie and that of national bourgeoisie, without however being able to draw up adequate criteria for distinguishing between them. See Poulantzas 1975, pp. 70 ff, pp. 34 ff.

Bibliography

Abbreviations

Gesellschaft = Gesellschaft. Beiträge zur marxschen Theorie.
Prokla = Probleme des Klassenkampfs.
SOPO = Sozialistische Politik.

AGNOLI, J. & BRÜCKNER, P. 1967: *Die Transformation der Demokratie*. West Berlin.
AGNOLI, J. 1975: *Überlegung zum bürgerlichen Staat*. Berlin.
A. K. MÜNCHEN, 1974: Warum scheitern Marxisten an der Erklärung des bürgerlichen Staates? *Resultate der Arbeitskonferenz* 1, 120.
ALMOND, G. 1966: Political theory and political science. *American Political Science Review* 60, 869– .
ALTVATER, ELMAR 1972: Zu einigen Problemen des Staatsinterventionismus. *Prokla* 3, 1–53. (translated in 1973a.)
     1973a: Some problems of state interventionism. *Kapitalistate* 1, 96–116; 2, 76–83.
     1973b: Zu einigen Problemen des 'Krisenmanagements' in der kapitalistischen Gesellschaft. In Jänicke, M., editor, *Herrschaft und Krise*. Köln & Opladen.
ALTVATER, ELMAR; HOFFMANN, JÜRGEN; SCHÖLLER, WOLFGANG; SEMMLER, WILLI 1974: On the analysis of imperialism in the metropolitan countries: the West German example. *Bulletin of the Conference of Socialist Economists* Spring 74, 1–24.
ARZINGER, RUDOLF 1966: *Das Selbstbestimmungsrecht im allgemeinen Volksrecht der Gegenwart*. East Berlin.
BACKHAUS, HANS-GEORG 1969: Zur Dialektik der Wertform. In Schmidt, Alfred, *Beiträge zur marxistischen Erkenntnistheorie*.
BAIROCH, PAUL 1973: Commerce internationale et genèse de la révolution industrielle anglaise. *Annales Économies, Sociétés, Civilisations* 2, 541– .
BARAN, PAUL A. & SWEEZY, PAUL M. 1966: *Monopoly Capital*. New York.
BISCHOFF, JOACHIM 1973: Gesellschaftliche Arbeit als Systembegriff. Berlin.

BLACKBURN, R. 1972: *Ideology in Social Science.* London.

BLANK, HANS-JOACHIM 1969: Verwaltung und Verwaltungswissenschaft. In Kress & Senghaas 1969, 368– .

BLANKE, B. 1973: Staat. In von Eynern, Gert, *Wörterbuch zur politischen Ökonomie.* Opladen.

BLANKE, BERNHARD; JÜRGENS, ULRICH; KASTENDIEK, HANS 1974: Zur neueren marxistischen Diskussion über die Analyse von Form und Funktion des bürgerlichen Staates. *Prokla* 14–15, 51–102.

 1975: *Kritik der politischen Wissenschaft.* 2 vols. Frankfurt.

BOCCARA, PAUL 1971: Zum Staatsmonopolistischen Kapitalismus. *SOPO* 11, 7– .

 1972: Übersicht über die Theorie der Überakkumulation – Entwertung des Kapitals und die Perspektiven der fortschrittlichen Demokratie. *SOPO* 16–18–19.

 1973: *Études sur le capitalisme monopoliste d'état.* Paris.

BRAUNMÜHL, CLAUDIA VON 1973: Weltmarktbewegung des Kapitals, Imperialismus und Staat. In Braunmühl *et al.* 1973.

 1974: Kapitalakkumulation im Weltmarktzusammenhang. Zum methodischen Ansatz einer Analyse des bürgerlichen Nationalstaats. *Gesellschaft* 1, 30–51.

 1976: Weltmarkt und Staat. *Gesellschaft* 8/9.

BRAUNMÜHL, FUNKEN, COGOY, HIRSCH 1973: *Probleme einer materialistischen Staatstheorie.* Frankfurt.

BRUHN, HERRMANN; WÖLFING, DIRK; KOCH, BERND 1974: Das Geld im Imperialismus. *Prokla* 11–12, 149– .

BUKHARIN, NIKOLAI 1972a: *Imperialism and the accumulation of capital.* London (orig. 1924).

 1972b: *Imperialism and world economy* (orig. 1915), London.

BUSCH, KLAUS 1973: Zur Diskussion über internationale Durchschnittsprofitrate, ungleichen Tausch und komparative Kostentheorie, Anhand der Thesen von A. Emmanuel. *Prokla* 8–9, 47– .

CARDOSO, FERNANDO HENRIQUE 1971: *Politique et développement dans les sociétés dépendantes.* Paris.

CARTELLIERI, WOLFGANG 1967: *Die Grossforschung und der Staat.* Munich.

COGOY, MARIO 1973: Werttheorie und Staatsaufgaben. In Braunmühl et al. 1973.

COLLETTI, LIBERTINI, MAITAN, MAGRI 1970: *Über Lenins 'Staat und Revolution' – Heute.* Berlin.

CORDOVA, ARMANDO 1973: *Strukturelle Heterogenität und wirtschaftliches Wachstum.* Frankfurt.

DEPPE, FREYBERG, KIEVENHEIM, MEYER, WERKMEISTER 1969: *Kritik der Mitbestimmung.* Frankfurt.

DOBB, MAURICE 1937: *Political economy and capitalism.* London.

 1959: The falling rate of profit. *Science & Society* XXIV No. 2. Published in German in Rolshausen (ed.) 1970.

 1963: *Studies in the development of capitalism.* London. (revised edition; original 1946).

EMMANUEL, A. 1972: *Unequal Exchange.* New York & London.

ENGELS, FRIEDRICH 1962: *Anti-Dühring*. Moscow. See also Marx.
FINE, BEN & HARRIS, LAURENCE 1976a: 'State expenditure in advanced capitalism': a critique. *New Left Review* 98, 97—112.
     1976b: Controversial issues in Marxist economic theory. *Socialist Register*, 141—178.
FLATOW, SYBILLE VON & HUISKEN, FREERK 1973: Zum Problem der Ableitung des bürgerlichen Staates. *Prokla* 7, 83—   .
FRAENKEL, ERNST 1966: Kollektive Demokratie. In Ramm 1966, 79—   .
FRANK, ANDRÉ GUNDER 1967: *Capitalism and underdevelopment in Latin America*. New York.
FREE UNIVERSITY BERLIN DKP PROJECT; RABEHL, B. 1969: *DKP — eine neue sozialdemokratische Partei*. (Parlamentarismus-debatte 2). Berlin.
FREUD, MICHAEL 1951: *Die grosse Revolution in England: Anatomie eines Umsturzes*. Hamburg.
FREY, RENÉ L. 1970: *Infrastruktur*. Tübingen-Zurich.
FUNKEN, KLAUS 1973: Überlegung zu einer marxistischen Staatstheorie. In Braunmühl *et al.* 1973.
FURTADO, CELSO 1970: *Economic development of Latin America*. Cambridge.
GALBRAITH, J. K. 1967: *The New Industrial State*. London.
GERSTENBERGER, HEIDE 1973a: Zur Theorie der historischen Konstitution des bürgerlichen Staates. *Prokla* 8—9, 208—   .
     1973b: *Zur politischen Ökonomie der bürgerlichen Gesellschaft: die Bedingungen ihrer historischen Konstitution in den USA*. Frankfurt.
     1975: Klassenantagonismus, Konkurrenz und Staatsfunktionen. *Gesellschaft* 3, 7—26.
     1977: Zur Theorie des bürgerlichen Staates — Anmerkungen zum gegenwärtigen Stand der Debatte. Forthcoming.
GILLMANN, JOSEPH 1957: *The falling rate of profit*. London.
     1969: *Das Gesetz des tendenziellen Falls der Profitrate*. Vienna.
GLYN, ANDREW & SUTCLIFFE, BOB 1972: *British capitalism, workers and the profits squeeze*. London.
GODELIER, MAURICE 1967: Structure and contradiction in 'Capital'. *Socialist Register*. Reprinted in Blackburn 1972.
GOLD, LO & WRIGHT 1975: Recent developments in Marxist theories of the capitalist state. *Monthly Review* vol. 27, nos. 5 & 6.
GOUGH, IAN 1975: State expenditure in advanced capitalism. *New Left Review* 92, 53—92.
GRAMSCI, ANTONIO 1971: *Selections from the prison notebooks*. Edited by Q. Hoare & G. Nowell-Smith. London, New York.
GROSSMANN, HENRYK 1970: *Das Akkumulations- und Zusammenbruchsgesetz des kapitalistischen Systems*. Frankfurt (Originally 1929).
GURLAND, A. 1928: *Produktionsweise — Staat — Klassendiktatur*. Leipzig.
HABERMAS, JÜRGEN 1973: *Legitimationsprobleme im Spätkapitalismus*. Frankfurt. Translated as:-
     1976: *Legitimation Crisis*. London, Boston.
HELLER, HERRMANN 1963: *Staatslehre*. Leiden. (Originally 1934).
     1971: *Gesammelte Schriften*. Leiden.

HENNING, HIRSCH, REICHELT & SCHÄFER 1974: *Karl Marx, Friedrich Engels: Staatstheorie.* Frankfurt.
HILFERDING, R. 1968: *Das Finanzkapital.* (Originally 1909). Frankfurt.
HIRSCH, JOACHIM 1973: Elemente einer materialistischen Staatstheorie. In Braunmühl et al. 1973, p. 199— .
　　1974: *Staatsapparat und Reproduktion des Kapitals.* Frankfurt.
　　1976: Bemerkungen zum theoretischen Ansatz des bürgerlichen Staates. *Gesellschaft* 8—9.
HIRSCH, J. & LEIBFRIED, S. 1971: *Materialien zur Wissenschafts- und Bildungspolitik.* Frankfurt.
HOBSBAWM, E. J. 1968: *Industry and Empire.* London.
HOCHBERGER, HUNNO 1974: Probleme einer materialistischen Bestimmung des Staates. *Gesellschaft* 2, 155— .
HODGSON, G. 1976: Exploitation and embodied labour-time. *Bulletin of the Conference of Socialist Economists*, No. 13.
HÖHME, HANS-JOACHIM 1971: Der Staatshaushalt der BRD. *DWI — Forschungshefte* vol. 6 No. 1, 44— .
HOLLOWAY, JOHN & PICCIOTTO, SOL 1976: A note on the theory of the state (A reply to Ian Gough). *Bulletin of the Conference of Socialist Economists* No. 14.
HUBERMANN, LEO n.d.: *Kapital und Proletariat. Ursprung und Entwicklung. Politisch-ökonomische Geschichte der Neuzeit.* New edition — no place of publication.
HUFFSCHMID, JÖRG 1969: *Die Politik des Kapitals.* Frankfurt.
HUISKEN, FREERK: see FLATOW, SYBILLE von.
Imperialismus der BRD. 1971. Berlin. (Collective work).
JELLINEK, GEORG 1905: *System der subjektiv öffentlichen Rechte.* Tübingen.
JOCHIMSEN, REIMUT & SIMONIS, UDO E. 1970: *Theorie und Praxis der Infrastrukturpolitik.* Berlin.
KADRITZKE, NIELS 1973: Faschismus als historische Realität und als unrealistischer Kampfsbegriff. *Prokla* 8—9, 103— .
KAEMMEL, ERNST 1966: *Finanzgeschichte.* East Berlin.
KAHN-FREUND, OTTO 1966: Das soziale Ideal des Reichsarbeitsgerichts. In Ramm 1966, 149— .
KATZENSTEIN, ROBERT 1967: *Die Investitionen und ihre Bewegung im staatsmonopolistischen Kapitalismus.* Berlin.
　　1973: Zur Theorie des staatsmonopolistischen Kapitalismus. *Prokla* 8—9, 1— .
KIDRON, MICHAEL 1968: *Western Capitalism since the War.* London.
KLEIN, DIETER 1967: Über die inneren Widersprüche des modernen Imperialismus. *Wirtschaftswissenschaft* 6, 975— .
KRESS, G. & SENGHAAS, D. 1969: *Politikwissenschaft.* Frankfurt.
KUCZYNSKI, JÜRGEN 1961: *Zur Geschichte der Lage der Arbeiter unter dem Kapitalismus.* Berlin.
　　1942—6: *A short history of labour conditions under industrial capitalism.* 4 vols. London. Reissued 1972—3.
KULISCHER, JOSEF 1929: *Allgemeine Wirtschaftsgeschichte.* Berlin.
LAPINSKI, P. 1928: Der Sozialstaat, Etappen und Tendenzen seiner Entwick-

lung. *Unter dem Banner des Marxismus* 2, 383—   . Reprinted in *Gegen den Strom* vol. 1 no. 1 Aug. 1969, 39—   .

LÄPPLE, DIETER 1973: *Staat und allgemeine Produktionsbedingungen.* Berlin.

LENIN, V. I. n.d.: *Selected works.* 3 vols. Moscow.

LEON, ABRAHAM 1970: *Judenfrage und Kapitalismus.* Munich.

LEONTIEF, B. WASSILY 1961: The economic problem of organised invention. *Rivista di politica economica* 51(12), 2167—2171.

LEUCATE, CHRISTIAN 1975: Internationalisation du capital et impérialisme. *Critiques de l'économie politique* 19, 88—127.

LINDNER, GUDRUN 1973: Die Krise als Steuerungsmittel. *Leviathan* vol. 1, no. 3, 342—82.

LUHMANN, NIKLAS 1968: Soziologie des politischen Systems. *Kölner Zeitschrift für Soziologie und Sozialpsychologie* 20, 722—   .
    1969: Komplexität und Demokratie. *Politische Vierteljahresschrift* 10.
    1973: Politische Verfassungen im Kontext des Verfassungssystems. *Der Staat* vols. 1 & 2.

LUKÁCS, GEORG 1971: *History and class consciousness.* London.

LUXEMBURG, ROSA 1899: *Social Reform or Revolution?* London edition n.d. Also printed in Howard (ed.) 1971: *Selected political writings of Rosa Luxemburg.* New York.

MACPHERSON, C. B. 1962: *The political theory of possessive individualism.* London.

MAGRI, LUCIO 1970: Für einen neuen Realismus. In Colletti et al. 1970.

MAITAN, LIVIO 1970: Notwendigkeit des revolutionären Bruchs. In Colletti *et al.*

MANDEL, ERNEST 1962: Marxist economic theory. (1968 reprint in one vol., same paging).
    1969: *Die deutsche Wirtschaftskrise.* Frankfurt.
    1975: *Introduction* to Trotsky, *The Struggle against Fascism in Germany.* London.

MARX, KARL: *Grundrisse. Foundations of the critique of political economy (Rough Draft).* 1973, London.
    Capital. Vol. 1, 1974, London. Vol. 2, 1966, Moscow. Vol. 3, 1966, Moscow.
    Results of the immediate process of production. Appendix to 1976 edition of *Capital,* London.
    Theories of surplus-value (cited as TSV). Vols. 1 & 2, 1969, London. Vol. 3, 1972, London.

MARX, KARL & ENGELS, FRIEDRICH: *Marx-Engels Collected Works* (cited as MECW). 1975—   . London, New York, Moscow. (Vols. 1—7 published by 1977.)
    Marx-Engels Werke 41 vols (cited as MEW) completed 1968, Berlin.
    Marx-Engels Selected Works in 3 vols (cited as MESW). 1969, Moscow.
    Political Writings. Vol. 1: The Revolutions of 1848. 1973, London.
    Vol. 2: *Surveys from Exile.* 1973, London.

MARXISTISCHE GRUPPE ERLANGEN 1972: *Zur Oberfläche des Kapitals.* Theoriefraktion Cirkular 3.

MASON, TIM 1966: Der Primat der Politik. *Das Argument* vol. 6, no. 41.
MATTICK, PAUL 1959: Value theory and capital accumulation. *Science & Society* vol. XXIII, no. 1. Reprinted in German in Rolshausen 1970.
    1969: Marx and Keynes. London.
MEISSNER, HERBERT 1967: *Bürgerliche Ökonomie im modernen Kapitalismus.* East Berlin.
MILIBAND, RALPH 1969: *The state in capitalist society.* London.
    1970: The capitalist state: a reply to Nicos Poulantzas. *New Left Review* 59, 53—60. Reprinted in Blackburn 1970.
    1973: Poulantzas and the capitalist state. *New Left Review* 82.
MILL, J. S. 1965: *Principles of political economy.* (7th ed.) New York.
MOORE, W. BARRINGTON 1967: *Social origins of dictatorship and democracy.* London.
MÜLLER, W. & NEUSÜSS, C. 1970: Die Sozialstaatsillusion und der Widerspruch von Lohnarbeit und Kapital. *SOPO* 6—7, 4—67. Reprinted in *Prokla* Sonderheft No. 1. Translated into English:—
    1975: The illusions of state socialism and the contradiction between wage-labour and capital. Telos 25.
NARR, WOLF-DIETER 1969: *Theoriebegriff und Systemtheorie.* Stuttgart.
NASCHOLD, FRIEDER 1968: Demokratie und Komplexität. *Politische Vierteljahresschrift* 9, 484—
    1969: Vernachlässigte Aspekte der Regierungs und Verwaltungsreform in der BRD. *Kommunikation* 4.
NEGRI, ANTONIO 1976: Sur quelques tendances de la theorie communiste de l'état la plus récente: revue critique. Paper given to meeting of ACSES (Association pour la critique des sciences économiques et sociales). Originally in *Critica dell Diritto* 3.
NEGT, OSKAR 1973: Thesen zur marxistischen Rechtstheorie. *Kritische Justiz* 1, 1— .
NEGT, OSKAR & KLUGE, ALEXANDER 1972: *Öffentlichkeit und Erfahrung. Zur Organisationsanalyse von bürgerlicher und proletarischer Öffentlichkeit.* Frankfurt.
NELSON, PECK & KALACHEK 1968: *Technology, economic growth and public policy.* Washington (2nd edition).
NEUES ROTES FORUM 1973: Imperialismus und Weltmarktbewegung. *Neues Rotes Forum* 4, 42— .
NEUMANN, FRANZ 1957: *The democratic and the authoritarian state.* (Edited Marcuse.) Toronto. Includes 1937: The change in the function of law in modern society.
NEUSÜSS, CHRISTEL 1972: *Imperialismus und Weltmarktbewegung des Kapitals.* Erlangen.
NIKOLAJEW, VADIM 1972: *Forschung und Entwicklung im Imperialismus.* Berlin.
O'CONNOR, JAMES 1973a: Summary of the fiscal crisis of the state. *Kapitalistate* 1, 79—83.
    1973b: *The fiscal crisis of the state.* New York.
OECD 1970a: *Gaps in Technology. Analytical Report.* Paris.
    1970b: *The growth of output 1960—70.* Paris.

1971: *The conditions of success in technological innovation.* Paris.

OFFE, CLAUS 1972: *Strukturprobleme des kapitalistischen Staates.* Frankfurt. The last chapter of this book is translated in:—
1975: Reply to Müller and Neusüss. *Telos* 25, 99—111.

OERTZEN, PETER VON 1974: *Die soziale Funktion des staatsrechtlichen Positivismus.* Frankfurt. (Originally 1953.)

PALLOIX, CHRISTIAN 1971: *L'économie mondiale capitaliste.* 2 vols. Paris.

PANNEKOEK, ANTON 1977: The theory of the collapse of capitalism. *Capital & Class* No. 1. (Reprint in translation of 1934 article.)

PANNEKOEK, LUKACS, FRIEDLÄNDER, RUDAS 1968: *Parlamentarismusdebatte.* West Berlin.

PASHUKANIS, EUGENE 1951: General theory of law and Marxism. In *Soviet Legal Philosophy by V. I. Lenin et al.* trans. by Hugh W. Babb, introduced by John N. Hazard. 20th Century Legal Philosophy series, No. 5, Harvard U.P. Reprinted 1968, Johnson Reprint Corp.
1966: *Allgemeine Rechtslehre und Marxismus.* Frankfurt. (Both 1951 and 1966 translated from Russian 1929 3rd ed.)

PETROWSKY, WERNER 1971: Zur Entwicklung der Theorie des staatsmonopolistischen Kapitalismus. *Prokla* 1.

POLACK, KARL 1968: Karl Marx über Staat, Eigentum und Recht. In *Karl Marx, Begründer der Staats- und Rechtstheorie der Arbeiterklasse.* East Berlin.

POULANTZAS, NICOS 1969: The problem of the capitalist state. *New Left Review* 58, 67—78. Reprinted in Blackburn 1972.
1973: *Political power and social classes.* London.
1974: *Fascism and Dictatorship.* London.
1975: *Classes in contemporary capitalism.* London.
1976a: The capitalist state: a reply to Miliband and Laclau. *New Left Review* 95.
1976b: *The crisis of the dictatorships.* London.

PREUSS, ULRICH K. 1969: *Zum staatsrechtlichen Begriff der Öffentlichkeit.* Stuttgart.
1973: *Legalität und Pluralismus.* Frankfurt.

PROJEKT KLASSENANALYSE 1971: Kritik der Sozialstaatsillusion. *SOPO* 14—15, 193— .
1972: *Zur Taktik der proletarischen Partei.* Berlin.
1973: *Materialien zur Klassenstruktur der BRD.* Berlin.

RABEHL, B. 1969: see Free University.

RADBRUCH, G. 1969: *Einführung in die Rechtswissenschaft.* Stuttgart.

RAMM, THILO 1966: *Arbeitsrecht und Politik. Quellentexte 1918—33.* Neuwied & Berlin.

REICHELT, HELMUT 1970: *Zur logischen Struktur des Kapitalbegriffs bei Karl Marx.* Frankfurt.
1974a: Einige Anmerkungen zu Sybille von Flatows und Freerk Huikens Aufsatz 'Zum Problem der Ableitung des bürgerlichen Staates'. *Gesellschaft* 1, 12—29.
1974b: Zur Staatstheorie im Frühwerk von Marx und Engels. In Henning *et al.* 1974.

RIEHLE, ECKART 1974: *Probleme und Elemente einer dialektischmaterialist-ischen Theorie des bürgerlichen Staates*. Thesis. Heidelberg.

RKW FORSCHUNGSPROJEKT 1970: *Wirtschaftliche und soziale Aspekte des technischen Wandels in der BRD*. Vol. 1, 7 reports.

RÖDEL, ULRICH 1972: *Forschungsprioritäten und technologische Entwicklung.* Frankfurt.

ROLSHAUSEN, C. 1970: *Kapitalismus und Krise*. (Reprints of articles from *Science & Society* on the tendency of the rate of profit to fall.)

ROBINSON, JOAN 1956: *The accumulation of capital*. London.

RÖMER, PETER 1972: Klassenkampf, Staat und allgemeines Gesetz. *SOPO* 19, 87— .

RONGE & SCHMIEG 1973: *Restriktionen politischer Planung*. Frankfurt.

ROSDOLSKY, ROMAN 1968: *Zur Entstehungsgeschichte des Marxschen 'Kapital'*. 2 vols. Frankfurt. (Forthcoming 1977 in English.)

    1974 Comments on the method of Marx's 'Capital' and its importance for contemporary Marxist scholarship. *New German Critique* 3, 62—72.

ROTE HILFE WEST BERLIN 1973: Staatsgewalt, Reformismus und die Politik der Linken. *Kursbuch* 31, 29— .

SACHVERSTÄNDIGENRAT ZUR BEGUTACHTUNG DER GESAMTWIRTSCHAFT-LICHEN ENTWICKLUNG 1967/8: *Stabilität in Wachstum*. Stuttgart/Mainz.

SCHMID, GÜNTHER 1973: *Funktionsanalyse und politische Theorie: Funk-tionalismuskritik, politisch-ökonomische Faktorenanalyse, genetisch-funktionale Systemtheorie*. Düsseldorf.

SCHMIEDE, RUDI 1973: *Grundprobleme der Marxschen Akkumulations- und Krisentheorie*. Frankfurt.

SCHRÖDER, DIETER 1971: *Wachstum und Gesellschaftspolitik*. Stuttgart.

SCHWARZ, WINFRIED 1974: Das 'Kapital im Allgemeinen' und die 'Kon-kurrenz' im ökonomischen Werk von Karl Marx. Zu Rosdolskys Fehlinter-pretation der Gliederung des 'Kapital'. *Gesellschaft* 1, 222—247.

SEIFERT, JÜRGEN 1971: Verrechtliche Politik und die Dialektik der marxist-ischen Rechtstheorie. *Kritische Justiz* 2, 185—200.

SEMMLER, W. & HOFFMANN, J. 1972: Der Zusammenhang von Kapitalakkumu-lation, Staatsangriffen und Lohnbewegung. *Prokla* 2, 1— .

SERING, P. 1935: Wandlungen des Kapitalismus. *Zeitschrift für Sozialismus* (Prague) 22—3, 717— .

SHONFIELD, ANDREW 1965: *Modern Capitalism*. London.

SOHN-RETHEL, ALFRED 1973: *Ökonomie und Klassenstruktur des deutschen Faschismus*. Frankfurt.

STEIN, LORENZ VON 1972: *Gesellschaft-Staat-Recht*. Frankfurt.

STOHLER, JACQUES 1965: Zur rationalen Planung der Infrastruktur. *Kon-junkturpolitik* 11, 279— .

STUČKA, P. 1969: *Die revolutionäre Rolle von Recht und Staat*. Frankfurt. (Original edition 1921, in Russian, Moscow.)

VOGT, WINIFRIED 1973: Zur langfristigen ökonomischen Entwicklung eines kapitalistischen Systems. *Leviathan* 2, 161— .

WEBER, MAX 1954: *Max Weber on Law in Economy and Society*. Edited by Shils & Rheinstein. Boston. (Reprinted 1966.)

    1964: *Wirtschaft und Gesellschaft* (Studienausgabe). Köln-Berlin.

1968: *Economy and Society*, 3-vol. selection edited by Roth & Wittich. New York.

WIRTH, MARGARET 1972: *Kapitalismustheorie in der DDR*. Frankfurt.

1973: Zur Kritik der Theorie der staatsmonopolistischen Kapitalismus. *Prokla* 8—9, 17— . (To appear in English in *Economy and Society* 1977.)

WYGODSKI, S. L. 1972: *Der gegenwärtige Kapitalismus*. Köln.

YAFFE, DAVID & BULLOCK, PAUL 1975: Inflation, the crisis and the post-war boom. *Revolutionary Communist* 3—4, 5—45.

ZELENY, J. 1968: *Die Wissenschaftslogik bei Marx und 'Das Kapital'*. Berlin-DDR.

ZIESCHANG, KURT 1956: Zu einigen theoretischen Problemen des staatsmonopolistischen Kapitalismus. *Wirtschaftswissenschaft* 5, 702— .

1965a: Grundfragen des ökonomischen Inhalts des staatsmonopolistischen Kapitalismus — dargestellt am Beispiel der ökonomischen Rolle der Staatsfinanzen. *Konjunktur und Krise* 9, 1— .

1965b: Probleme des Haushaltsstruktur und des Haushaltsvolumens in Westdeutschland und ihre Bedeutung für den Rekonstruktionsprozess. *Konjunktur und Krise* 9, 295— .

1969: Zu den Entwicklungstendenzen des kapitalistischen Grundwiderspruchs unter den Bedingungen der wissenschaftlich-technischen Revolution. *Wirtschaftswissenschaft* 6, 872— .

Indices

In references to footnotes the chapter number is given first.

Author Index

Subject Index